CONVICTED

CONVICTED

LANDMARK CASES
IN BRITISH
CRIMINAL HISTORY

GARY POWELL

AMBERLEY

First published 2018

Amberley Publishing
The Hill, Stroud
Gloucestershire, GL5 4EP

www.amberley-books.com

Copyright © Gary Powell, 2018

The right of Gary Powell to be identified as
the Author of this work has been asserted in
accordance with the Copyrights, Designs and
Patents Act 1988.

ISBN 978 1 4456 7052 2 (paperback)
ISBN 978 1 4456 7053 9 (ebook)

British Library Cataloguing in Publication Data.
A catalogue record for this book is available
from the British Library.

Typesetting and Origination by Amberley
Publishing.
Printed in the UK.

CONTENTS

INTRODUCTION

Great Britain has one of the oldest judicial systems in the world. Our common law can be traced back to the Middle Ages, and at its cornerstone is the jury system, with the basic tenet that a person is innocent until proven guilty. The law, of course, cannot stand still and has to move with the times to be fit for purpose in relation to Britain's ever-changing social and economic traits, even to the point of questioning the effectiveness of the jury system in some cases. This book reflects on those changes and the landmark cases throughout our criminal history that have strengthened this country's reputation for fairness and justice.

Starting as far back as the late eighteenth century, the examination and preservation of crime scenes had become ever more important, coinciding with the emergence of specific forensic methods and sciences. Fingerprinting, entomology, ballistics, facial reconstruction, forensic dentistry/odontology and of course DNA, to name some but not all, have aided the police in their ultimate aim to convict those guilty of some of the most horrendous crimes imaginable. But for these and other sciences to be accepted as reliable and admissible evidence, they have to be tested in our judicial system. The court has to accept their legality, and a jury their credibility. When this is first achieved, the cases in question become notable, resulting as they do in landmark convictions.

Mistakes have been made along the way, resulting in miscarriages of justice; for instance, the untested use of ear-print comparisons led to the wrongful conviction and imprisonment of an innocent man. Cases such as these are quite correctly deemed to be *as* ground-breaking as those with happier outcomes.

This book examines one hundred such examples of what must be considered, in varying degrees, landmark convictions. They may be of note for the preparatory work carried out during the investigation, for representing the first conviction under a new piece of legislation, or indeed for the court case itself. Many of the cases are quite bizarre – a twentieth-century witch, a defendant sentenced on his mobile telephone – or cruel. As one chapter shows, we are a nation of animal lovers; dogs, rabbits, and bats all feature. Examples of the bravery of our police officers and the despicable way they have been treated through history are alluded to, alongside several coppers who behaved rather badly.

All the cases featured have in some way significantly affected the manner in which laws governing our lives today are interpreted and administered. We proudly consider ourselves to be one of the most just, civilised societies in the world, but it's been a long, bumpy path riddled with mistakes and injustice – and it is a journey far from completion. Who knows how technological developments will evolve to mould the landmark cases of the future?

G. Powell

2018

1. THE KING'S HEAD (1649)

On the morning of 30 January 1649, the diminutive King Charles I walked from the first floor of the Banqueting House, Whitehall, London, onto a specially constructed scaffold on which he would die at the hands of his own people. He was tried and convicted by a court of justice in Westminster Hall and sentenced to death in the only case of regicide in British history.

Charles was born on 19 November 1600 in Dunfermline Palace, Fife, Scotland. He was the son of James VI of Scotland, later James I of England, Scotland, France and Ireland. He succeeded to the English throne as King Charles I on 27 March 1625, being crowned at Westminster Abbey on 2 February 1626. From day one Charles was at loggerheads with the Puritan-dominated House of Commons; this would lead to the emergence of Oliver Cromwell and the English Civil Wars, ending in the defeat of the monarch's armies at Preston on 17 August 1648 and the eventual abolition of the monarchy by Parliament in March 1649. The two civil wars caused the deaths of an estimated 85,000 English men and women, with a further 100,000 dying through war-related disease – approximately 3 per cent of the population. Charles I was held responsible for the terrible casualties in his war against Parliament, and in particular the treasonable implications of his secret 'Engagement Treaty' with the Scots. Oliver Cromwell ranted that Charles' actions were 'a more prodigious treason than any that had been perfected before because the former quarrel was that Englishmen might rule over one another; this to vassalize us to a foreign nation'.

A bill was passed creating a High Court of Justice in order to try Charles I for high treason in the name of the people of England. John Cook, who held the position of Solicitor General, was appointed as prosecutor. In all, 135 commissioners were empowered to try Charles (although only sixty-eight ever sat in judgement). The indictment stated that Charles 'for accomplishment of such his designs, and for the protecting of himself and his adherents in his and their wicked practices, to the same ends hath traitorously and maliciously levied war against the present Parliament, and the people therein represented...'[1]

---

1   *Notable Historic Trials* (Folio Society) Vol: II

The trial of Charles I commenced at Westminster Hall on 20 January 1649. The indictment was read out by John Cook amid unprecedented scenes – the king, standing just to his right, continuously interrupted the Solicitor General as he spoke, first tapping him on the shoulder with his silver-tipped cane to bring the court's attention to the fact that he wished to address them. Cook ignored the king, who repeatedly struck him with the cane; one such blow was delivered with such force that the silver tip fell to the ground. At the completion of the official arraignment Charles was allowed to speak; he refused to enter a plea, insisting that the court had no jurisdiction over a monarch. Charles was of the opinion that his own authority to rule had been due to the divine right of kings, given by God, and that the king can do no wrong. The trial continued on the basis of *pro confesso* (a decree entered by a court based on a defendant's default and therefore the presumption that the allegations are confessed). Witnesses were heard outside the main courtroom, with Charles denied the opportunity to cross-examine their testimonies. The trial lasted eight days; on Saturday 27 January 1649, the king was declared guilty of the charges and sentence passed:

> That the court being satisfied that he, Charles Stuart, was guilty of the crimes of which he had been accused, did judge him a tyrant, traitor, murderer and public enemy to the good people of the nation, to be put to death by the severing of his head from his body.

The sixty-seven commissioners present at the sentencing stood to show their solidarity with the sentence passed – fifty-nine of them signed Charles Stuart's death warrant. At 10 a.m. on the morning of 30 January 1649, surrounded by halberdiers, King Charles I was escorted by his custodian, Colonel Francis Hacker, from St James's Palace to the Banqueting Hall, Whitehall, after saying his last goodbyes to his children and pulling on an extra shirt – it was a cold morning, and he didn't wish his enemies to see him shivering and mistake it for fear.

John Rushworth (*c.* 1612–90), an English lawyer, historian and politician – and later private secretary to Oliver Cromwell – extensively recorded these most turbulent times in English history and provided an eye-witness account of this unique and traumatic episode:

The scaffold was hung round with black and the floor covered with black, and the axe and block laid in the middle of the scaffold. There were divers companies of foot and horse on every side the scaffold and the multitudes of people that came to be spectators were very great. The king making a pass upon the scaffold, looked very earnestly on the block, and asked Colonel Hacker if there were no higher [the usual execution block had been mislaid, replaced by a block usually used for the dismembering of traitors, and was only a few inches from the ground, meaning Charles had to be prone], and then spoke thus, directing his speech to the gentlemen on the scaffold.

Charles intended to deliver his final speech to the people, emphasising the principles that he believed in and would die for and affirming his loyalty to the Church of England. This proved impossible as Parliament, fearful that sections of the crowd loyal to the king would attempt to break him free, had surrounded him with soldiers. His speech was recorded by reporters close by instead. The king then turned and spoke to the executioner, Richard Brandon: 'I shall say but very short prayers and then thrust out my hands.' The last words King Charles I uttered were, 'I go from a corruptible to an incorruptible crown, where no disturbance can be.' John Rushworth describes the final moments:

The king took off his cloak and his George [the jewelled pendant of the Order of the Garter], giving his George to Dr Juxon [Bishop of London] … After which the king stooping down, laid his neck upon the block. After a little pause, stretching forth his hands, the executioner at one blow severed the head from his body. As the king's bloody head was held up to the crowd the celebratory shouts of the soldiers were nullified by the desperate groans of the crowd.

Charles I still commanded a following in England after his death. Cromwell feared that his grave would become a pilgrimage site, so he ordered the former king's body to be buried inside St George's Chapel within the confines of Windsor Castle.

Richard Brandon was the latest in a long family line of executioners; he was rumoured to have prepared for his calling by decapitating domestic animals as a child. Presumably a Royalist, Brandon had refused to carry out the sentence on his king when the judgement was passed. However, on the fateful morning Brandon was summoned from his bed by a troop of horse and escorted to Whitehall and instructed to carry out the punishment. He was paid £30 and rewarded with an orange crammed with cloves (which he later sold for 10 shillings) and a handkerchief from the king's pocket. The reality of what he had done on that cold January morning stayed with Brandon; he sank into a downward spiral of depression and remorse and died just six months later.

Diarist John Evelyn wrote, 'I was struck with such horror that I kept the day of his martyrdom a fast, and would not be present at that execrable wickedness, receiving a sad account of it from my brother George.'

The execution of King Charles I is the only example of regicide in British history – a ruling monarch was tried by a British judicial body and executed at their behest. This chapter changed the course of a nation's history. English poet, satirist and politician Andrew Marvell captured this sense of change in his work *Horatian Ode* (written 1650, published in 1681):

> The royal actor born
> The tragic scaffold might adorn,
> While round the armbands
> Did clap their bloody hands.
> He nothing common did or mean
> Upon that memorable scene:
> But with his keener eye
> The Axe's edge did try:
> Nor called the gods with vulgar spite
> To vindicate his helpless right,
> But bowed his comely head
> Down, as upon a bed.
> This was that memorable hour
> Which first assured the forced power.

2. WHERE'S THE BODY? (1660)

The village of Chipping Campden is situated in the Cotswolds in southern England. In the 1660s this small village was at the centre of an extraordinary case in British criminal history. Dubbed the 'Campden Wonder', the case eventually resulted in an historic ruling that would survive well into the twentieth century.

On 16 August 1660, businessman William Harrison left his home in Chipping Campden intending to walk 2 miles to the nearby village of Charingworth. When the seventy-year-old did not return home later that evening, his wife sent their manservant John Perry to look for him. To her dismay, neither her husband nor John Perry returned that night. The following day William's son Edward set out to look for his father, tracing his steps to Charingworth; on the way he bumped into John Perry, who was returning home. Perry informed Edward that he had not found his father; the two decided to walk on to the village of Ebrington and visit a tenant whom they knew William would have called upon. This tenant did confirm that William Harrison had been there the previous night but had left that morning. They then moved on to the village of Paxford, but failed to find any trace of Harrison. During the return journey they were stopped and informed that some items of clothing and personal property, believed to belong to William Harrison, had been found dumped on the roadside. These items included a hat that had been slashed with a knife or a sword, plus a shirt and tie – all were identified by Edward as belonging to his father. Worryingly, the shirt and tie were covered in blood, and there was no sign of his father.

Suspicion fell on John Perry, who was questioned by a local Justice of the Peace about the disappearance of William Harrison. Inexplicably Perry told the justice that he was aware that his master had been murdered but had played no part in his slaying, directing the blame to his mother Joan and brother Richard, whom he accused of killing the old man before stealing his money and disposing of the body in a millpond. Of course Joan and Richard strenuously denied the allegations; the millpond was dredged but no corpse was found.

As no body had been found, on the allegations sworn by John Perry his mother and brother were charged with theft from William Harrison. The jury listened carefully to John's evidence and decided that he was telling the truth; at this stage the defendants changed their pleas to guilty of an offence of theft (even though they may well have been innocent) – as first-time offenders they would be granted a free pardon under the Indemnity and Oblivion Act of 1660. This act was a general pardon for everyone who had committed crimes during the Civil War and Interregnum with the exception of the most serious of offences, such as murder, piracy, buggery, rape and witchcraft.

The judge decided not to go ahead with a trial for murder as no corpse had been found at this stage. In early 1661 the court reconsidered the evidence, probably at the behest of the deceased's close family, and decided to proceed with a charge of murder against not only Joan and Richard but also John Perry. All three denied the charge; John Perry said the earlier accusations he had made against members of his family were false as he had been suffering from a mental illness at the time. Nevertheless, the jury listened carefully to the circumstantial evidence and found all three guilty of the murder of William Harrison, whose body was still missing, and they were sentenced to death. The mother and two sons were hanged together on Broadway Hill, Gloucestershire, pleading their innocence to the last.

A year after the Perrys were executed, a very much alive William Harrison returned to England and the village of Chipping Campden from Lisbon, Portugal, with an extraordinary tale. He claimed on the afternoon he disappeared – presumed murdered – that he had walked to the village of Charingworth to collect rent due to his employer Lady Campden. The tenant he was to collect from was working in the fields, thereby delaying Harrison's departure; he left the village late that evening after he had collected £23. As he was walking home past the village of Erbrington in the pitch blackness of night he was met by a horseman who enquiringly said, 'Are you there?' Afraid that the horse was going to stamp on him, Harrison hit the horse across the nose; according to Harrison, this prompted the rider to attack him with his sword. He declared that a second man appeared and stabbed him in the thigh before they were joined by a third. Robbery seemed an unlikely motive as they did not initially steal his money but secured his hands together and flung a coat over his head before carrying him away. He was taken to the port of Deal and put on a ship; during the journey he was transferred to a Turkish ship and sold into slavery. Following the death of his elderly master he escaped and hid aboard a Portuguese ship which carried him home to the Port of Dover.

Following this incredible miscarriage of justice, which resulted in the execution of three innocent people, British courts followed a principle of 'no body, no murder'; this principle would last for nearly 300 years.

3. WELL DONE THAT MAN (1670)

A Crown Court judge is an arbiter of the facts and provides direction and ruling in regards to points of the law; he should have no say in the deliberation of the jury, nor their eventual verdict.

Quakers William Penn (the founder of Pennsylvania) and William Mead were arrested in Gracechurch Street in the City of London in August 1670 for violating a law which forbade the religious assembly of more than five men of any other faith outside the Church of England. The two men denied the charges; the jury returned a verdict of guilty in relation to 'speaking in Gracechurch Street' but refused to find them guilty of speaking to an unlawful assembly. This verdict did not impress the trial judge, who, ignoring the dictum above, let his feelings be known. The jury reconsidered and reworded their verdict to 'guilty of speaking to an assembly', stopping short of saying 'unlawful'. This would not do; the jury were ordered to be locked up with no food, water or heat until they came to their senses. William Penn objected and was ordered to be bound and gagged. The jury were in fact incarcerated for two days before returning a verdict – not guilty! The judge, astounded by their obstinacy, found the jury guilty of contempt of court and fined each member; they were to be confined in prison until the fine was paid.

One member of the jury, Edward Bushel, defied the judgement and refused to pay the fine. While incarcerated he applied for a writ of *habeas corpus* (a writ requiring a person to be brought before a judge or into a court, especially to investigate the lawfulness of their detention). Sir John Vaughan, Chief Justice of the Court of Common Pleas, ruled that a jury could *not* be punished simply on account of the verdict it returned. William Penn was acquitted and Edward Bushel released. If the ruling had gone a different way and Penn found guilty, it is unlikely that the United States of America would have a state called Pennsylvania today. Vaughan's ruling guaranteed the independence of the jury system from this point on. A plaque remains on display at the Central Criminal Court, Old Bailey, commemorating the bravery of Edward Bushel.

4. THE WEIGHT OF JUSTICE (1721)

A form of legal torture known as *peine forte et dure* (a phrase in French Law meaning 'hard and forceful punishment') was introduced into English law by the Standing Mute Act of 1275 during the reign of King Edward I. Before this point, if a defendant pleaded either guilty or not guilty to a capital charge and was then executed, all of their property would be escheated (a common law doctrine that transfers the property to the state). Defendants who were charged with capital offences therefore often refused to enter a plea so that their family would be entitled to keep their estate if they were found guilty. Refusal to enter a plea, whatever the outcome, guaranteed the property passed to the rightful heirs. It would appear the initial intention of *peine forte et dure* was that a defiant defendant would serve time under extremely harsh conditions until they changed their minds and entered a plea, but this changed under the reign of Elizabeth I when it took the form of 'pressing' the accused with weights until they pleaded either guilty or not guilty or simply died.

One infamous case which highlighted this practice was that of William Spigget (alias Spiggot) and Thomas Phillips, tried at the Old Bailey in January 1721. William Spigget was a highwayman who led an eight-strong gang robbing victims of money and jewellery along the roads leading from London out to Middlesex, Surrey and Hertfordshire. Spigget and other members of his gang, including Phillips (aka Cross), were arrested in a Westminster tavern following a violent shootout. At their trial at the Old Bailey both men refused to plead to the numerous charges of robbery they faced. The trial records[2] state that:

William Spigget alias Spiggot, and Thomas Phillips alias Cross, having had several Bills of Indictment for Robbing on the High Way, found against them by the Grand Jury, were brought to the Bar to be Arraigned and take their Trials, but they stood Mute, and refused to Plead till they should have the Money, Horses, Accoutrements, and other things which were taken from them when they were Apprehended returned to them; But the Court told them that could not be granted, and for their Satisfaction order'd a Clause in an Act of Parliament made in the 4th and 5th Years of the Reign of King William and Queen Mary, intituled An Act for Encouraging the Apprehending of Highway Men, to be read unto them, which is as follows: That the Prisoner shall be sent to the Prison from whence he came, and put into a mean House, Stopped from Light, and there shall be laid upon the bare Ground without any Litter, Straw or other Covering, and without any Garment about him, saving something to cover his Privy Members and that he shall lie upon his Back, and his Head shall be covered, and his Feet bare, and that one of his Arms shall be drawn with a Cord to one side of the House, and the other Arm to the

---

2   *Old Bailey Online*

other side, and that his Legs shall be used in the same manner, and that upon his Body shall be laid so much Iron and Stone as he can bear, and more, and that the first Day after he shall have three Morsels of Barley Bread, without any Drink, and the second Day he shall drink so much as he can three times of the Wa`ter which is next the Prison Door, saving running Water, without any Bread: and this shall be his Diet until he die. And he, against whom this Judgment shall be given, forfeits to the King his Goods.

Even after such threats both Spigget and Phillips remained mute – refusing to plead to the charges. They were returned to Newgate Prison for the punishment to be carried out. Phillips was the first to crack and asked to be returned to the court in order that he may enter a plea. Spigget was more obstinate. As he lay with his legs and arms stretched and secured by cords, 350lb of iron was placed on his chest; apart from a few groans and the occasional gasp of 'pray for me' he kept his silence. Another 50lb was added to the weight after half an hour, and finally William Spigget could take no more and asked for the weights to be removed and that he be returned to the court to enter a plea. Both Spigget and Phillips entered pleas of not guilty in answer to the charges and were tried in the normal manner. Both men were found guilty and sentenced to death. They were executed at Tyburn on 11 February 1721 with five other men. A supportive crowd carried off Spigget's body to save it from being dissected by the surgeon's knife.

Peine forte et dure was rarely used – the Spigget case was one of the last examples – before it was abolished from British law in 1772. For a period of time refusing to plead to a charge was deemed to be equivalent to pleading 'guilty'; this was changed in 1827 to being deemed a plea of 'not guilty', a practice that continues, of course, to this day.

5. CUT UP IN THE NAME OF SCIENCE (1752)

The Murder Act of 1751 decreed that in order to deter people from the horrid crime of murder the law of the land would add further terror and infamy to the punishment by not allowing a Christian burial of a convicted murderer's body, instead directing that it be either publicly dissected (the body would be sent to the Royal College of Surgeons for such – a process called anatomisation) or hanged in chains until it rotted. The first person to fall foul of this new legislation was Thomas Wilford, executed and sent for anatomisation on 22 June 1752.

Fulham-born Wilford was up against it from the time of his birth; he was born with only one arm to very poor parents and soon found himself in the workhouse. However, at the age of seventeen he met twenty-two-year-old Sarah Williams. They soon got married and moved into lodgings in the rough district of St Giles. The honeymoon was short-lived; on the Sunday after the ceremony Sarah went out to meet an old friend, and when she got back after midnight a jealous Wilford asked her where she had been. She replied, 'To the park.'[3] A violent quarrel took place in which Wilford seized a knife and cut his wife's throat with such force that he almost severed her head. He ran from their room in a distressed state, confessing to a fellow lodger that he had taken the life of his new bride: 'I have murdered my poor wife,' he cried, 'whom I loved as dearly as my own life.' He was led to the landlord, John Underhill, and again confessed to the slaughter. Underhill would give evidence at Wilford's trial describing the killer standing at the foot of his bed: 'I saw the blood run off his arm to his breeches; he was bloody as high as his elbow.'[4]

Wilford was charged with murder and appeared at the Old Bailey. He pleaded guilty, but the court refused to accept his plea and his case was put aside. When he appeared again he re-affirmed

---

3   *The Newgate Calendar* (1752)
4   *Old Bailey Online*, 25 June 1752

his guilt, but was prevailed upon to elect trial by jury. The trial, which lasted less than a day, ended with the expected verdict of guilty as charged. In sentencing Wilford to be hanged, the judge added, '... after which your body is to be publically dissected and anatomised, agreeable to an act of Parliament in that case made and provided'.

6. OUCH! THAT HURTS (1782)

The last man in British criminal history to suffer the most bestial of executions – being hanged, drawn and quartered – was David Tyrie in 1782. Tyrie worked in the Royal Naval office in Portsmouth as a clerk; the Scotsman was arrested and accused of treason for passing intelligence regarding the state of the Royal Navy to the French. He stood trial at Winchester Assizes on 10 August 1782. The *Scots Magazine* of August 1782 recorded that 'the indictment was laid for giving intelligence to the enemy of the fitting, failing and destination of His Majesty's ships and fleet, and for hiring William James to convey the said information to the French King and his subjects'.

Tyrie had been found in possession of over fifty documents that he had copied from the naval office, some on his person and some at his address. The documents contained details of the stores aboard ships at Woolwich, the state of the national debt and a list of the ships in commission at the Portsmouth Royal Naval Dockyard. William James gave evidence of Tyrie requesting him to deliver the said documents to the French via Cherbourg. A naval colleague of Tyrie, James Mayelstone, who had served an apprenticeship with the defendant in Leith, Scotland, gave evidence to the court that Tyrie, during the previous November 1781, had gained employment for him (Mayelstone) to buy livestock for the

East India ships at Portsmouth; the evening before he set out Tyrie asked him to send an account of all ships of war that came in or went out and what convoys sailed and arrived. When Mayelstone expressed surprise at the request, Tyrie told him that he did not send any such advices he received forward without the relevant ministry seeing them. Mayelstone was suspicious of Tyrie's unusual request, and although he did send some reports on some insignificant ship movements he decided against sending information on Admiral George Rodney's fleet (the fleet would go on to defeat the French fleet in the Battle of Saintes in April 1782 during the American Revolutionary War).

The jury took only a few minutes to convict David Tyrie of treason. The trial judge pronounced the dreadful sentence: 'That you David Tyrie are to be led to gaol, and from thence are to be drawn upon a hurdle to the place of execution and there be hanged by the neck; and being alive, are to be cut down, and your bowels being cut out and burned, and your head to be cut off, and your body to be divided into four quarters; your head and quarters to be disposed of as his Majesty shall think fit.' The sentence was carried out in front of an estimated crowd of 10,000 on Southsea Common on 24 August 1782. Following his dreadful death Tyrie's corpse was placed into a coffin and buried under the pebbles, but some reports state that as soon as the officials had left, sailors dug up the traitor's coffin, removed the body and cut it into many pieces which they kept as souvenirs. Several other felons were sentenced to the same fate after Tyrie, including four of the Cato Street conspirators, who planned to murder the British cabinet ministers and Prime Minister Lord Liverpool in 1820; however, in each subsequent case this barbaric sentence was commuted to merely being hanged and posthumously beheaded; this more 'civilised' form of execution formally replaced hanging, drawing and quartering in 1814.

7. YOU PUT YOUR FOOT IN IT (1787)

Following the brutal murder of nineteen-year-old Elizabeth Hughan in Kirkcudbright, Scotland, in 1787 a smart piece of detective work – one of the first recorded examples of a recognisable crime scene examination – led to the identification and conviction of her killer.

William Richardson had cut the throat of his secret lover Elizabeth, who was pregnant at the time. Doctors had examined Elizabeth's corpse and concluded the fatal wound had been inflicted by a left-handed man due to the cut traversing the neck from right to left. Footprints were found leading from the murder scene across a local bog; the distance between each footprint led investigators to believe the killer had run from the scene and slipped over in his haste to escape undetected, so was likely to be covered in mud. Plaster-cast impressions were made of the footprints, revealing the assailant's footwear had been shod with iron nails; there were also unique wear-and-tear marks to the soles that rendered them identifiable. All investigators had to do was find a left-handed male, perhaps covered in mud, with boots that compared favourably with footmarks lifted from the scene. Later, a local constable had the astuteness to examine the shoe casts from the scene and compare them with the footwear of all those men who attended the funeral; William Richardson's shoe fitted perfectly, including the distinct wear-and-tear marks. He was also left-handed. However, he had a solid alibi for the estimated time of the murder, corroborated by his peers.

Further questioning of witnesses revealed that, in fact, Richardson had left the company of those who gave him an alibi on the day of the murder. He had left to visit the blacksmith, and they recalled him being absent for some considerable amount of time; on returning, his clothes were muddied and he displayed a deep scratch to his cheek. Richardson's relationship with the dead girl soon came to the fore. His house was searched and his dirty stockings, which he hadn't had the sense to discard, were discovered; the sand on them could only be found locally in the bog near to the victim's cottage, which the killer had waded through to make good his escape. Richardson confessed to his crime and was executed on 30 June 1787.

8. WHO WOULD BE A WOMAN? (1788)

Burning at the stake was reserved for the fairer sex as an alternative to being hanged, drawn and quartered until it was abolished as a method of execution by the Treason Act of 1790. The last female to be officially burnt at the stake was Catherine Murphy, convicted with her husband at the Old Bailey on 18 September 1788 for the offence of coining – counterfeiting coins of the realm or shaving the edges off genuine coins to melt down and produce more coins. They were sentenced to death. The sentence was carried out on the morning of 8 March 1789 at Newgate Prison. Catherine's husband was hanged with seven other condemned men guilty of differing offences; however, because of her sex, the law directed Catherine be burnt at the stake.

Her punishment was to be the last of the day. Catherine was escorted from her cell past her husband, who was still dangling at the end of a rope, and on to a platform in front of the stake to which she was secured with rope and an iron ring. The Sheriff of London, Sir Benjamin Hammett, watched the procedure with utter abhorrence; he ordered the executioner, William Brunskill, to strangle Catherine Murphy before he lit the fire. A noose was duly placed around her neck and the platform on which she stood removed; she was left to hang for thirty minutes before Brunskill lit the flames, engulfing her body in fire. Sir Benjamin Hammett's criticisms of this barbarous form of punishment were the driving force behind its abolition the following year.

9. FORGET JUSTICE, LET'S HAVE A FIGHT (1817)

In the year 1817, Erdington was a small village 5 miles east of Birmingham in the county of Warwickshire, bordering the larger town of Sutton Coldfield. On the evening of 26 May 1817, Mary Ashford, a twenty-year-old housekeeper who lived with her uncle in Langley Heath, went with best friend Hannah Cox to a local dance at the Three Tuns public house – better known locally as the Tyburn House – situated in the nearby district of Tyburn, 2 miles from Erdington.

Mary had left work earlier in the day to go into Birmingham; she had with her clothes for the evening which she later changed into at Hannah Cox's house. The dance was truly a local affair, the attendees mainly farm girls and labourers, although one young man stood out from the crowd – Abraham Thornton, the twenty-four-year-old son of a well-to-do builder from Castle Bromwich.

Thornton was a confident, if somewhat arrogant, sexually experienced man who, when informed of Mary's surname, purportedly commented, 'I have been intimate with her sister three times and will with her or I'll die for it.' Mary was smitten with Thornton, and they danced together for most of the night. Neither Hannah nor Mary had intended to stay late, and by 11 p.m. Hannah was getting concerned – Mary seemed to be enjoying herself too much, and was reluctant to leave when Hannah drew her attention to the time. They agreed that Hannah would wait for her outside by the canal bridge. Hannah met up with neighbour Benjamin Carter, who had kindly agreed to see her home. Sometime later Cox asked Carter to go back into the dance and bring Mary out, as it was now getting very late. Carter obliged but returned without Mary, stating that she would be out very soon; a few minutes later she emerged with Thornton.

All four headed along the Chester Road toward Erdington – Mary and Thornton led the way, followed a few paces behind by Hannah and Carter. As they neared Hannah's house, Carter left and returned to the dance. Hannah continued home after Mary assured her she was fine and would stay at her grandfather's house, leaving her and Thornton to continue towards Erdington. Cox was woken at 4 a.m. by Mary pleading that she be allowed to get changed into her working clothes, which she had left there the previous evening, as she had to get home to her uncle's house before he woke and left for work. She told Cox that she had spent the last few hours at her grandfather's after leaving Thornton, who had gone home. Mary left in a hurry with her party clothes in a bag; she was seen by several men who knew her from the local area. She was last seen alive by a fellow party-goer returning from the same dance in Tyburn at 4.30 a.m. He commented that she was walking very swiftly along Bell Lane.

As the early summer sun rose, gun-barrel borer George Jackson was walking from Birmingham to Erdington seeking work. Just after 6 a.m. he crossed the stile out of Bell Lane heading towards Penns Mill Lane, where he spotted what appeared from a distance to be discarded clothing near to a water-filled pit; a closer examination revealed a woman's white bonnet and a pair of white shoes. His concerns increased when he saw that one of the shoes had bloodstains on it. He looked around for any sign of another, possibly injured, person, but, finding no sign, and unfamiliar with the location, he left the scene to raise the alarm. Within minutes he met a local man called Mr Lavell. Jackson relayed what he had seen and both returned to the pit; Jackson found, upon searching, more blood between the pit and the nearby lane. Further assistance arrived and they were joined by labourer William Simmons, who fetched a rake and some reins; he dredged the pit with this makeshift dredging implement and on the third occasion pulled to the surface the body of a young woman whom he and Lavell recognised as Mary Ashford. A search of the local area commenced for any evidence that could shed light on the circumstances surrounding her death.

Mr Lavell and a colleague, Mr Bird (both worked at a local factory), entered a recently ploughed field nearby and discovered two sets of footprints in the soil – one a man's, one a woman's. Lavell and Bird concluded from the pattern of the footprints that the male had been chasing the woman as the prints frequently crossed over each other; they then discovered the male footprints trailing away from the pit in a different direction. On returning to the pit Lavell made a further discovery – a male footprint turned sideways and embedded in the soil much deeper, as if casting something heavy into the pit. A much larger pool of blood was discovered roughly 40 yards from the pit under a tree, where the outline of a human body could clearly be seen in the dewy grass.

Many of the men present were aware that Mary Ashford attended the dance the previous evening; Daniel Clarke, the landlord of the Tyburn House, was summoned and he recalled that she left the dance in the company of Abraham Thornton. Clarke rode out towards Castle Bromwich to find Thornton and came across him on the roadside; he questioned him about Mary and told him she had been murdered. Thornton admitted that he had been with her until 4 a.m., but denied killing her. Thornton was detained at the Tyburn House until the arrival of assistant constable Thomas Dales from Birmingham. Dales arrived at the Tyburn House mid-morning, and although given instructions by local magistrate Mr Bedford, who had summoned him, to await his arrival before speaking to the suspect, Dales disregarded this request and with little knowledge of what had taken place proceeded to interview Thornton. Rather amateurishly, he failed to record the crucial answers in reply to his questions; this would result in him being severely criticised at the later court trial.

In the meantime, Bedford had been very busy at the scene of the crime, securing evidence and interviewing Hannah Cox at her home before arriving at the Tyburn House at midday. Bedford had Thornton brought before him and proceeded to examine the suspect, recording the explanation proffered by Thornton. The prisoner told Bedford that after Hannah Cox left them they had walked together, crossing a stile and wandering across several fields before ending back at the stile. Thornton declared they were seen and spoken to by a male passer-by who wished them a good morning.

A short while later they started to walk towards Erdington; he knew Mary wished to return home, and while she did so he waited for her on the village green until 4 a.m. When she didn't return, he left to make his way home to Castle Bromwich, arriving about 4.40 a.m. During his walk home he met several local male acquaintances. Thornton signed the statement and was taken to a different room and searched thoroughly by Constable Dales on the instructions of Bedford. Dales asked Thornton to strip off his clothes, and noticed bloodstains on his underclothes. When questioned about presence of blood Thornton immediately confessed to Dales and then in turn to Bedford that he had been 'concerned' with Mary – a virgin – but the sexual act had been consensual and he knew nothing of her death.

An initial medical examination of the victim revealed two lacerations to her groin, believed to have been inflicted during sexual intercourse against her will. A full post-mortem examination two days later by Birmingham surgeon Mr Freer revealed that the stomach contained approximately half a pint of fluid mixed with duckweed, and therefore concluded Mary Ashford had been thrown into the pit semi-conscious and then drowned. Freer was also satisfied that the victim had been a virgin prior to her attack and that the lacerations were indeed caused during a violent sexual encounter. The inquest into the death of Mary Ashford took place at Penns Mill on 30th May 1817. Several witnesses were summoned to give their evidence substantiating Thornton as the last person to be seen in the company of the deceased. The inquest jury returned a verdict of 'Wilful Murder' and Abraham Thornton was committed in custody to stand trial at the next assizes.

The trial date was set for 8 August 1817 at the County Hall, Warwick. The public interest was immense, the whole area around the hall being swamped with onlookers hoping to claim a space in the public gallery. Local opinion weighed heavily against the defendant; pamphlets circulated around the county virtually convicting Abraham Thornton of the murder of Mary Ashford before a word of evidence had been uttered. The defence team were extremely concerned about the impartiality of any local jury, but a jury was nonetheless empanelled and the trial started at 8 a.m., presided over by Mr Justice Holroyd. *The Times* of 11 August 1817 describes the scramble to secure a place when the doors were opened as 'tremendous, the court being crowded to excess throughout the day'. Ladies were excluded – the evidence that was to be presented during the trial was deemed unfit for a lady's ear. The paper goes on to paint a detailed picture of the defendant, Abraham Thornton: 'The prisoner was short of stature, about five feet seven inches in height and of so stout a build that his corpulence amounted almost to a deformity. His limbs seemed well proportioned, but his face, which surmounted a short thick neck, appeared swollen and shining … He was well-dressed in a long black coat, yellow waistcoat, coloured breeches and stockings and remained unmoved during the whole of the trial.' Thornton pleaded not guilty to the two charges contained on the indictment: the wilful murder and rape of Mary Ashford.

The prosecution believed they had a strong circumstantial case that, when knitted together, pointed to an irresistible conclusion of guilt. The condition of his clothes, his admission to having sex with the victim and that his shoes fitted the footprints left at the scene were all cited as absolute proof of Thornton's guilt. The prosecution alleged that, having had his sexual advances rebuffed by the deceased, Thornton lay in wait for her to return along the path and that on seeing him she attempted to escape but he caught her, raped her and threw her into the pit in a semi-conscious state before abandoning her to drown. The prosecution called their witnesses; among the first were Lavell and Bird, who had discovered the footprints to which they matched the defendant's shoes. Under cross-examination they had to admit that the impressions may well have been affected by a heavy burst of rain on the morning in question. The defence established a solid alibi for Thornton, introducing evidence that he was seen by a milkman 2½ miles away at 4.30 a.m. and at 4.50 a.m. by gamekeeper John Heydon at his father's home in Castle Bromwich. The defence suggested to the jury that logistically, due to the sightings, for Thornton to have been able to commit the offences charged he would have had to chase and catch Mary, rape her and then carry her to the pit before walking the 3 miles to his Castle Bromwich home all in just eleven minutes.

Mr Justice Holroyd summed up the case, following ten hours of uninterrupted evidence, with what can only be described as 'a leaning toward the defendant'. Holroyd was at the time an inexperienced judge – indeed this was his most important trial to date. During his two-hour summation he urged the jury not to be prejudiced by the defendant's reprehensible behaviour toward the victim; they were there to determine if he raped and murdered her. He highlighted the fact Thornton had never tried to pretend that he had not been with Ashford that morning, freely admitting that they had consensual sex and that he had remained in her company until 4 a.m. when she returned to her uncle's house. His Lordship urged the jury to consider if they believed the offence of murder had been committed before or after Thornton had left the victim, emphasising the point that it would not be possible for him to commit the alleged offences and have time to get to Castle Bromwich and be seen by Heydon at 4.50 a.m. The judge concluded with a biased and damning statement that it was better a murderer go free than an innocent man be convicted. The jury sat in the courtroom discussing the case for only six minutes before returning a verdict of not guilty.

Locally the verdict was met with disbelief and anger; the people of Erdington had made up their minds that Mary Ashford was murdered and Thornton was the killer. Accusations circulated, mainly by the press, that witnesses for the defendant had been bribed and the jury and judge hoodwinked by perjured evidence. Newspapers, in particular the *Lichfield Mercury* and the London based *Independent Whig*, spurred on by their readership, published letters and comments against Thornton and his family. A campaign was waged by local and national papers to raise funds to appeal the acquittal. As the law stood in 1817, a defendant acquitted by a jury could, in some circumstances, be charged under a process of 'appeal of murder' with the same offence for a second time. In the case of unlawful killing it was open to the heir-in-law of the deceased to lodge an appeal of murder within a year and a day of the completion of the felony by death. The plea of *autre fois acquit* (in which the defendant claims to have been previously tried and acquitted for the same offence) was no bar to such an appeal.

Mr Bedford was the main instigator behind what *The Times* (25 August 1817) described as a group of 'independent gentlemen in the neighbourhood of Sutton Coldfield' who would before long dispel the 'oppressive cloud on the unappeased sense of public justice'.

Mary Ashford's heir-in-law was her elder brother, twenty-two-year-old labourer William Ashford; although illiterate and timid, he was deeply affected by his sibling's murder and willing to have the appeal launched in his name. There was a concern that Thornton – whether due to the abuse and intimidation he was receiving or, indeed, having heard the rumours that an appeal was to be launched – may well leave the country and travel to America. A writ of appeal was issued on 1 October 1817 and Thornton was arrested on the evening of 9 October and incarcerated in Warwick jail.

Thornton would stand trial for the second time on 6 November; the case would be heard in the Court of the King's Bench in Westminster Hall, London. Thornton was transferred to London and placed in the custody of Marshalsea Prison. Thornton faced an indictment that read, 'For that he did feloniously and of malice aforethought cast, throw and push Mary Ashford into a pit of water, situated in the Parish of Sutton Coldfield, wherein the said Mary Ashford was choked, suffocated and drowned and then and there did instantly die.' Following the arraignment Thornton's barrister, Mr Reader, rose to his feet asking for an adjournment as he had only recently been given the brief and needed time to take instructions from his client on what was an extremely rare case. The case was adjourned until 17 November. Reader had in mind a piece of English legislation unused since the reign of Charles I.

Thornton was to be advised by his counsel to exercise his right to 'wage battel'. This was a legitimate form of defence in appeals to murder by way of resorting to arms between the appellant (William Ashford) and the defendant (Thornton). There were exceptional circumstances that deprived the defendant of such a privilege – if the appellant were a peer of the realm, a priest, a citizen of the City of London, a female, an infant, blind or lame. Ashford, although weak of character, did not fall into any of these exemptions.

Should the challenge be issued, then, a judicial combat must ensue in lists 60 feet square. Should Thornton be defeated in the contest, he would be hanged immediately; however, if he were the victor he would be acquitted.

On hearing of Reader's intentions, Mr Bedford, now acting as William Ashford's solicitor, was troubled; he wrote a note to his clerk expressing his concerns:

> I am sorry to say that difficulties have been started likely to occasion much trouble and perhaps ultimate defeat. It seems the Appellee has the option of waging battle and of challenging the Appellor in single combat which if not accepted by the Appellor the suit is lost and, if accepted, and the Appellee can hold out from sunrise to sunset then he wins the contest and claims his discharge, otherwise his election subjects him not only to a good threshing but also the pain of death into the bargain. It is rumoured here that is the plea intended to be set up by the Def[endant] and unless we can devise any means by argument to induce the court not to allow it I am very apprehensive our poor little Knight [William Ashford] will never be able to contend the Battle with his brutish opponent.

The court re-adjourned on the morning of 17 November 1817. Westminster Hall was a throng of people pushing and shoving in an attempt to see Thornton and Ashford. The indictment was re-read and Thornton asked for his plea; he responded, 'Not guilty and I am ready to defend the same with my body.' Thornton was handed a pair of leather gauntlets by Reader, one of which he pulled on, the other he threw theatrically to the floor in the direction of William Ashford, inviting him to pick it up and thus accept the challenge – William declined. Ashford's counsel, Nathaniel Clarke, stood to his feet and argued that Thornton should not be able to compound the murder of his client's sister with an attempt to murder the brother. Lord Ellenborough simply pointed out that 'it is the law of England Mr Clarke; we must not call it murder'. Clarke turned his attention to his client's youth and lack of strength as a reason why he should not face the older, stronger Thornton. Reader stood on behalf of

Thornton and argued that this was not sufficient a reason to decline the trail by battle and that he had advised Thornton that this, after all the 'extraordinary and unprecedented prejudice' against him was the only way he could receive a fair trial. The case was adjourned until 22 November for legal arguments, following which Lord Ellenborough delivered his ruling:

> The general law of the land is in favour of the wager of battle, and it is our duty to pronounce that law as it is, and not as we may wish it to be. Whatever prejudices may exist therefore against this mode of trial, still as it is the law of the land, the court must pronounce judgement for it.

William Ashford's counsel declared to the court that his client would not take part in the battle and that he would not object to Thornton's full dismissal on the charge he faced as long as no action would be taken against his client; this was agreed and Abraham Thornton was released from custody. In June 1819 Lord Eldon, the Lord Chancellor, introduced a bill unanimously passed by Parliament abolishing the right to private appeals following acquittals and the right to trial by battle. Thornton emigrated to the United States and worked as a bricklayer; he died in the early 1860s.

The village of Erdington featured in another landmark case in December 2016 when former lorry driver Ralph Clarke was convicted at Birmingham Crown Court of twenty-one historic sex offences against children between 1974 and 1983. When found guilty, he became the oldest man, at the age of 101, to be convicted by a jury in this country.

10. TRIAL BY MEDIA (1823)

The trial of John Thurtell and Joseph Hunt was the first British trial to be covered extensively by the media, leading to clashes between newspaper editors and the judiciary, with the possibility of the defendants not receiving a fair trial as a result.

This whole case revolved around the seedy world of illicit gambling and prize fighting; link this environment with murder and you have a story that journalists turned into an unprecedented public frenzy. The main protagonist was a son of the Mayor of Norwich, a former Royal Marine officer, prize-fighting amateur boxer, sports promoter and serious gambler called John Thurtell. Thurtell had a major disagreement with solicitor William Weare, whom he accused of cheating him out of a large sum of money during a card game. Thurtell was not going to let the debt pass as a matter of principle, and set about planning Weare's murder. He invited Weare up to Hertfordshire on the pretence of spending the weekend gambling with other acquaintances.

The destination was a cottage owned by a gambling associate named William Probert in Radlett, Hertfordshire. Thurtell and Weare travelled up from London together on the night of 24 October 1823 in Thurtell's horse-drawn gig. As they neared Radlett, Thurtell confronted Weare about his behaviour in the recent card game and pulled out one of a pair of loaded single-shot muskets, firing at Weare's head; the bullet glanced off Weare's cheek. The injured and very frightened Weare managed to escape from the gig and literally ran for his life. Thurtell chased and caught him. Weare pleaded for his life, promising to pay the money back to him, but Thurtell slid a knife from his pocket and slit Weare's throat, placing the body in a sack and completing the journey to Probert's cottage. Probert and an actor friend called Joseph Hunt assisted Thurtell, firstly to strip the body of any valuables (Thurtell made a gift of Weare's gold chain to Probert's wife), including the victim's clothes, before dumping the unfortunate William Weare's body in the lake adjoining the cottage. They then changed their minds and transported the corpse overnight to another lake in Elstree, a few miles away. However. Thurtell's meticulous planning was let down when he carelessly discarded the murder weapons – the bloody knife and the pistol – near to Probert's cottage; these items were found by a labourer, who reported his find to the local authorities.

Probert was questioned about the weapons and soon panicked, implicating Hunt, who in turn blamed Thurtell before leading them to the Elstree where they recovered the body of William Weare from the lake. Thurtell was quickly tracked down and arrested in possession of the matching pistol. The media furore soon started, dubbing the murder – depending on which paper you read – the 'Radlett Murder' or 'Elstree Murder', together with the witty verse:

> They cut his throat from ear to ear,
> His head they battered in.
> His name was Mr William Weare,
> He lived in Lyons Inn.

All three men were placed on trial for the murder of William Weare at the Hertford Assizes in January 1824. Although it appears to have been Joseph Hunt who gave most assistance to the authorities, it was Probert who was offered the chance to 'turn King's Evidence' and became a prosecution witness. It was the first duty of the jury, on the direction of the trial judge Mr Justice Park, to find Probert 'not guilty'. Probert turned to the court and bowed before being let out of the dock.

The barrister for the prosecution, Mr Gurney, stood and addressed the jury about the delay in the trial due largely to the interference of the press: 'I trust you are now assembled in that calm and temperate state of mind which will enable you to administer fair and impartial justice.'[5] Detailed facts of the case were presented to the jury before Thurtell, who was legally unrepresented, stood to give his side of the story in his defence. He blamed both Probert and Hunt, followed by the media circus; he referred to previous cases where the lives of the innocent had been sacrificed to cases based on circumstantial evidence. He finished up by appealing to the jury through a flood of tears: 'Gentlemen of the jury – my existence is in your hands. If there

---

5   *Lancaster Gazette*, 10 January 1824

be a doubt give me the benefit of it. Cut me not off in the summer of my days. Render not the once happy bosom of my father desolate. If there be one among you who thinks me capable of the crime, I say to him, in the words of the apostle, "I would to God you were in all things such as I am, save these bonds." Gentlemen of the jury remember these my last words – I am innocent of this crime, so help me God.'

Joseph Hunt, also unrepresented, was unable to utter his defence due to the anxiety of facing the gallows and submitted a written statement to the court in which he stated he had been induced to make his confession on the pretence that he may turn king's evidence. He had not been present when the crime was committed and knew nothing of any premeditated plan to murder the deceased. He admitted to the concealment of the body but in no other respect had he been guilty. He accused Probert of inventing falsehoods to save his own life.

The judge summed up the case, during which he made known his contempt for the reporting in the newspapers when he commented, 'If these statements of evidence before trial which corrupt the purity of the administration of justice in its source are not checked, I tremble for the fate of our country.' The jury returned guilty verdicts against both men. John Thurtell was sentenced to death; Joseph Hunt, in view of the cooperation he had given in the recovery of the body and the identification of Thurtell, was sentenced to transportation to Australia. He was sent to Botany Bay, settling in the country after his sentence lapsed; he married and started a family, winning the respect of his peers, who made him a police constable. He died in 1861. Probert became a social outcast, having turned against his criminal associates and suspected of being the main source of the media's information. He couldn't find a job to support his family so reverted to crime, and was executed the following year for stealing a horse.

John Thurtell's execution took place on 9 January 1824. Having previously denied the commission of the crime of which he was accused, he admitted his guilt just before he was hanged. After his body had hung for one hour it was taken down and the corpse handed over to the medical profession for dissection. William Weare was buried in the grounds of St Nicholas parish church in Elstree.

II. JUSTICE – BUT NOT FOR YOU, OFFICER! (1830)

The newly formed Metropolitan Police Force of 1829 was not popular with the people of London – many thought they were just spies or agents of the government in uniform, and not to be trusted. Two very early cases in the Met's history underline the lack of acceptance and tolerance of a force established to protect London's population.

The first recognised police constable to be murdered (although the forerunners of the police force, the Bow Street Runners and the Marine Police, also suffered fatalities in the execution of their duties) was PC 169 'S' Division Joseph Grantham, who was killed on 29 June 1830. A married man with twins born to his wife the day before his death, he had only joined the force six months previously. PC Grantham was on patrol in the Somers Town district of London (near to Euston station) when he intervened in a drunken argument between two Irish bricklayers, one of whom had severely beaten his wife. They took exception to the interference of PC Grantham and one of the men, bricklayer Michael Duggan, turned and viciously assaulted the officer; the *Morning Post* of 29 June 1830 describes the events under the headline 'Cruel Murder of a Police Constable in the Execution of his Duty'.

> Last evening between seven and eight o'clock Joseph Grantham a police constable No. 196 letter S Division was savagely murdered in the execution of his duty whilst endeavouring to quell a di[s]turbance in Thornley Place, Skinner Street, Somers Town, occasioned by a fight between two Irish bricklayers. The fight continued for some time until one of the neighbours called for the assistance of the police. PC Grantham, on whose beat it was, came up and endeavoured to part the combatants; but he had no sooner attempted to interfere than [Michael] Duggan the most furious of the combatants knocked him down with a blow from his fist. His head coming into contact with a large paving stone, he was stunned and whilst in that state Duggan, who was

perfectly outrageous, kicked him in the groin and the left side several times with great violence.

PC Grantham died a few minutes later. A coroner's inquest heard the evidence relating to the young constable's death, and following testimonies from two doctors that Grantham had died of apoplexy (a stroke), the jury returned a verdict: they exonerated Michael Duggan. They came to the conclusion that PC Grantham had brought about his own demise 'by over-exertion in the discharge of his duty'. Duggan could not now be charged with murder, and instead faced a charge of assault against the deceased officer and PC Bennett, who had come to his assistance. Duggan appeared in front of the Middlesex Sessions on 10 July 1830 and was found guilty of assault and sentenced to six months imprisonment.

***

The National Union of the Working Classes was frustrated with the limitations of the Reform Act of 1832. A public protest was organised by the union's secretary, John Russell. The protest was to take place on the Calthorpe Estate, Cold Bath Fields, Clerkenwell, London at 2 p.m. on 13 May 1833. The event was extensively advertised via posters and placards. However, Home Secretary Lord Melbourne had issued an order declaring the meeting illegal and instructed the newly formed Metropolitan Police, backed up by the 1st Regiment of the Life Guards, to quell any demonstrations. This was new territory for the Metropolitan Police – a public order situation on a scale never before handled by police, with little or no guidance as far as the legality of the Home Secretary's order and little in the way of leadership. Some 300 people congregated at the meeting site, met by a large detachment of uniformed police officers with instructions from their senior officers to show restraint. It wasn't long before a palpable tension grew between the two sides; the crowd started to shout abuse and threw rocks and stones at the police lines. No risk assessments or strategic public order plans existed at this time; the officers would claim they reacted in self-defence, but the crowd and the media present described the officers' behaviour as overbearing and aggressive. One reporter for *The Times* wrote,

The police furiously attacked the multitude with their staves, felling every person indiscriminately before them; even the females did not escape the blows from their batons – men and boys were lying in every direction weltering in their blood and calling for mercy.

It is quite probable that both sides were guilty of acts of violence toward each other. Three officers were badly injured during this period, one fatally; at no time during the subsequent judicial hearings was any evidence of wrongdoing presented to any court about the conduct of these particular officers.

PC Robert Culley, a policeman for a little over three years, became detached from his colleagues during the maelstrom of bricks and rocks and found himself alone among the hostile crowd in Calthorpe Street heading toward Gough Street. Culley's colleagues reported seeing him holding bloodied hands to his chest: 'I am stabbed, I am done' were his last words. PC Culley, with assistance from other officers, managed to struggle to the Calthorpe Arms public house on Gray's Inn Road before collapsing and dying from his injuries. The inquest into the officer's death opened in the very same pub, with the body of the deceased officer still on the premises for the jury to examine if they wished.

The jury seemed to have made up their minds before the inquest commenced and were overtly hostile to the police. The coroner, to his credit, attempted to complete the due process of the law, but was hindered by the antagonistic jury, who decided that as there was no proof that the Riot Act had ever been read, the police action was unlawful and indeed an illegal assault on the crowd. Their verdict of 'justifiable homicide' in relation to the murder of PC Culley was strongly opposed by the coroner, but at the jury members' insistence was recorded with an added rider that described the police actions on the day as 'ferocious, brutal and unprovoked'. The verdict was overturned by the Court of the King's Bench, but no finding of wilful murder was ever recorded. PC Culley was buried in St Anne's Church, Soho, in the presence of his pregnant wife and a 300-strong jeering mob.

Following the verdict, members of the inquest jury were treated with celebrity status. One anonymous donor had a number of pewter medallions struck to commemorate their momentous decision; they were delivered to Samuel Stockton, the jury foreman, to hand out to the other jury members. On one side it recorded the name of the individual with the inscription 'We shall be recompensed, the resurrection of the just', and the reverse side was inscribed: 'In honour of the men who nobly withstood the dictation of the coroner; independent and conscientious in the discharge of their duty, they promoted a continued reliance upon the laws under the protection of a British jury.'

Two further officers received stab wounds during the disturbances: Constable John Redwood and Sergeant John Brooks, a military man who served twenty-five years with the 1st Grenadier Guards and fought at the Battle of Waterloo. The offender was a man called George Fursey, who stood trial at the Old Bailey on 8 July 1833. At the same time that PC Culley was being stabbed and ultimately murdered, Sergeant Brooks attempted to prevent poles and banners from being used by members of the crowd as offensive weapons. He grabbed one flag, reportedly of the United States, which was being waved around by George Fursey. Fursey pulled out a knife and stabbed Brookes in the chest – fortunately the blade struck a rib, deflecting it away from the heart and saving his life. Brooks fell backwards into his colleague, PC John Redwood. Redwood attempted to wrestle the flag from Fursey, probably unaware of the severity of the assault on Brookes; he too was stabbed by Fursey, taking a wound to the forearm. Redwood responded by striking Fursey with his baton several times before dragging him back behind police lines to be detained by his colleagues. Fursey was charged with the malicious wounding of Sergeant Brookes and PC Redwood; even though overwhelming evidence was produced by the Crown, including the evidence of the injured officers, Fursey was found not guilty and carried shoulder-high from the court by his supporters.

***

The first conviction for the murder of a police officer was that of PC John Long, stabbed to death six weeks after the murder of PC Joseph Grantham. Just after midnight on 16 August 1830, PC John Long noticed three men acting suspiciously in the vicinity of Gray's Inn Road, King's Cross. Believing them to be burglars surveying properties to break into, the thirty-six-year-old officer approached them and asked, 'What have you been after?' The officer was surrounded by the suspected offenders; one stabbed him with a long, pointed shoemaker's knife; the blade, delivered with such force it broke off inside the officer's body, slid through his ribs and into his heart. Several witnesses came forward naming the killer as William Sapwell.

One of these witnesses had spoken to PC Long several minutes before he was fatally injured; she was Mary Ann Griffiths, a local prostitute who remembered the kindness shown to her by the constable, who had given her a penny. She knew Sapwell as a man who had run a local brothel in which she had previously plied her trade. After her conversation with PC Long she was entertaining a client in a local pub when she saw Sapwell run past at the relevant time. Another witness, who saw the attack, chased down Sapwell – importantly, he never lost sight of him – shouting out, 'Stop, thief, murderer!' His cries drew the attention of a watchman, who grabbed Sapwell and detained him.

Sapwell protested that he had spent the evening in the Bedford Tea Gardens in Camden Town until 11 p.m. playing skittles: 'I then walked home and saw a man (referring to PC Long) in pursuit of three others in Gray's Inn Road, but I wasn't involved in the chase or the stabbing.' Sapwell's defence team could not produce any witnesses to back up his alibi, and he was found guilty of the murder of PC Long and sentenced to hang on 20 September 1830. He maintained his innocence until the very end, claiming that when he met his maker he would be asked what crime he had committed, and on hearing his answer God would shake his head and say, 'They sent you wrongfully.'

There was no facility in the police force of the 1830s for pensions, or compensating the families of police officers killed in the execution of their duties; often it would be down to the generosity of the public, and, as alluded to, the police of the day were not exactly popular. PC Robert Culley's wife was awarded £200 (a substantial amount of money at the time), an unprecedented award by a shamed government of the day. In today's society we often hear the minority shouting louder than the silent majority, particularly when the police get it wrong – as they sometimes do. But policing in this country has always been with the consent of the British people, and will hopefully always be so. Much of nineteenth-century British society, together with its government, was waking up to the fact that a police force was needed to protect the public and people's property, and the public was willing to back it, as demonstrated in an article and letter published in the *London Courier and Evening Gazette* of 25 August 1830:

> We have great pleasure in announcing that the government have ordered an allowance of 10s. per week to be paid in support of the widow and children of Long the police constable who was murdered in the performance of his police duty. Several private donations towards the same benevolent object have been received. The following letter appears in the *Morning Herald* of this day:
>
> MR. EDITOR – Your Journal of yesterday contains a long list of subscriptions for the benefit of widows and orphans of *foreigners*, who fell in their own countries, fighting for *their national rights*. It contains likewise an affecting account of the funeral of the murdered police officer, who fell endeavouring to *prevent* crime. Now, Sir, this faithful servant of the public has left a distressed widow and five orphans, who need pecuniary assistance. I will therefore, through you, request my countrymen (who think with me) not to forget those of our own land, whose husbands or parents may fall in defending the persons or property of their neighbours, either in a civil or any other capacity. I request that you insert this letter, and to except the inclosed for the widow and five orphan children of the cruelly murdered Long.

12. THE M'NAGHTEN RULE (1843)

British history has only witnessed the assassination of one prime minister: Spencer Perceval, shot by John Bellingham in the lobby of the House of Commons in 1812. Another prime minister had a close shave just thirty-one years later. Sir Robert Peel, the founder of the Metropolitan Police, had often travelled with Queen Victoria in her carriage during her Scottish tour the preceding year, leaving his private secretary, Edward Drummond, to travel in the commissioner's official carriage. This led to Peel's would-be-assassin, Daniel M'Naghten, mistakenly identifying Drummond as his would-be target during his reconnaissance.

On the afternoon of 20 January 1843, M'Naghten made his move. Having travelled down to London, he waited at the Charing Cross end of Whitehall for his target to pass by; he did not realise that Prime Minister Robert Peel, whom he did not recognise, had walked past him thirty minutes before the arrival of the unfortunate Drummond. Edward Drummond was related to the Drummond banking dynasty, and had been visiting his brother at the family bank at No. 49 Charing Cross; he left to make his way back to Downing Street when M'Naghten broke cover and coldly shot him in the back. As he drew a second pistol from a breast pocket to finish the job he was tackled by PC James Silver and detained after a struggle in which the pistol discharged into the pavement but injured no one. The wounded Drummond was carried by passers-by back to Drummond's Bank. Richard Jackson, an apothecary and surgeon, attended and advised that the injured man be removed to his house in Grosvenor Square.

M'Naghten, in the meantime, was taken to a police station, having stated to the arresting officer that 'he or she, I cannot say which, shall not break my peace of mind any longer'. It was discovered M'Naghten had been a successful businessman, selling his woodturning business in 1840. He was a regular attendee at the Athenaeum Debating Society and the Glasgow Mechanics Institute and could speak fluent French; on his arrest he was found in possession of two £5 notes, £4 in gold and a deposit receipt from the Glasgow and Shipping bank for the sum of £750.

The killer was interviewed by the Commissioner of the Metropolitan Police, Richard Mayne, but little was forthcoming and he was charged with 'attempting to assassinate, by shooting at him with two loaded pistols, near Charing Cross, Mr Edward Drummond, the private secretary of Sir Robert Peel'.

Surgeons operating on Drummond initially discovered that the pistol ball had travelled around the body and lodged in the fleshy part of the thigh near the groin, missing all major organs – the ball was removed and the prognosis was good. The following day Drummond's condition deteriorated and surgeons discovered that the pistol ball had in fact shattered one of the lower ribs, causing increased inflammation and infection. They attempted to 'bleed' the patient by opening the temporal artery. Drummond's condition worsened, and he died of his injuries on 24 January 1843. The inquest was held in the Lion and Goat tavern in Grosvenor Street and a verdict of wilful murder returned.

M'Naghten appeared at Bow Street Magistrates' Court, now charged with murder, and was committed to stand trial at the Central Criminal Court, Old Bailey. It was during this committal hearing at the lower court that concerns which had previously simmered below the surface came to the fore when M'Naghten made a statement to the court in which he described how persecution by the Tories had driven him to this act: 'The Tories in my native city have compelled me to do this. They follow, persecute me wherever I go, and have entirely destroyed my peace of mind ... It can be proved by evidence.' Drummond's body was released to his family and buried in St Luke's Church graveyard in Charlton, south-east London – curiously enough, the very same graveyard as the assassinated Prime Minister Spencer Perceval.

M'Naghten's trial commenced at the Old Bailey on Friday 2 March 1843 in front of Chief Justice Tindal. The indictment for the murder of Edward Drummond was put to the defendant, and when asked for a plea to the charge he replied, 'I was driven to desperation by persecution – I am guilty of firing.' Because of the concerns over the mental state of the defendant, the case proceeded on the basis of a not guilty plea. M'Naghten's mental health was central to both the prosecution and defence cases, with both sides agreeing the defendant suffered from delusions of persecution. The Solicitor General, Sir William Follett, representing the Crown, argued that in spite of his 'partial insanity' he was responsible for his actions as he was capable of distinguishing right from wrong and was therefore guilty of murder. The defence barrister, Alexander Cockburn, opened his defence by underlining the difficulties in the practical application of the principle in English law that held an insane person exempt from legal responsibility and legal punishment; in other words, there was no satisfactory template, no set of guiding principles that a court could refer to in such cases of obvious mental instability.

The defence called several eminent psychiatrists who testified to the state of M'Naghten's mental health, concluding that the delusions of persecution had deprived him of 'all restraint over his actions'. Follett was unable to call upon any such credible witnesses to rebut the conclusions of the expert witnesses for the defence, and the trial was halted at this point. Chief Justice Tindal stressed to the jury that the medical evidence strongly supported the defence's argument. He informed the jury that should they find the defendant not guilty on the grounds of insanity he would still be detained but in an appropriate institution where he would receive proper care. The jury retired to consider their judgement before returning a verdict of not guilty of murder on the grounds of insanity.

The verdict caused a great public outcry – it appeared M'Naghten, who had admitted shooting the prime minister's private secretary, had simply walked away from the hangman's rope. Her Majesty Queen Victoria, a victim of several attempts on her own life, became involved in the case, writing to the prime minister expressing her concerns at the verdict and the precedent it set for the future. The House of Lords, under pressure to act, revived an ancient right to question the judges. They constructed five pertinent questions in relation to serious crimes committed by individuals suffering from mental illness. The answer to one of these questions, delivered by Chief Justice Tindal, would define the law on criminal responsibility for over a century. The result, dubbed the M'Naghten rule, decreed:

To establish a defence on the ground of insanity it must be clearly proved that, at the time of committing the act, the party accused was labouring under such a defect of reason from disease of the mind, as not to know the nature and quality of the act he was doing, or if he did know it, that he did not know that what he was doing was wrong.

Following his acquittal Daniel M'Naghten was incarcerated in the State Criminal Lunatic Asylum, Lambeth, south London (now the Imperial War Museum) for twenty-one years before being transferred to a new facility – Broadmoor – where he died on 3 May 1865.

13. FASTER THAN A SPEEDING TRAIN (1845)

A formidable quiz brain on ITV's *The Chase* was asked to name the first person arrested for murder in Great Britain as a result of telecommunications? 'Hawley Harvey Crippen,' he fired back confidently before his face crumpled into an expression of shock when informed the answer was incorrect.

The Crippen case did indeed create British criminal history, but it was not the first murder to come to justice under such circumstances; that dubious honour fell to Norfolk-born forger and murderer John Tawell, whose fate was sealed by the chief technical advance of the Victorian era: the electric telegraph.

John Tawell was born in the small south Norfolk village of Aldeby in 1783; his mother and father were shopkeepers. He left the family home in the late 1790s, travelling north to the Norfolk seaside town of Great Yarmouth where he gained employment as a shop assistant. It was here that he first discovered the Quaker faith – a path which would take him through life's highs and lows and ultimately contribute to his violent, premature death. In the early years of the nineteenth century, Tawell fuelled his business ambitions by travelling to London where he obtained a position with a Quaker drapery company before moving on to making furniture and then umbrellas.

John Tawell remained on the periphery of his faith, never fully committing until 1807 when he applied to become an official member of the movement, which was approved. Sadly this journey was to last only a year when he was disowned by the Quakers for marrying outside the order, having tied the knot with Mary Freeman at St James's Church of England church on London's Piccadilly. Tawell earnt his living as a commercial travelling salesman; he flitted from one company to another selling various products including medicines for a drug company – although a natural salesman, he became frustrated with a lack of opportunities to make his fortune and turned to crime; he was arrested and convicted for forgery when he attempted to pass counterfeit banknotes of the realm in 1814, a capital offence for which he received the death penalty, a sentence profoundly opposed by the Quaker bank he had attempted to deceive; following an appeal by the sect, his sentence was commuted to fourteen years' transportation to Australia.

Tawell's life in Australia was as eventful as in his home country. When he arrived in Sydney he told his captors that he was a 'druggist'; he was sent to work in the dispensary of a Sydney hospital, but couldn't keep his hands to himself and was caught stealing from the hospital's stores, which resulted in his incarceration in a penal settlement in Newcastle, New South Wales, for one year. On his release he buckled down and was joined by his wife Mary, who bore him two sons, William and John. By 1820, as a result of good behaviour, Tawell received a ticket-of-leave allowing him his freedom with a proviso that he was not to leave Australia. Shortly after being granted his partial freedom he opened Australia's first retail pharmacy and at last made his fortune. He remained in Australia until the end of his full sentence before returning to England with his family – now a very rich man.

Tawell returned to Australia and built the first Quaker meeting house in New South Wales (although still shunned by the movement);

he also invested vast amounts of money in the growing Australian infrastructure until he and his family finally returned to England for good in 1838, settling in a house on the periphery of Regent's Park. Tawell's life took yet another disastrous turn when Mary died of tuberculosis later the same year; the disease also claimed the lives of their two sons. During Mary's illness she was attended by a young nurse called Sarah Hart, with whom Tawell had an affair which produced two children by March 1841. He never married Hart but supported her and the two young children with a weekly allowance of £1, having moved them well out of London to a cottage in a small village called Salt Hill near Slough in Berkshire.

Tawell met his second wife, a widowed Quaker also called Sarah, whom he married in 1841. They set up home in Berkhampstead, where they had a son in 1843. The worldwide depression in the 1840s had a serious effect on Tawell's investments in Australia; while awaiting a sum of £700 from his business interests he was overdrawn at his bank, leaving him in deep financial difficulties. Tawell decided he was no longer able to support Sarah Hart and travelled by train from Paddington station to Slough, a journey he made at the beginning of each month to pay Sarah her maintenance. He completed the journey to the small cottage in Bath Place, Salt Hill, by foot on New Year's Day 1845. Dressed in a Quaker outfit of tall hat and long, dark brown coat, he was a familiar figure. On his arrival Sarah went and purchased some beer to share with her visitor; Tawell laced Sarah's beer with prussic acid and left her to die the most excruciating of deaths.

As Sarah lay dying, her death throes were heard by a neighbour, Mrs Mary Ann Ashlee, who crossed paths with the departing John Tawell at the gated entrance to Hart's cottage; she noted he was looking agitated and in a great hurry; she asked after the health of Hart but Tawell made no comment. Mrs Ashlee found Sarah frothing at the mouth and in great pain. She summoned a local doctor, Henry Champnes, who rushed to Bath Place only to find Miss Hart in the last moments of an agonising death. He sent a messenger back to his house to inform his cousin the Reverend Edward Champnes to attend as the woman was in need of spiritual comfort – he was too late. The clergyman suggested that he search the local area and the road to Slough armed with the description provided by Mrs Ashlee in order to locate the man dressed as a Quaker who, at the very least, was a material witness to the circumstances surrounding the death of the unfortunate victim, if not indeed her killer. He returned to Bath Place a few minutes later to report to his cousin that he could not locate him, and suggested that both of them travel in his pony and trap to Slough station in order to intercept him before the departure of the next London-bound train. The cousins acted quickly, racing to Slough; on their arrival they spoke to a railway official asking if he had seen a man fitting the description and dressed in Quaker attire, and he told them he had just directed such a man to the London-bound train; all three watched as John Tawell boarded the 7.42 p.m. service bound for London Paddington at the very last moment as it slowly gathered speed – frustratingly, they had missed their chance.

The station manager took them into the station office, explaining that all was not lost as they were operating a revolutionary piece of telecommunications equipment invented by the Englishmen Sir Charles Wheatstone and William Fothergill Cooke called the electric telegraph. They announced that it was capable of sending signals down a wire from Slough to Paddington. The operator, Richard Home (whose brother Thomas was the licensee of the world's first commercial electric telegraph and stationed at the Paddington end), painstakingly pieced together a message. This entailed manipulating levers to point to letters of the alphabet which passed along the wire and replicated the same actions and thus the same message on an identical machine at the other end. There were fundamental limitations to the system, as only selected letters of the twenty-six letter alphabet were included. The message sent read:

A murder has just been committed at Salt Hill and the suspected murderer was seen to take a first-class ticket to London by the train that left Slough at 7.42 p.m.

He is in the garb of a Kwaker with a brown great coat which reaches his feet; he is in the last compartment of the second first-class carriage.

At first there was some confusion about what 'Kwaker' referred to (the letter 'Q' was one of the missing letters); this was quickly overcome as operators frequently abbreviated such messages (a little like we do today with text messages). At the Paddington end Thomas Home rushed the message to the station supervisor, who in turn passed the message to Detective Sergeant William Williams of the Great Western Railway Police (the forerunners of the modern-day British Transport Police). Williams placed a civilian coat over his uniform and observed passengers alight from the relevant train and picked out the suspect easily; John Tawell was fairly at ease for a man who had allegedly just committed murder, unaware a description of him had been forwarded with such speed to his destination. The facts regarding the incident were very sketchy, so Sergeant Williams decided not to initiate an arrest immediately but follow the suspect; a message was sent back to Slough reporting that

> The up train has arrived and a person answering in every respect the description given by the telegraph came out of the compartment mentioned. The man got into a New Road omnibus and Sergeant Williams into the same.

Sergeant Williams stuck to his man, who evidently still suspected nothing as he mistook the policeman for the conductor, giving him his fare as he alighted. Williams followed the suspected murderer around the City of London in what is probably the first recorded example of a covert surveillance operation, shadowing him as he visited a confectioners' and a coffee house before retiring to lodgings in Scott's Yard off Birchin Lane.

The following day, when the facts surrounding the death of Sarah Hart and the mysterious Quaker's possible involvement had been substantiated, Sergeant Williams attended Paddington Green police station and spoke to a colleague, Inspector Wiggins of the Metropolitan Police. Both returned to the Scott's Yard lodgings but Tawell had left earlier. They then visited the coffee house he had been seen in the previous day, and there the suspected murderer was found nonchalantly drinking his morning beverage. He was arrested for the murder of Sarah Hart and cautioned, to which he replied, 'I wasn't at

Slough yesterday.' Williams informed Tawell, 'Yes you were, sir, you got out of the train and got onto an omnibus and gave me sixpence.' Tawell was charged with the murder of Sarah Hart and his trial commenced at Aylesbury Courthouse on 12 March 1845. With the extraordinary events of Tawell's life and the circumstances leading to his arrest, the trial of this cold-blooded killer was never going to be straightforward; Tawell's defence didn't disappoint.

Tawell was represented by an experienced barrister, Sir Fitzroy Kelly. Kelly listened attentively to the prosecution case. Witnesses placed his client at Slough both at Sarah Hart's home and at the station on the day in question. Sergeant Williams gave evidence of the defendant alighting the Slough train at Paddington; a post-mortem examination (and further tests by toxicologists – a relatively new profession) revealed that the victim had been poisoned by ingesting at least one grain of prussic acid. This was followed by evidence of Tawell purchasing such a poison from a chemist on Bishopsgate on the morning of the murder, which he reportedly mixed with a potion for treating varicose veins. Kelly got to his feet, looked at the judge and jury, took a firm grip of his robes and simply said, 'Apple pips.'

He explained to the jury that apple pips produce prussic acid in its natural form and the probable cause of her death was not down to his client poisoning her but the victim consuming too many apples over the festive and New Year periods. During the trial, evidence was produced that Tawell had in fact attempted to murder Sarah Hart the previous September in a similar fashion but failed in his endeavours. The defence was dismissed by the jury and they returned a guilty verdict. Tawell was sentenced to death. Sir Fitzroy was the butt of many jokes for the remainder of his career, and often referred to as 'apple pip Kelly'. He wasn't very popular with the English fruit farming industry either, as the sale of apples plummeted.

John Tawell was hanged on 28 March 1845 on the first-storey balcony of Aylesbury courthouse, where he had been convicted. His execution was conducted with an estimated crowd of 10,000. He was hanged by the infamous public executioner William Calcraft. As he dangled from the end of a rope too short to cleanly break his neck, the crowd stood in morbid silence as the condemned man fought for his life, eventually succumbing to his fate following several minutes of appalling suffering; he was left for an hour before being cut down and buried in the grounds of the nearby gaol. The prison governor informed the local press that Tawell had made a written confession before his execution admitting his culpability in the murder of Sarah Hart.

The nationwide media attention given to the trial of John Tawell publicised the communicative power of the new electric telegraph; indeed, the manufacturers often used the case of John Tawell to promote their product. Within four years telegraph wires would stretch across most of the country alongside railway lines, reaching 200 destinations.

The Tawell case is also recognised in British criminal history as the first example of a murderer escaping the scene of his crime by steam train, and the first recorded use of prussic acid as an instrument of murder.

14. GOOD PLAN, BUT ... (1848)

On the evening of 28 November 1848, local police were alerted to an incident in which gunshots had been fired at Stanfield Hall Estate in Wymondham, Norfolk. A police officer arrived at 9.20 p.m. to what he described as a 'scene of utter dismay'. The landowner, Isaac Jermy, had been shot on the porch of the house and his son of the same name, who heard the commotion, met the same fate at the hands of an intruder armed with two pistols; he also shot and injured a maidservant and the pregnant wife of Jermy Jnr.

The following day, police officers arrested a problematic local tenant farmer named James Blomfield Rush; Rush had mortgaged and re-mortgaged his home – Potash Farm, situated on the estate – with the Jermy family, but found himself in a deep financial mire; final payments were due to be paid within two days of the murders. If he didn't make the repayments, he, his two youngest children and his pregnant governess Emily Sandford faced eviction. Rush hatched a devious plan which involved the murder of the landlord, his son and the son's pregnant wife. He was aware that the Jermys were in some dispute with other family members about their claim to the estate, but it seemed unlikely that Isaac Jermy Snr, who was an important local businessman and the Recorder of Norwich, would lose the battle. Rush believed that following the murders other members of the family involved in the dispute would be blamed. Rush disguised himself using a wig and false whiskers and wore a mask but his mistake was not killing Isaac Jermy's young wife and the servant Elizabeth Chestney, who would later identify him. Rush was also relying on his mistress Emily Sandford to provide his alibi by telling the police that he had left the house for only ten minutes – as he was in the habit of doing each evening, to search for poachers – and that otherwise he had been home at the farm for the rest of the night, but she ultimately refused to perjure herself.

Rush was charged with two murders and two attempted murders. The initial court proceedings to establish a *prima facie* case were held almost immediately, but a problem arose: the two main witnesses, Mrs Jermy and the servant Chestney, were both resting at the hall, recovering from their wounds and unable to travel. It was decided by the magistrate that the proceedings would go to them. The prisoner was taken to the hall where the two witnesses repeated their allegations and formally identified Rush as the killer; this identification was backed up by another maid and the cook. Back in the courtroom the following day, Emily Sandford was called; although she initially backed her husband's story that he had only left Potash Farm for ten minutes, she changed her story after cross-examination and admitted that she had been reading a book and was unsure how long he had been absent.

The committal proceedings were adjourned for a couple of days; when the court reconvened Emily Sandford, who was again called to the witness box, having had a little more time to consider her own future, was much more frank with her account. She informed the court that Rush had been absent from the farm for over one and a half hours and that he had asked her to lie on his behalf. During Sandford's re-examination Rush became so irate – indeed violent – that he had to be removed from the courtroom. Further witnesses gave evidence of Rush making enquiries as to the Jermys' movements on the night of the murders and it was stated that a disguise used during the murderous attack had been found in his house. The magistrate, satisfied that there was a case to answer, committed Rush to stand trial.

The trial commenced in the courtroom of the Shire Hall in the grounds of Norwich Castle on 29 March 1849. He defended himself over the six days of the trial without any prior knowledge of the law or court procedure and completed his defence with one of the most notable closing speeches ever seen at a British criminal trial which lasted for fourteen hours. But he would often become confused, with the judge often pointing out that he repeatedly called witnesses who rebutted evidence of other defence witnesses he relied on; on the whole, though, it was an incredible effort for a man who, if he failed to convince the jury of his innocence, knew he would be executed, making this trial remarkable. The jury were less impressed and took just ten minutes to return a verdict of guilty to the charges and Rush was sentenced to death.

The execution date was set for 21 April 1849 at Norwich Castle, a location described by Charles Dickens as a 'grand place for a scoundrel's exit'. The trial had attracted nationwide interest, and the execution would follow suit, with between 12,000 and 20,000 people travelling to Norwich via the new train links from around the country. The media frenzy continued unabated; the words of the trial judge and reports of the execution headlined the nation's papers. The *Norfolk Chronicle* set the scene:

Coaches are crowded and carts laden with passengers … rain, hail and sleet fell rapidly yet the country people flocked into the city … and great numbers came by the different trains. Numerous portraits of the murderer, accounts of his life and reports of the trial were sold on the streets … the scaffold built high above the bridge ... many journalists were allowed to climb the steps to the top of the bridge for the best view of the execution.

The *Chelmsford Chronicle* of 27 April 1849 continues:

On the morning of the execution from the turret immediately over the castle gate hung an immense black flag, indicative of the solemn event which was to close the career of him who then sat within those walls, to which he was to return a lifeless cor[p]se, and within whose precincts his body was to be consigned to earth, far removed from the bones from whom he sprung ... The engine of death was raised on the bridge leading from the castle hill to the castle meadow. This spot is a circular mound, on the top of which stands the ancient castle of Norwich.

Rush was led out from Norwich Castle, hands bound behind his back, to the place of his execution at twelve noon; following a short prayer he was hanged. His body was interred within the grounds of the castle along with sixteen other murderers who had met their ends in a similar way. A death mask was taken of the executed man's face and his wax effigy featured as an attraction in Madame Tussaud's Chamber of Horrors up until the 1970s. The *Chelmsford Chronicle* published a rhyme as a header to their execution report:

Listen to that low funeral bell,
It is tolling alas! A living man's knell!
And see – from forth that opening door
They come – *he* steps that threshold o'er
Who shall never tread upon threshold more.
– God! 'tis a fearsome thing to see
That pale wan man's mute agony,
The glare of that wild despairing eye,
Now bent on the crowd, now turned to the sky,
As though 'twere scanning in doubt and fear,

The path of the spirit's unknown career;
Those pinioned arms, those hands that ne'er
Shall be lifted again – not even in prayer;
That heaving chest! –Enough – 'tis done!
The bolt has fallen! – the spirit is gone –
For weal or for woe is known but to One!
Oh! 'twas – a fearsome sight! Ah me;
A deed to shudder at, – not to see.

15. NOT A WIFE, JUST A PUNCHBAG (1853)

The Aggravated Assaults Act of 1853 was ahead of its time and akin to contemporary domestic violence acts. The act was aimed at stemming the tide of violent assaults by men against women and children under the age of fourteen. Henry Fitzroy, MP for Lewes and the architect of the bill, stated to Parliament that aggravated assaults on women and children were increasing so fast that they were a 'blot on the nation's character'. He went on to point out that he was only asking them (the all-male House of Commons) to 'extend the same protections to defenceless women as they already extended to poodles and donkeys (under the Cruelty to Animals Act)'. The act increased the punishment for aggravated assault to £20 or six months' hard labour. The first man to succumb to the new act, and in particular to the increased sentencing guidelines, was Henry Davidson.

Davidson was described in the *Bells New Weekly Messenger* of 26 June 1853 as a tall, muscular man. As he stood in the dock facing the magistrate his wife was in the witness box, her face greatly disfigured with both of her eyes shockingly blackened and swollen. She stated that she had been married to the defendant for seven years; they had three children and in consequence of his repeated acts of brutality they had been rendered a complete burden to her. She told the magistrate of a previous incident that occurred ten weeks before when he had beaten her in such an unmerciful manner that she was compelled to give him into custody and he was sentenced to two months in the house of correction with a further six months on bail with a condition of good behaviour. On his release Henry Davidson quickly returned to his bad old ways of drinking and violence, leading to her present physical state and Henry appearing yet again in the magistrates' court. She explained that a few days earlier she had sat up at home waiting anxiously for her husband to return home. She eventually retired to bed and was asleep between two of her children when he returned home in a drunken state. Mrs Davidson was awoken by a violent blow to the back of her head and found her husband standing over her. She tried to convince him that he should go and eat his supper, but, fuelled by alcohol, he wanted revenge for the two months he had spent inside at her behest. He hit her around the face until her eyes were so swollen she could hardly see; her nightdress and bedcover were covered in blood.

In his defence to the charge he admitted to assaulting his wife, but in mitigation submitted he had been greatly provoked yet was deeply sorry for his actions. Mr Hammill, the magistrate, referred to the now greater sentencing powers bestowed on him by the new legislation with the discretion to either fine the maximum £20 or send the defendant to prison for six months with hard labour. To Mrs Davidson's great relief, he decided on the latter.

16. PRINCE OF POISONERS (1855)

Charles Dickens described Doctor William Palmer as 'the greatest villain that ever stood in the Old Bailey';[6] however, if it hadn't been for a landmark piece of legislation, Palmer may well have been able to escape the end that he so richly deserved.

Palmer lived in Rugeley, Staffordshire, where he was suspected of killing several people, including his own brother, mother-in-law and, most tragically, four of his own children. Following detailed reports in local papers describing his alleged actions, the 'Rugeley Poisoner', as he was dubbed by the press, was so hated in his own county that it was thought impossible for him to receive a fair trial from his peers, giving him, should he be found guilty, automatic grounds for a retrial. An Act of Parliament was passed (the Central Criminal Court Act 1856) to allow crimes such as Palmer's to be tried in London at the Central Criminal Court; the act became popularly known as Palmer's Act.

Palmer was born in Rugeley in 1824 and by the time he was seventeen already in trouble when he was sacked from his first job – an apprenticeship in a pharmacy in Liverpool – for stealing. He was fascinated by medicine and remarkably graduated as a doctor from the prestigious St Bartholomew's Hospital in London, returning to Staffordshire to set up his own general practice. In 1845 he met his future wife, Anne Thornton, an heiress to the sixteenth-century Noah's Ark hostelry in Crabbery Street, Stafford. When Palmer first proposed she turned him down, having been warned off by her guardian; however, Palmer never gave up. Anne eventually made the fatal mistake of agreeing to his proposal, marrying in 1847.

Palmer was in fact an unsuccessful gambler and a heavy drinker, and had growing debts. He started to borrow money from his mother-in-law, who hated him but loved her daughter; it is believed

---

6 *Old Lamps For New Ones, And Other Sketches And Essays Hitherto Uncollected* (1856)

that he decided to murder his mother-in-law so that his wife could inherit her wealth. They invited her to stay, and within two weeks of her arrival, on 18 January 1849, she was dead. A local doctor signed a death certificate recording the reason for death as apoplexy. Palmer was disappointed with the inheritance, believed to be in the region of £8,000. He began to take even more of an interest in horse racing, attending meetings far and wide; at one such meeting he met a man called Leonard Bladen, who lent him £650. Bladen died at Palmer's house on 10 May 1850; the death certificate recorded that he had succumbed to an abscess on the hip and that Palmer – who, let's not forget, was a doctor – was present. Mysteriously, Bladen was found to have no money on him despite having recently won a large sum. In addition, all his betting books had disappeared, and with them details of any loans he had made.

William and Anne had five children. The first, a son christened William, was the only one to survive; the four younger siblings all died in infancy, Elizabeth (aged two and a half months) in 1851, Henry (one month) and Frank (seven hours) both in 1852 and John (three to four days) in 1854. The cause of death in each case was recorded as 'convulsions'. There were no insurance policies in force, so it was presumably just an attempt to reduce his financial burden.

In 1854, his betting and his losses were out of control. He began to forge his mother's signature in order to pay off some of his many creditors, and took out a life insurance policy on his wife with the Prince of Wales Insurance Company for the sum assured – £13,000, for which he paid a premium of £750. Anne only survived for a short period of time before she conveniently died on 29 September 1854; the death certificate recorded cholera as the reason. The insurance payout on his wife's death still didn't satisfy his creditors – two in particular were owed a total £23,000.

Palmer had a brother named Walter who spent most of his life drunk. In his search for more revenue streams, Palmer attempted to insure Walter's life for the incredible sum of £84,000. All the companies he approached turned him down, so he returned to the Prince of Wales, who agreed to insure Walter for a much reduced amount – £14,000 for a premium of £780. Palmer took it upon himself to care for his brother's welfare, often supplying him with the very thing he needed to avoid: copious amounts of alcohol. Walter duly died in August 1855, but the insurance company refused to pay out this time and appointed investigators to delve deeper into the claim. During the enquiry the investigators discovered Palmer had also attempted to initiate a life insurance policy on a man called George Bate, a former employee, in the sum of £10,000. Palmer's financial burden increased around the time of his brother's death when his housemaid, Eliza Tharme, with whom he had been having an affair, gave birth to his sixth child, a son called Alfred. Desperate for money following the lack of a payout on Walter's policy, Palmer turned his attention to a horse racing associate called John Parsons Cook.

William Palmer befriended John Parsons Cook through their love of betting on horses. Cook was a wealthy man who had previously inherited £12,000. In November 1855, Palmer and Cook went to a race meeting in Shrewsbury where Cook had a very successful few days, betting on the eventual winner of the Shrewsbury Handicap Stakes and collecting winnings of £3,000. Palmer's bad luck had continued; he had lost heavily. Both men went to a local hostelry to celebrate Cook's good fortune. It was during this evening that Cook complained that the brandy he had been drinking had burnt the back of his throat, and following a later bout of sickness he confided to two associates that 'I believe that damn Palmer has been dosing me'.

It was later revealed that during this period Palmer had received a letter from a creditor threatening to reveal his criminal use of her funds to his mother and demanding payment to settle the debt immediately, which had resulted in Palmer placing virtually all he had on a horse that lost. The ever-desperate Palmer met Cook a few days later for coffee, during which time he administered a poison to some soup, causing Cook to fall extremely ill with bouts of violent vomiting. While Cook was in bed as a result of Palmer's action, the good doctor began collecting bets amounting to £1,200 on behalf of his 'friend'. He also purchased three grains of strychnine, which he introduced to medicine he gave to Cook. On 21 November 1855, Cook died in agony.

A post-mortem examination and coroner's inquest was demanded by Cook's father-in-law, William Stevens. The post-mortem took place at the Talbot Arms public house in Rugeley a few days later. The examination was wholly inadequate, carried out by a medical student and a drunken assistant with the ever-helpful Dr William Palmer conveniently available to look after the stomach contents of the deceased. As expected, the quality of the stomach contents (if indeed they were even Cook's) sent by Palmer to Dr Alfred Swaine Taylor for analysis were of little use; Taylor ordered a second post-mortem. Palmer wrote to the coroner requesting that the cause of Cook's death be recorded as 'death by natural causes'; the letter was accompanied by a £10 note. Following Dr Taylor's examination during the second post-mortem he reported that although he could find no evidence of poison in what was left of the stomach contents he believed poisoning to be the cause of death. The inquest jury agreed with him, deciding that the poison had been administered by Dr William Palmer. Palmer was arrested and charged with Cook's murder and forgery offences in relation to his mother's bank account.

Due to the new Act of Parliament being rushed on to the statute books so that the case could be tried at the Central Criminal Court, Palmer faced his destiny at last on 14 May 1856, accused on indictment of the murder of John Parsons Cook. The public gallery was full to capacity with lords and ladies, gentlemen, noblemen and the odd commoner. Attorney General Mr Edwin James QC set out the prosecution's case in a powerfully delivered four-hour opening speech in which he laid out the facts of the defendant's rise and fall from professional physician and surgeon to desperate gambler and then gripping the rail at the Old Bailey.

The prosecution evidence was convincing; witnesses at the Shrewsbury race meeting gave evidence of how Cook was violently sick and the allegations he made that Palmer had poisoned him. His financial situation was examined in minute detail, including the purchase of insurance policies. The chemist Mr Salt recalled the selling of strychnine to the defendant (although none was ever found in the stomach, but the fact that Palmer had taken control of the stomach contents shortly after the post mortem was evidence in itself). Medical men argued on both sides as to the cause of death;

Dr Taylor for the prosecution believed that death was caused by tetanus as a result of strychnine poisoning. Following a mammoth summation by the trial judge lasting eight hours, the jury took just one hour to return a verdict of guilty and Palmer was duly sentenced to death.

William Palmer was publicly executed at Stafford Prison on 14 June 1856 in front of an estimated 30,000 people. The *Rugby Advertiser* reported Palmer's last moments:

> When the fatal hour arrived, and the melancholy procession was formed, he marched along with a jaunty air and a tripping gait, and though the distance was considerable, he maintained this bold front to the last. He stepped lightly up to the gallows, took his place on the drop, and confronted the vast multitude below, not without emotion, but without anything like bravado. The work of the executioner was coolly and skilfully performed, and the culprit died in a few minutes and without a struggle.

Palmer was buried within the prison walls; the rope from which he had hung was sold off for 5s per inch.

17. WHAT'S MINE IS YOURS (1858)

The Divorce Act (officially the Matrimonial Causes Act 1857) was introduced by Parliament in order to create a unifying court to handle all issues of family separation. The act reformed the law on divorce and took it away from the jurisdiction of the ecclesiastical courts, transferring it to the civil courts and therefore allowing the process of divorce to be made available to all rather than only those who could afford it. The act also created the Court of Divorce and Matrimonial Causes and abolished the criminal offence of adultery. It also dealt with the problem of marital property – who keeps the dog, and so on.

The first conviction under the Divorce Act came in relation to marital property. As reported in the *Berkshire Chronicle* of 29 May 1858, under the headline 'First Conviction for Felony Under the New Divorce Act':

> A man named Owen Owens has been committed to prison for three months by the Stockport magistrates for stealing nine table knives, the property of his wife, who had previously obtained protection for her property under the new Divorce Act.

18. QUACK QUACK (1859)

The advance of the medical profession and its clinical practices throughout the reign of Queen Victoria was remarkable, but the lack of regulation and scrutiny opened the door for imposters with questionable qualifications – if any. This was a particularly dangerous time for patients, especially those from the poorer sections of Victorian society who cared little about a doctor's credibility when they had a sick child at death's door. The Medical Act of 1858 (an act to regulate the qualifications of practitioners in medicine and surgery) created the statutory body named the General Council of Medical Education and Registration of the United Kingdom, the forerunner of what we know today as the General Medical Council. Their main role was to establish and maintain a register of doctors either provisionally or fully qualified as medical practitioners in order to protect, promote and maintain the health and safety of the general public. The Medical

Act also recognised foreign medical degrees, allowing the first woman, Elizabeth Blackwell, to be entered on the medical register in this country. But the act also tightened up on the unscrupulous and deceitful – the quacks.

The first conviction under the 1858 act came from the prosecution of Samuel Nunn, described by the *Morning Post* of 22 July 1859 as a 'chemist, druggist and dentist carrying on business at No. 8 Mount Terrace, Hercules Buildings, Lambeth'. He was accused by the court of 'having unlawfully, wilfully and falsely taken and used the name and title of "surgeon" not being duly authorised to take and use the same' in contravention of S.40 of the 'Qualifications Act'. Evidence was presented by officials that Samuel Nunn had presented himself, by way of signage displayed outside his premises, as a fully qualified surgeon; this was backed up by a member of the Medical Council producing a copy of the General Practitioners Register, on which Samuel Nunn's name did not appear. Nunn became the first man to be convicted under the act and was fined £1. This act remained on the statute books for one-hundred and twenty-five years until the updated Medical Act of 1983 became law.

19. A BIT OVER THE TOP, SIR! (1860)

Many people of a certain age will remember standing, petrified, outside the headmaster's office awaiting a guaranteed rap across the knuckles or the buttocks for insolence or bad behaviour toward a teacher or our peers. Did we have more respect for our elders because of the possibility of the severe discipline we faced? Does corporal punishment have a role in our society? It is a matter of personal opinion in the politically correct culture in which we live, which in the author's view criminalises *reasonable* parental admonishment. In 1860 severe corporal punishment was very much accepted, even encouraged, by Victorian parents even though its severity could cast a shadow over a child's life for many years. One such extreme case came before the British courts in 1860, and would set a legal precedent limiting the level of corporal punishment enforced in British schools.

Headmaster Thomas Hopley ran a boarding school from his home at 22 Grand Parade in the seaside town of Eastbourne. In October 1859 Hopley was offered £180 a year to educate a fifteen-year-old adolescent called Reginald Cancellor, described as robust, stolid and stupid and deemed to be uneducable. Cancellor was placed in the care of Hopley by his affluent father, John. Some months later, having experienced disciplinary difficulties with his charge, Hopley asked John Cancellor's permission to administer a more severe form of corporal punishment in order to steer the boy back on track. Cancellor agreed, believing it would make a man of his boy. This gave Hopley the authority to proceed with an evil and brutal regime of beatings that would lead to tragic consequences.

Hopley did not avail himself of the traditional cane but an array of weapons including a skipping rope and a walking stick. On the morning of 22 April 1860, Reginald Cancellor was found dead in his bedroom. His legs were stockinged and his hands were gloved, disguising his many injuries; only his face was visible when a naïve doctor declared, without proper examination, that young Cancellor had died of natural causes. Hopley suggested that the most likely explanation for his premature death was heart disease and wrote to his father recommending his son be buried at once. John Cancellor viewed the covered body of his son and agreed that he should be interred as quickly as possible.

However, Reginald's older brother, John Cancellor Jnr, was not so trusting; on his arrival in Eastbourne he identified ambiguities between the accounts given by employees of the school and heard rumours that Hopley and his wife had conspired to cover up what in fact amounted to homicide. John Cancellor Jnr demanded an autopsy be performed on his brother. An inquest was convened and an autopsy ordered. When stripped, the young victim was found to be covered in blood; he had been subjected to the most severe of beatings, resulting in the appalling injuries described in the *Dover Express* of 28 July 1860: 'wounds an inch deep ... his cellular membranes [turned] into a perfect jelly'. The wounds recorded on the victim's legs were so deep in places that Robert Willis, the surgeon who performed the examination, was able to touch bare bone.

Willis ruled out the cause of death as 'natural causes' following his examination of the boy's major organs. A witness – servant girl Ellen Fowler – reported to police that she had heard Cancellor screaming in pain as he was beaten between 10 p.m. and midnight on the night of his death. She also noticed traces of blood on a candlestick left outside the deceased's bedroom and that both Hopley and Cancellor's clothes were washed shortly after he was found dead.

Thomas Hopley stood trial at Lewes Assizes on 23 July 1860; he was charged with the manslaughter of Reginald Cancellor (the prosecution felt they did not have enough conclusive evidence to prove Hopley intended to kill his victim). This was a contentious point in the media, fuelled by a public who vented their anger by sending large sacks of hate mail. The trial was big news; the court issued daily tickets for the public gallery, which filled to capacity an hour before the commencement of each day's proceedings. Hopley's defence claimed he was initially reluctant to use corporal punishment but that the behaviour of Cancellor legitimised his use of such force, although he claimed to have cried when administering it. The catalogue of terrible injuries, outlined by Robert Willis in his evidence, shocked the jury; Willis had formed the opinion that the beating had taken place over a period of several hours before death. Hopley was convicted of the manslaughter of Reginald Cancellor and sentenced to four years' penal servitude at Millbank Prison. The *Dover Express* of 28 July 1860 summed up the feelings of a nation:

Corporal punishment may or may not be a legitimate part of scholastic discipline; but surely it is foully abused when enforced at the dead of night in the solitude of the victim's bedroom, and when the strokes of the lash and the cudgel are only intermitted for hours together for the purpose of – prayer! There is something almost incredible in the fanatical consistency with which Hopley carried out his merciless system. The four years' penal servitude which his relentless cruelty has brought upon him will, it is hoped, open the eyes of the other wrong-headed and passionate pedagogues to the danger of giving effect to their inhuman and draconian theories.

The case of *R* vs. *Hopley* was credited with a swell of public opinion against corporal punishment in schools, but the practice would not be outlawed by Parliament in state-run schools until 1986 and in public schools in England and Wales until 1998 (Scotland 2000 and Northern Ireland 2003). Thomas Hopley went into private tutoring following his release and died in London on 24 June 1876.

20. IS THAT A RABBIT IN YOUR POCKET, SIR? (1862)

In 1862 the Poaching Prevention Act was made law, and within weeks it claimed its first catch. Reported in the *Cambridge Independent Press* on 23 August 1862 was the first conviction of a person under this legislation. A police officer in Malvern in Worcestershire stopped the defendant, Thomas Freeman, in pursuance of his new powers (whereby a constable can search any person he may have good cause to suspect had come from any land where he shall have been unlawfully in search or pursuit of game) and searched him, having heard gunshots coming from nearby private land. The police officer told magistrates that he opened the defendant's coat and found a dead rabbit. It was reported – not without a little sarcasm and a great deal of annoyance – that the magistrates (whose names the paper unashamedly published)

> fined the defendant, Thomas Freeman, one pound and costs, and ordered the gun be destroyed! Such a law is monstrous and un-English and unworthy of modern legislation.

21. WHO REALLY KILLED JESSIE MCPHERSON? (1862)

The 'Sandyford Mystery' involved the brutal murder of a young live-in house servant called Jessie McPherson (*nee* Richardson) in the city of Glasgow in 1862. The case was notable for being the first trial in which forensic photography had played a significant role in the Scottish courts, the first murder investigation carried out by the newly formed Glasgow Detective Branch, and one in which the convicted woman named the prosecution's chief witness as the real killer.

Jessie McPherson was employed within the household of accountant John Fleming at 17 Sandyford Place, Glasgow. Fleming lived at the address with his young son and his eighty-seven-year-old father James Fleming. During the absence of John Fleming and his son over the weekend of 4/5 July 1862, McPherson was murdered in her basement room. The two people that detectives suspected of the murder were in the house during this period – they were James Fleming and Jessie's close friend Jessie M'Lachlan, who regularly visited her. Following an investigation by the newly formed Detective

Branch of Glasgow's police, M'Lachlan was charged with the murder of her close friend and appeared in front of Glasgow Autumn Circuit Court in September 1862. The *Greenock Telegraph and Clyde Shipping Gazette* of 20 September 1862 describes the accused as she took her place in the dock:

> ... the prisoner came up the trap and took her place in the dock. A young woman with an air of superior manners, modest-looking, plainly but neatly attired in a mauve barege dress, a black barege shawl, a straw bonnet trimmed with white ribbon and having a short black veil depending over her face, she took her seat without any apparent mark of timidity or apprehension, save that she was deathly pale. She was attended by the matron of the prison and a female turnkey, who sat beside her. She exchanged a few words with the Governor of the jail, and with her leading counsel, by whom she was successively accosted; and then the trial began.

John Fleming was the first to give evidence, stating that he and his son John Jnr, with whom he worked, had been away for the weekend in question; they had travelled to Dunoon, where the rest of his family were gathered, via his office on the Friday and did not return to their Glasgow office in Vincent Street until Monday morning. At 4 p.m. both father and son left the office and headed home to Sandyford Place. On the way John Fleming went into a butcher's shop near to their home and ordered some meat to be delivered for their tea, whilst John Jnr carried on to the house. When John arrived home, both his son John Jnr and his father James were standing in the lobby. The meat had been delivered, but the son remarked to his father that 'there is no use of sending anything here for dinner as the servant is run off and there is nobody to cook it'. Nodding to his grandfather, he commented that James had last seen Jessie McPherson on Friday night, adding that 'her door is locked'.

Fleming went down to the pantry and found a spare key to the locked bedroom door. On entering Jessie's room, he found the maid lying dead on the floor. Her clothes had been removed from the waist down and her upper torso, including her head, were covered by dark clothing and a piece of carpet. Fleming enlisted the help of a neighbour to summon a local constable to the house. A doctor examined the body of the girl and confirmed life extinct; the cause of death was multiple blows to the head, and there was severe bruising to her wrists and back. Although detectives didn't believe an outsider was involved, as there was no sign of a forced entry, they asked John Fleming to return to the house later that evening to identify anything that may be missing; he told the officer that a large amount of silver cutlery, which had been in the charge of the victim, had disappeared – this, the police believed, firmly indicated M'Lachlan as the guilty party.

Fleming informed the court that the defendant had been in his service as a housemaid at the same time as the victim and that they had become friends, but she had left his employ four years previously; he had seen her off and on over that period as she regularly visited the victim. John Fleming Jnr corroborated his father's recollection of the circumstances before James Fleming gave evidence that he had heard a noise and a squeal coming from the kitchen area at 4 a.m. but went back to sleep.

James Fleming had originally been arrested on suspicion of the murder but was released when items of personal property belonging M'Lachlan were found in the house, despite the fact that they could have been left during the numerous visits she had previously made to her friend. The jury retired with photographs and detailed plans of the crime scene to consider their verdict; they took less than fifteen minutes to find Jessie M'Lachlan guilty of her friend's murder. She was sentenced to death.

M'Lachlan continuously proclaimed her innocence, openly blaming the eighty-seven-year-old James Fleming during the proceedings (could she really have physically inflicted such injuries? And what of the evidence of sexual interference?). Following a public outcry and serious doubts raised by senior government officials about the reliability of the verdict, an unprecedented step was taken in appointing a court commission to examine the evidence presented during the trial. Although the commission's findings did not exonerate M'Lachlan, the death sentence was commuted to life imprisonment. She served fifteen years in Perth General Prison before being released in October 1877. She emigrated to the United States of America, where she married. She died in Michigan on New Year's Day 1899.

22. THE FIRST RAILWAY MURDER (1864)

Great Britain's first passenger railway service was rolled out in 1825; rail travel would grow in popularity as networks spread across the country, allowing the population to travel freely. Today it is Great Britain's preferred method of public transport, with a reported 1.6 billion passenger journeys made during 2014/15.[7]

Vast crowds of people will always attract a criminal element, and the railway system was no different, becoming a magnet for bag thieves and pickpockets; however, surprisingly, the first murder on Britain's rail network did not take place until the middle of the nineteenth century.

On Saturday 9 July 1864, two bank clerks entered an empty first-class carriage on the 9.50 p.m. North London Railway departure from Fenchurch Street station in the City of London's financial district, which travelled north-east, arriving at Hackney Station at 10.11 p.m. They were shocked to discover copious amounts of blood spread over the seats and carriage interior. A black beaver-skin hat, a walking stick and a bag had been abandoned. The shocked bank clerks called a railway official, who realised the seriousness of the situation and, sensibly, sealed the compartment. The train then carried on its journey to its final destination, Chalk Farm,

---

7   *Office of Rail and Road*

where the sealed carriage was detached and pulled to Bow for closer examination by the police.

Minutes after the train had departed Hackney for Chalk Farm, a driver of a London-bound train saw an object at the side of the tracks near Hackney Wick station; closer examination determined it to be an unconscious and badly injured man. He was taken to a nearby public house, where he later died of his injuries. He was Thomas Briggs, a sixty-nine-year-old chief clerk at a London bank who lived in Clapham Square, a few hundred yards from Hackney station.

The walking stick and bag belonged to the deceased man, but the hat was the killer's, probably discarded in his haste to escape (taking Mr Briggs's hat by mistake) after the attack; detectives believed robbery was the most likely motive as Briggs's gold watch, chain and eye-glasses were missing. Given that this was the first case of homicide on Britain's railways, great concern was expressed among the travelling public and the media. A reward was offered by the government and Briggs's employees in the City of London.

A week later, John Death, a Cheapside jeweller, came forward with some important information. He gave a description of a German who called at his shop in Cheapside on 11 July and exchanged a gold chain, later identified by Briggs's family as belonging to the deceased. A week later, a cabman told police that he found a small cardboard box bearing the name 'Death' in his home. It had been given to one of his children by a young German named Franz Muller who was engaged to his eldest daughter. Inquiries into the German's whereabouts revealed Muller had disappeared; he was traced to a ship that had sailed for New York on 15 July. The cabman also informed detectives that the black beaver-skin hat found in the carriage, which had a maker's label from a shop in Crawford Street, Marylebone, was one he had purchased on behalf of Muller. He gave police a photograph of Muller, and Death, the jeweller, identified him as the man who had exchanged the gold chain.

A warrant was issued for the arrest of Franz Muller at Bow Street Magistrates' Court on 19 July 1864. Two Metropolitan Police officers, Inspector Tanner and Sergeant Clarke, were tasked with reaching New York before the suspect and detaining him for the murder of Thomas Briggs. They travelled by train from Euston to Liverpool, boarded a fast steamship and arrived in New York on 5 August, three weeks before Muller. When Muller stepped from the ship on to American soil, he was arrested. At the time of capture he was wearing Briggs's hat and was in possession of the banker's gold watch. He was extradited back to London to face trial for murder, and on 27 October 1864 appeared at the Central Criminal Court, the Old Bailey. His defence rested on a sketchy alibi, and strong prosecution evidence secured a guilty verdict. Muller was sentenced to death.

The execution of Franz Muller took place in front of 50,000 onlookers outside Newgate Prison on 14 November 1864. The *North London News* of 19 November 1864 records the scenes in Old Bailey the night before the execution:

> On Sunday night people begun to assemble, and the crowd gradually increased until daybreak, when there were 3,000 to 4,000 persons present. Nearly all night it rained heavily, but the people kept their ground regardless of all consequences. The proprietors of the houses on the side of the Old Bailey opposite the gaol reaped a rich harvest from letting their windows, the lowest price for a seat being five shillings, while others which commanded a clear view of the drop, let for as much as a guinea. The execution of the wretched man took place in front of the Old Bailey on Monday morning and it is satisfactory to state that before leaving the world he made a confession of his crime to the protestant clergyman who had afforded him spiritual assistance during the time he had been under the sentence of death.

As a direct result of the murder of Mr Thomas Briggs by Franz Muller, the railway companies installed cords within each railway carriage, enabling communication with the train staff.

23. WHY DIDN'T YOU SPEAK UP, DOC? (1865)

The Hippocratic Oath is taken by physicians at the start of their career. In it they swear to uphold the traditions of the medical profession and do everything in their power to treat their patients to the best of their ability. We Britons admire and respect our doctors and our wonderful National Health Service, but there is a bad apple in every barrel and in this case, the trial of Dr Edward William Pritchard, there are two – one a murderer and the other, shall we say, a little misguided.

Born in Southsea, Hampshire, Dr Pritchard came from a naval background. His father was a captain in the Royal Navy. He finished his medical degree at King's College, London and returned to the south coast, serving in the Royal Navy as an assistant surgeon for four years. After travelling around the world, he resigned from the Navy after meeting his future wife, Mary Jane Taylor, the daughter of an Edinburgh-based silk merchant. Pritchard and Mary were married in 1851 and they produced five children. During these early years of the marriage Pritchard had taken a job as a general practitioner in Yorkshire before moving the whole family even further north to Glasgow in 1859. By 1863 the Pritchards lived at 11 Berkeley Street, Glasgow; it was in May of this year that a suspicious fire occurred at the house. When the fire had been extinguished, the body of the Pritchard family maid, Elizabeth McGrain, was found in her room. The investigation concluded that the fire had actually started in the maid's bedroom, and that she had apparently made no attempt to escape; this led to the reasonable conclusion that she was already deceased, unconscious or insensible when the fire was started. A police investigation, under the direction of the procurator fiscal, revealed no evidence appertaining to foul play.

By 1865 the family were living in Sauchiehall Street, Glasgow. Pritchard's mother-in-law, Jane Taylor, developed symptoms of sickness and severe stomach cramps that proved fatal; she died on

28 February. Shortly after this, Pritchard's wife Mary started to develop similar symptoms as her mother. Pritchard and another physician, Dr Paterson, were treating Mary. Paterson became suspicious and thought Mary was perhaps being poisoned by her husband, but, disgracefully, said nothing and took no further action. Mary died on 18 March 1865, aged just thirty-eight. Paterson, although refusing to sign the death certificate, still sat on his hands and made no effort to confront Pritchard or report his suspicions to the authorities.

The allegation that William Pritchard had in fact murdered his wife and mother-in-law did not surface until an anonymous letter was sent to the authorities (perhaps by Dr Paterson). The two bodies were exhumed, and, following a more in-depth examination, traces of the poison antimony were found. Pritchard was arrested and charged with murder.

The trial commenced on 3 July 1865 in a packed High Court of Justiciary in Edinburgh. Pritchard was indicted on two charges. The first was that he administered tartarised antimony, aconite and opium to his mother-in-law, Jane Cowper Taylor, in tapioca, porter beer and a medicine called Bateley's Sedative Solution between 10 and 25 February 1865. The second charge was of a similar nature, but with his wife as the victim this time. The *Carlisle Patriot* of 8 July 1865 describes the prisoner's entrance:

> The prisoner entered the dock at 10 o'clock dressed in deep mourning. He was calm and self-possessed, and looked coolly around the court when he had taken his seat. He is a stout, well-built man, prepossessing in appearance, and with sharply defined features. He wears his hair long and has a large bushy beard, but no moustache.

Catherine Lattimer, a cook in the Pritchard household, gave evidence about the weeks leading up to the death of Dr Pritchard's wife Mary Jane. She stated that Mrs Pritchard had been frequently sick during the month of February, retching violently and suffering from severe pains or cramp in the stomach, normally after she had drank some tea made by her husband. On one occasion, following such a bout of sickness, Mrs Pritchard had been laid up in bed with her husband in attendance; she looked at him and said, 'Don't cry, for if you do so, you are a hypocrite.' She continued, referring to the medical profession in general: 'You are all hypocrites.' Dr Edward William Pritchard was found guilty by the Edinburgh jury and sentenced to death. Several newspapers nationwide reported on the execution, which took place on 28 July 1865 at the Saltmarket end of Glasgow Green. The *Sheffield Independent* of 29 July 1865 echoed many other similar reports:

> Dr Pritchard was executed this morning a few minutes after eight o'clock. He slept from half past eleven last night until half past five, when he arose and dressed himself in the suit of black in which he buried his wife. He was perfectly calm and collected, and acknowledged the justice of his sentence. He made no further confession. He submitted with perfect composure to the pinioning, and walked to the gallows with a firm step, muttering prayers with his face uplifted. No demonstration of feeling was shown by the public [numbering 80,000]. He placed himself under the drop, which in a minute afterwards fell. The culprit appeared to die hard.

24. NOT ENOUGH ROOM TO SWING – WELL, ANYTHING (1866)

Life in the overcrowded slums of London and many other major towns and cities in Victorian England was a filthy, intolerable and degrading state of affairs. Following the introduction of the Public

Health Act 1866, the nuisance authority of any parish was able to make regulations for 'fixing the number of persons who may occupy a house or part of a house which is occupied or let in lodgings'. The first conviction came about at Clerkenwell Magistrates' Court in north London. Landlord Frederick Barlow of 41 Payne Street, Islington, was summoned to appear at the court in August 1866 to answer a complaint by Mr William Mayes, an inspector of nuisances and sanitation. He accused Barlow of keeping premises 'so overcrowded as to be dangerous and prejudicial to health'.[8] It was noted by the magistrate that these were the first proceedings under this act, which had only received royal assent on the 7th of the month.

Mr Mayes, the sanitary inspector, informed the court that he had visited 41 Payne Street in company with a local physician, Dr Ballard, and found it to be occupied by five families. In the two kitchens there were a man, a woman and four children; in the front parlour there was a man, a woman and four children; in the back parlour, one woman; in the first-floor front room one man and three children; and in the back room of the first floor there was one woman. Mr Mayes commented that 'from the first floor a woman was taken away very ill and died. The house was filthy dirty and the stench from the front parlour was fearful.' The magistrate, who was profoundly shocked at the inspector's evidence, commented that this was 'downright cruelty to the poor persons in the house'. He imposed a fine of 20s and ordered Barlow to pay £1 3s costs, reminding him that if he were brought before the court under similar circumstances the full penalty would be imposed.

---

8   *Burnley Gazette*, 25 August 1866

25. GOT THE NEEDLE (1868)

The concept of vaccinating children, as any parent will testify, has always led to a certain amount of soul-searching and is a very emotive subject. The controversy surrounding the MMR (Measles, Mumps and Rubella) vaccine in the late 1990s caused a great deal of concern and worry for parents following a report in *The Lancet* that lent support to the discredited claim that the vaccine was linked to colitis and autism spectrum disorders. Today, parents have the freedom to make an informed choice as to whether or not they should vaccinate their children. However, this has not always been the case.

The Vaccination Act of 1867 stated that within seven days of a child's birth being registered the registrar was to deliver a vaccination notice. If the child was not presented within three months of the notice being served, or brought for inspection after the expiration of this time, the parents or guardians were liable to a summary conviction and fine of 20s.

The first instance of a parent being taken to court and convicted of such an offence was recorded in the *Nottinghamshire Guardian* of 4 September 1868 sourced from the London papers:

> We copy the following report of a conviction under the new Vaccination Act from the London papers of Tuesday; and we would advise our readers of the humbler classes, more especially, to take warning from it, and not refuse, as we understand some are doing, to have their children vaccinated as the law directs.

The paper reported that on 29 August 1868 a poulterer named as James Bovingdon, living in Merton, Surrey, was summoned to appear before magistrates at the Wandsworth Police Court by Mr Edward Bailey, the registrar of births and deaths for the Mitcham district, to face a charge under the new vaccination act, in that he neglected to have his daughter Emily vaccinated within the statutory three months after her birth. Bovingdon claimed that he had in fact had his daughter vaccinated on the very day he received the court summons, having first objected to it on principle.

Bailey informed the court that the child had been born on 3 December 1867 and that the notice of vaccination had been served on the child's mother on 8 January 1868, when the birth had been registered. He had seen Mr Bovingdon since that date when Mr Bovingdon stated that he would rather send the child to Australia then have it vaccinated. The defendant was asked by the magistrates why he had not complied with the act, and replied that he had listened to a lot of opinion on the subject and had been informed that he was not compelled to have his child vaccinated – it was the first time he had heard of the new law. He went on to argue that several otherwise healthy children had broken out in sores since having the vaccination. The magistrate found him guilty, adding that vaccination was required to maintain not only *his* child's safety but that of his neighbours' children also. Bovingdon was fined 10s plus the same amount again towards the court costs; if he did not pay he was liable to fourteen days' imprisonment.

26. THE LAST PUBLIC EXECUTION (1868)

Irish Republican Michael Barrett was the London-based leader of a group of terrorists known as the Fenian Brotherhood. His murderous attack in a heavily populated area of north London would lead to his execution – the last to be carried out in public view.

The Fenian Brotherhood was an Irish Republican terrorist group formed in the United States in 1858 by James Stephens and John O'Mahony, who had fled after a failed armed rebellion in 1848. The Irish branch of the group was known as the Irish Republican Brotherhood (IRB). On 20 November 1867, two members of this group – Richard O'Sullivan-Burke and Joseph Casey – were arrested in Woburn Square, London, and charged with arms offences; they were remanded in custody at the Middlesex House of Detention, also known locally as Clerkenwell prison. Deemed to be impregnable, the prison was a grim, menacing place surrounded by a 25-foot-high brick wall. Police informers warned that an attempt would be made to break O'Sullivan-Burke and Casey out of the prison; extra armed guards were placed on the roof of the prison and police officers stationed in nearby streets observing all who entered the area.

Around 3.30 p.m. on the afternoon of 12 December 1867, a man – whom the prosecution stated was Michael Barrett – wheeled a costermonger's handcart up Corporation Row and came to a stop adjacent to the prison's exercise yard. Precariously balanced on the cart was a large barrel, which he unloaded after some exertion and placed next to the prison's outer perimeter. A white ball was thrown over the wall – a pre-determined signal to warn O'Sullivan-Burke and Casey that the attempt to break them free was about to take place. A prison guard reportedly saw the ball being cast but suspected nothing – in fact, he placed the ball in his pocket to take home for his young son. O'Sullivan-Burke and Casey retreated to the corner of the prison yard, awaiting the expected explosion, but it never happened.

The bomber attempted to light the fuse on two occasions; each time he ran for cover, and each time the fuse went out. He then decided it was too dangerous to attempt to light the now shortened fuse again, so the barrel was put back on the handcart and removed from the area – all under the watchful eye of the police, who suspected nothing. The following day, another attempt was made; the barrel was returned to the same position and this time successfully detonated with a destructive, devastating force that could be heard all over London. The objective was achieved when a sixty-foot section of the wall was destroyed, but so were an adjacent row of houses, resulting in fifty of the tenants being buried in rubble. Five died immediately, and another seven would succumb to their injuries over the following days.

Michael Barrett and four others were arrested and placed on trial at the Old Bailey, but following acquittals and deals with the prosecution, Barrett stood alone in the dock to face justice. Following a guilty verdict, he was sentenced to death. It looked as if Barrett might escape the hangman's noose when his sentence was suspended for seven days on two separate occasions in order for the authorities to investigate new evidence of an alibi that placed him in Glasgow at the time of the explosion, which is now widely known as the 'Clerkenwell Outrage'. No foundation to the alibi claim was substantiated, and Barrett was duly hanged on 26 May 1868 by William Calcraft outside Newgate prison and in front of a vast crowd, the last to witness a public execution. The *Clare Journal and Ennis Advertiser* of 28 May 1868 recorded:

> The Fenian convict Michael Barrett was hanged in front of Newgate Jail ... The murderous outrage for which he died seemed to be forgotten. The maimed women, the crippled children, the countless agonies inflicted upon the aged, the helpless and the weak; the honest breadwinners reduced to a life of cheerless, painful pauperism. All faded out of sight; and hand-clapping, 'Bravo, Barrett', 'Goodbye Barrett', were mixed up with cheers as hearty as ever followed a hero to the battlefield.

On the 29 May 1868, three days after Barrett was hanged, the British Parliament passed the Capital Punishment within Prisons Bill, ending the practice of public executions and directing that all such future punishments take place privately within the prison walls. Executioner William Calcraft – infamous for his shortened drop, which resulted in a slow and painful death – would officiate over the first hanging under the new legislation when he executed railway carriage cleaner Thomas Wells on 13 August 1868 at Maidstone prison for the murder of his stationmaster.

27. THE DARK ANGEL OF THE NORTH (1872)

At what stage does a young dressmaker, nurse and housekeeper turn from innocent, respected young lady into Britain's first serial killer? In the case of Mary Ann Cotton, was there a trigger point in her young life that led her to kill as many as twenty-one people (although only convicted for one count of murder), including her own young children? Or was it just down to plain old greed? One can only report the facts of this disturbing case from contemporary records[9] and leave you to come to your own conclusions.

Mary Ann was born in 1832 at Low Moorsley, on the outskirts of Sunderland in the north-east of England with the maiden name Robson; she was one of three siblings. Her mother and father moved the family to the village of Murton in Durham when Mary Ann was eight years of age. Soon after the move, in February 1842, tragedy struck the family when Mary Ann's father Michael fell to his death down a mineshaft at Murton Colliery. Her father's body was delivered to their small miner's cottage in a coal sack for burial. The family now faced eviction from the company's cottage but Margaret, Mary Ann's mother, quickly remarried coalminer George Stott, securing some sort of future for her family.

Mary Ann started to earn her way when she left home at the age of sixteen to take up a position as a nurse to the three children of the Murton Colliery manager Edward Potter in the nearby village of South Hetton. It was a short-term appointment – the children in her charge were soon off to boarding school – and she subsequently returned home and trained as a dressmaker.

Mary Ann, now aged twenty, married colliery worker William Mowbray in 1852 and they started a new life hundreds of miles away in Plymouth. They had several children – an exact figure is unknown, as the requirement to register births and deaths did not become compulsory until the Births and Deaths Act 1874. A number of the

---

9   In the main the *Northern Echo* of 1872–73

children – four is the consensus figure – died in infancy. Mary Ann and her husband moved back to the north-east; William worked first as a fireman aboard a steamship out of Sunderland and then as a colliery foreman. Children were born, and some died; Isabella was born in 1858, but another daughter, Margaret Jane, died in 1860. Another daughter, also named Margaret Jane, was born in 1861, followed by a son named John Robert William in 1863; baby John died from gastric fever a year later.

William died in January 1865, the cause recorded as an intestinal disorder; his life and those of the children had been insured by the British and Prudential Insurance Office, and Mary Ann received a sum of £35 in relation to the death of her husband and smaller amounts for the children. No suspicion was raised around the circumstances of the deaths of any of the deceased.

Within a short period of time Mary Ann had started a relationship with a married man called Joseph Nattress. During this period her eighth child, Margaret Jane, whom she had with William Mowbray, died; she now had only one surviving child, daughter Isabella, whom she sent to live with her mother and stepfather.

Mary Ann returned to Sunderland and took up a position at the Sunderland Infirmary, House of Recovery for the Cure of Contagious Fever, Dispensary and Humane Society. This is where she met her next husband, an inpatient called George Ward who was an engineer by trade. They were married in August 1865; within fourteen months Ward was dead. His death certificate recorded the reason as English cholera and typhoid. Once again Mary Ann collected an insurance payout.

Within one month of the death of husband number two, Mary Ann met a recently widowed shipwright called James Robinson who lived in the Pallion area of Sunderland and (according to the *Northern Echo* of 12 October 1872) already had five children from his previous marriage. He hired Mary Ann as a housekeeper, and a month later his youngest child died of gastric fever. Robinson, distraught by the death of his wife and now his youngest child, turned to Mary Ann for solace, which resulted in Mary Ann conceiving another child.

Mary Ann soon returned home, having received news that her mother had contracted hepatitis. After some time she seemed to be in recovery, but her condition deteriorated within a few days of her daughter's homecoming. Margaret died following severe abdominal pains aged fifty-four in the early months of 1867.

Mary Ann returned with eldest daughter Isabella to James Robinson's house, and within a few weeks Isabella and two of the Robinson children, Elizabeth and James, succumbed to severe stomach pains and died. All three were buried in the space of two weeks in April/May 1867. Robinson, apparently blinded by love, never appeared to suspect that the return of Mary Ann, still expecting their child, could be connected to so many deaths in the family; he married her in August 1867, and this was followed by the birth of their first child, Mary Isabella, in November 1867. Mary Isabella only survived for four months before becoming ill and passing away. They had a second child, a son called George, in June 1869.

Robinson's suspicions were at last raised when family members asserted that the deaths must be more than just an unlucky, though tragic, consequence, coupled with the fact that Mary Ann had become ever more insistent that he take out life insurance. The last straw for Robinson was the discovery that Mary Ann had been stealing from him and forcing his older remaining children to pawn many household items. Robinson disowned his wife and cast her out on to the streets.

Now homeless, she turned to childhood friend Margaret, who in turn introduced her to her brother, widower Frederick Cotton, who lived in Walbottle, Northumberland. At this point Mary Ann saw her chance to claw back some respectability – and some wealth. Margaret looked after Frederick's two surviving children, Frederick Jnr and Charles, but it would appear that she was an obstacle to Mary Ann's plans – she died of an undetermined stomach complaint in late March 1870. The way was clear, and within six months of Margaret's death the pregnant Mary Ann bigamously married pitman Frederick. Their son Robert (her twelfth child) was born in the early months of 1871.

During this time Mary Ann rekindled her relationship with her former lover Joseph Nattress, who was recently widowed and living in the village of West Auckland in County Durham. She persuaded Frederick to move the family roughly 30 miles so that she could be near Joseph. Within months of the move Frederick followed the others, dying of gastric fever after having insured the lives of himself and their sons. Following the death, Nattress moved in with Mary Ann as her lodger. In March 1872 Frederick Jnr died, quickly followed by Robert, her only child with Frederick Cotton, leaving only her stepson Charles surviving. Mary Ann started another relationship with a poorly excise officer called Quick-Manning who had previously employed her while he recovered from smallpox; it wasn't long before she fell pregnant with her thirteenth child. Meanwhile, Joseph Nattress died of gastric fever having altered his will in favour of Mary Ann. When Mary Ann took out life insurance on stepson Charles, his fate was sealed; however, this would be one death too many.

Parish official and assistant coroner Thomas Riley offered the pregnant Mary Ann a nursing position to attend to a local woman who was suffering from smallpox. She agreed, but rather callously told Riley that her one remaining child, stepson Charles Cotton, was a hindrance and would only get in the way of her carrying out her duties. She therefore asked him if he could arrange for Charles to be admitted to the local workhouse. Riley told her that she would have to attend the workhouse with the boy, at which point she reconsidered, telling Riley that 'I won't be troubled long' as he will 'go like all the rest of the Cottons'.

The following week, Charles Henry Cotton died. Riley was suspicious of the circumstances around the boy's death, coupled with the comments his mother had made and probably the sudden deaths of husband Frederick Cotton and his children. He reported his suspicions to the local police constable and strongly suggested to the doctor that he delay the completion of a death certificate so the circumstances of the death could be fully investigated. This frustrated Mary Ann, as she could not claim the insurance money until a death certificate had been issued.

It seemed that this evil woman would escape justice again when an inquest decided that Charles had died of natural causes; Mary Ann claimed to have used arrowroot whilst nursing her sick child and accused Riley of falsifying the claims in retaliation for her rejecting his sexual advances. The inquest generated a lot of local media interest, which led to the unearthing of the catalogue of deaths left in her wake: three husbands, twelve children, her mother, a lover and a childhood friend, all dying of stomach related illnesses. This prompted the law into much-needed action; the doctor who performed the post-mortem examination on Charles had luckily kept tissue samples and stomach contents which, when tested, revealed the presence of the poison arsenic. The doctor reported his findings to the police who arrested Mary Ann Cotton on suspicion of the murder of her stepson Charles, whose body was exhumed and examined, confirming the results of the earlier tests.

Mary Ann, charged with the murder of her twelfth child, gave birth to her thirteenth on 10 January 1873 whilst on remand at Durham Gaol. At her committal proceedings at Bishop Auckland Magistrates Court in February 1873 she was described as 'about forty years of age, rather above the ordinary height, swarthy in complexion and is said to be possessed of a pleasant and agreeable manner'.[10]

Mary Ann Cotton's trial began on 5 March 1873. She faced only one charge on the indictment – the murder of her stepson Charles Cotton. Her defence was that Charles had died from inhaling arsenic used as a dye in the wallpaper of their home. The prosecution proved that Cotton had purchased arsenic on the pretence that she wished to deep-clean her house. The defence counsel proposed that the chemist had in fact mistakenly prepared the bottle of arsenic rather than a requested bottle of bismuth powder used for the treatment of diarrhoea as he had been distracted by his conversation with other customers. The jury rejected Mary Ann's defence and convicted her of the murder by poisoning of her stepson Charles.

Following several fruitless petitions to the home secretary, Mary Ann Cotton was executed at Durham Gaol on 24 March 1873, still protesting her innocence. The *Lloyd's Weekly Newspaper* of 30 March 1873 reported her final moments:

> ... the miserable creature flinched visibly when suddenly brought face to face with death and the warders, who had hitherto supported her lightly at each elbow, had to help her along. In another moment she was placed upon the folding boards beneath the dangling noose, and Messrs. Calcraft and Evans

10 *North Devon Journal*, 27 February 1873

were at work. Never was this dreadful business transacted with such celerity, whilst the condemned woman ejaculated, as well as convulsive tremors would permit her, 'Lord have mercy upon me ... Oh Lord receive my soul.' Calcraft slipped the white cap over her head and face, and put the noose around her neck. The assistant in the meantime manacled her ankles and retired to the 'bolt' that was fixed at the back of the drop. Calcraft then stepped onto the side planks within a couple of feet of the doomed woman and instantly afterwards the assistant pulled the lever and the drop fell. The jerk was terrific and the victim of the law spun around and twisted from side to side in a horrible manner. Calcraft however took hold of her by the shoulder and held her steady, and in a few seconds the facial contortions ceased. The sight was dreadful and few were but unmanned by it. The Under-sheriff fainted. For just three minutes twitchings, more or less violent, were discernible in the body and it swung slowly around; but at the expiration of that time the motion ceased, and Mary Ann Cotton had paid the full penalty exacted by the English law for whatever crimes she may have committed.

The Reverend Bennett, who spent the last few hours of Mary Ann Cotton's life with her, reported that although he encouraged her to confess she would only say that she was indeed the poisoner, but that it had been accidental. A rather black nursery rhyme emerged shortly after her death which cannot be attributed to any one person and reads:

> Mary Ann Cotton, she's dead and she's rotten
> Lying in bed with her eyes wide open.
> Sing, sing, oh what should I sing?
> Mary Ann Cotton she's tied up with string.
> Where, where? Up in the air.
> Selling black puddings, a penny a pair
> Mary Ann Cotton, she's dead and forgotten,
> Lying in bed with her bones all rotten.
> Sing, sing, what can I sing?
> Mary Ann Cotton tied up with string.

28. WE ARE A NATION OF ANIMAL LOVERS AFTER ALL! (1876)

Us Brits have always been a nation of animal lovers, and those who would inflict cruelty or suffering on our wild or domestic creatures have the Royal Society for the Prevention of Cruelty to Animals (RSPCA) to answer to. The RSPCA today have extensive powers to deal with animal cruelty; in some extreme cases they have the power, when accompanied by a police officer, to enter a private dwelling and seize the suffering animal and prosecute the heartless and/or neglectful owner. The RSPCA was formed in 1824 and is therefore the oldest and largest animal welfare organisation in the world, although it didn't receive its royal status from Queen Victoria until 1840. The society was given its teeth with the passing of the Cruelty to Animals Act 1835, amended and updated with a similar act in 1876 (also known as the Vivisection Act), which included new laws to control animal experimentation.

A landmark case following the passing into law of the 1876 act was the conviction of Dr Abrath in Sunderland just seven weeks after the act entered the statute books. Dr Abrath had created a large placard on which he headlined 'The Balham Mystery', announcing that he intended to deliver a lecture in Sunderland on antimony (a brittle, silvery-white metallic element), during which he would perform experiments on animals to show the effects of poisons, and to demonstrate his theory that one 'Mr Bravo' had not been killed by that particular drug. 'The Balham Mystery' was a case of great interest to the media and the murder mystery-loving Victorian public. It surrounded the death of Charles Delaney Turner Bravo in suspicious circumstances – he was thought to have been poisoned with antimony in his room at the Bedford Hotel in Balham, London, in 1876. An inquest jury returned a verdict of wilful murder, concluding that

He had not committed suicide – that he did not meet his death by misadventure – but wilfully murdered by the administration of tartar emetic, but there is not sufficient evidence to attach guilt to any one person or persons[11]

The Sunderland branch of the RSPCA contacted their head office in London and action was taken to prevent the experiments taking place. By publicising his intentions to perform such experiments on animals, Dr Abrath had already contravened S.6 of the act and he was therefore summoned to appear before magistrates in Sunderland at the behest of the RSPCA. He was found guilty and, as reported in the *Paisley Herald and Renfrewshire Advertiser* of 7 October 1876, 'fined 1s and costs for publishing the illegal placard alluded to, the Society [RSPCA] only asking for a nominal penalty in vindication of the law'. Dr Abrath regularly delivered lectures around the country for several years, presenting his theories about the death of Mr Bravo in 1876 – but never using animal experimentation.

29. MORGAN'S NOSE SAVES THE DAY (1876)

The first official use of a police dog and the setting up of Britain's first police dog section were both carried out by the North Eastern Railway Police[12] in November 1907 following the success of police dogs in

---

11 *Tamworth Herald*, 12 August 1876

12 One of many forces that later formed the modern-day British Transport Police (BTP), although never officially credited with such as the railway police were not a recognised Home Office force. The BTP were also the first force in the UK to employ police women.

Belgium. Airedale Terriers were the favoured breed, acknowledged as strong working dogs with a keen sense of smell. The dogs were deployed initially at Hull Docks in 1908; this was extended to the Hartlepool, Middleborough and Tyne docks; they were utilised on night duty only. The dogs were trained to attack any person not wearing a police uniform, even growling at their own handlers when they were in civilian clothes. However, the earliest recorded instance of a dog being used to assist in the capture of a murderer actually took place thirty or so years earlier.

There are sketchy records of a bloodhound being used to track down a murderer in Luton, Bedfordshire, in 1859. The first properly documented case was in Blackburn, Lancashire, in April 1876. William Fish, a town barber, was accused and convicted of the horrendous murder of seven-year-old Emily Holland. The *Blackburn Standard* of 29 July 1876 reported:

> Another act in the tragic drama of the Blackburn murder has been performed. One more only needs to be played out, when the law will exercise its extreme mission, and then we hope the Blackburn murder case, in which Fish has committed the worst crime in modern times, will be consigned to the limbo of forgotten things.

On 28 March 1876, little Emily Holland went missing after telling a friend that she was going 'to fetch half an ounce of tobacco for a man in the street'. Emily Holland was never seen alive again. The following morning, a child's torso was found wrapped in two copies of the *Preston Herald* newspaper minus the head, arms and legs. A little later the same day a child's legs were found similarly wrapped in copies of the same newspaper. During a post-mortem examination the pathologist noticed that several strands of hair of different colours were found on Emily's body. Detectives came to the conclusion that she had been murdered and mutilated in a barber's shop. Two local barbers were the chief suspects, in particular William Fish. He was cooperative with the police, allowing them to search his home on several occasions; Fish was a collector of old local newspapers, in particular the *Preston Herald*, and detectives found that four copies in the sequential collection were missing, these corresponded to the copies wrapped around the body parts of young Emily. This was good circumstantial evidence, but when Fish told officers that he had used these particular copies to start a fire they were stumped; with no further evidence to rely on, they were in no position to charge him with murder.

The story was extensively covered in local and national media, which attracted an extraordinary offer from dog owner Peter Taylor. He claimed that his bloodhound, Morgan, could track down the missing remains of Emily Holland. A rather under-pressure chief constable agreed that a search should take place at relevant locations, led by Taylor and his canine companion. On 16 April the areas of Bastwell and Lower Cunliffe, where the torso and legs had been discovered, were searched with a negative result. They then searched William Fish's home, and Morgan started to bark in front of a bedroom fireplace. Police discovered a package wrapped in a copy of the *Manchester Courier* in a small recess of the chimney; it contained a human skull, hands and a forearm. Fish was charged with murder. The killer made a chilling confession:

> A few minutes after five in the evening I was standing at my shop door in Moss Street when the deceased child came past ... I asked her to bring me half ounce of tobacco from Cox's shop. She went and bought it for me and I asked her to go upstairs and she did. I went up with her and tried to abuse her, and she was nearly dead. I then cut her throat with a razor. This was in the front room near the fire. I carried her body down to the shop, cut off the head, arms and legs, wrapped up the body in newspapers on the floor, wrapped up the legs also in newspaper and put those parcels in a box in the back kitchen. The arms and head I put in the fire ... I took a part of the head that was unburnt and put it up the chimney in the front bedroom.

Fish was executed at Kirkdale Prison on 14 August 1876 by William Marwood; just before the trapdoor was sprung and he dropped to his death, Fish was heard to exclaim, 'Lord receive my soul. Lord have mercy on me.'

30. DOCTORS TO THE RESCUE (1877)

The 1877 murder of Harriet Staunton and her young son became one of the most sensational and scandalous crimes ever committed in Victorian London, and there were plenty of contenders. The trial was not only notable for the evil nature of the crime, but also because of the actions (some may say interference) of a section of the nation's most respected citizens, namely doctors. The case resulted in the jury-appointed death sentence for the guilty parties being commuted to imprisonment; it was the first such instance in British criminal history outside of cases where insanity was involved. It split the nation and the media, with some newspapers supporting the lawyers and leading physicians while other papers took a very strong view on the opposite side, questioning if this decision would lead to the abolishment of capital punishment and discredit a jury system which had stood at the very heart of British justice for centuries.

This wicked tale started when a mentally deficient clergyman's daughter met a twenty-three-year-old auctioneer's clerk from Streatham in south London. Harriet Richardson's father had died when she was twelve, and she was left a large sum of money (£5,000) in her early adult life by a great-aunt. When Harriet met Louis Staunton she was ten years older but vulnerable and mentally immature, and Staunton was already in another relationship with a fifteen-year-old called Alice Rhodes. Patrick Staunton, Louis's younger brother, was married to Alice Rhodes's older sister Elizabeth. Harriet and Louis married at Clapham in 1875, very much against the wishes of Harriet's remarried mother, who, thinking Louis was after her daughter's money, attempted unsuccessfully to have Harriet committed as a lunatic.

The couple moved into a house in the affluent south London suburb of Brixton. As soon as she was married, her property automatically came under the control of her husband – a fact Staunton would have been very aware of. Harriet's concerned mother visited the address shortly after but was not welcome; she received a letter, purporting to be from her daughter (although the spelling was far beyond the literary capabilities of Harriet), asking her not to visit again. In March of the following year Harriet gave birth to the couple's first and only child, a son whom they called Thomas.

Louis Staunton showed little interest in his new child, and continued his relationship with Alice Rhodes. He used some of Harriet's money to purchase a farmhouse called Little Grays in the small village of Cudham in Kent, just south of Orpington. Louis moved Alice Rhodes into the farmhouse and they lived as man and wife whilst he kept his wife Harriet and son Thomas in an upstairs room at his brother's home, Frith Cottage, twenty minutes away. The room was effectively a cell in which Harriet and Thomas were incarcerated, with no curtains, washing or toilet facilities, no proper bed and no communication with the outside world. All Harriet's belongings were taken from her, including her fine clothes and jewellery, and given to Alice. She was not allowed to leave the room; the Stauntons' maid, Clara Brown, was threatened with violence if their instructions were not strictly obeyed.

Over the next few weeks and months Thomas and Harriet were effectively murdered by Louis, Patrick, Alice and Elizabeth, who neglected the two to the point of starvation. Whilst this incredibly cruel turn of events was playing out, Harriet's mother was desperately trying to locate her daughter and by chance bumped into Alice Rhodes at London Bridge station. Noticing Alice wore one of Harriet's favourite brooches, she confronted Alice, demanding to know where her daughter was and why she was wearing such a personal piece of Harriet's jewellery. Alice told her that she had been given it as a gift by Harriet. Unconvinced, Harriet's mother managed to track the Stauntons' charwoman down and learnt that they had moved to the farmhouse in Cudham. She located the property and went to find her daughter; on her arrival she was confronted by Louis, who refused to let her see Harriet, who of course was at her brother-in-law's property a short distance away with her son, slowly starving to death.

The winter of 1876/7 came and went, with Harriet and Thomas weakening until little Thomas could survive no longer; now eighteen months old, pitifully he had remained the size of a baby. Patrick and Elizabeth Staunton took the infant, suffering from bruising to his face and malnutrition, to Guy's Hospital in April

1877; he died later the same evening. The next day, Louis Staunton instructed a local undertaker to bury the body of his son without any ceremony.

A few days after her son's death, having suffered the mental anguish of not being able to attend his burial, Harriet gave up all hope of her own survival. Louis Staunton, not wanting Harriet to die in Cudham, transported his wife 12 miles away to a lodging house at 34 Forbes Road, Penge. She died soon after; a local doctor naively believed the Stauntons' deceitful account of her symptoms before death and declared that she had died of apoplexy.

It was only through an incredible coincidence that the Stauntons and Alice Rhodes faced justice for their terrible crimes. Louis Staunton went into a local post office to inquire about where he could register the death of his wife, unaware that standing behind him in the queue waiting patiently to buy a stamp was Louis de Casabianca – Harriet's brother-in-law. He had been in the area on other business and was made curious by Staunton's description of the deceased woman, although he didn't catch her name. On hearing the mention of Cudham, a location he recognised from conversations with his mother-in-law, he thought it could be Harriet. He made further enquiries in the area and discovered that the dead woman was indeed his sister-in-law. Louis de Casabianca raised the alarm with local police, who recovered the body. A local doctor gave evidence to the inquest into Harriet's death; she was 'in a filthy state from dirt and vermin', and in his opinion 'death was caused by want of nourishment and starvation'.[13] At the time of her death, Harriet weighed just 5 st. 4 lb. Louis, Patrick and Elizabeth Staunton and Alice Rhodes were duly charged with murder, and appeared at the Old Bailey in September 1877 to stand trial.

The defence attempted to suggest Harriet's death was down to self-neglect and mental instability, trying to convince the jury that Harriet had been an alcoholic and refused to eat or allow her young son any nourishment. Conflicting evidence suggested the cause of death could have been anything from meningitis to tuberculosis. Following the evidence, and a particularly strong summation of the

---

13 *Leicester Journal*, 18 May 1877

facts from Judge Henry Hawkins in which he leaned towards the prosecution's case, the jury returned a verdict of guilty against all four defendants. Hawkins sentenced them to death by hanging, as required by law.

Public interest in the case was huge, and it didn't end with the verdicts. An unprecedented letter appeared in *The Lancet* some days after the trial, signed by many eminent physicians and protesting that, in their opinion, much of the expert evidence given during the trial had been ignored by the trial judge. A campaign was led by novelist Charles Reade (even then you couldn't keep a publicity-seeking celebrity away from a *cause celebre*), leading to a review of the case by Home Secretary Richard Cross. Alice Rhodes was pardoned and released immediately, and Louis, Patrick and Elizabeth had their death sentences commuted to life imprisonment.

There followed a national outrage. It was clear that the general public, who had taken a great interest in this terrible crime and followed the trial in the media, were overwhelmingly of the opinion that all four defendants were guilty of the most obscene crime imaginable – no cut throats or stabbings, no shooting at point-blank range or clubbing to death, but a pre-meditated and utterly cruel crime committed over an extended period of time. Most importantly, the lenience shown to the offenders was an affront to British justice and fairness. Many newspapers of the day had their say, but none so eloquently as the *Dundee Evening Telegraph* of 15 October 1877:

> The brothers Staunton, Mrs Staunton and Alice Rhodes, condemned to death for the murder of Harriet Staunton, have been reprieved. We hope the convicts are duly thankful, and the medical and legal critics, who have been the means of saving their lives, are satisfied. We do not believe the country generally will be so. Ordinarily intelligent people who followed the trial had no difficulty in endorsing the verdict of the jury and the sentence of the judge, who both heard the evidence and saw the demeanour of the witnesses. The same may be said without exception of the newspapers. So

far as we can remember not one of those who now applaud the remission of the sentence had a word to say against the verdict, which was certainly unexpected against Alice Rhodes. The *Daily News*, which had been the principal receptacle of the amateur legal and medical criticisms which poured into the press immediately after the trial, promptly changed front a couple of days after it had endorsed the verdict. The mass of papers, however, who this morning profess satisfaction with the clemency exercised by Mr Cross, have continued to write as if the execution of the male prisoners would be the least that would satisfy justice. We did so ourselves, and we see no reason to change our view. If capital punishment is not to be totally abolished – if trial by jury is not to be discredited – if evidence which satisfies the average intelligence of a community is not to be put aside at the bidding of a few amateur professional critics, then we cannot help saying that the respite of the brothers Staunton is a matter of surprise. The verdict that lumped together Alice Rhodes, who was not proved to have more than a guilty knowledge of the foul act that was being committed, and Mrs Staunton, who might have been to some extent coerced by her husband was certainly a matter for surprise. The logic however, which would spare all the prisoners because the jury wanted sense to discriminate in favour of some of them is still more surprising. So far as the convicts are concerned, everyone will be glad that they have had their lives spared and their period for repentance lengthened. But there can be no doubt that trial by jury, common justice, and the moral sentiment of the country, have received a serious shock by the message conveyed on Saturday evening to the Penge murderers.

Patrick Staunton died in prison. Louis served twenty years, and Elizabeth was out in six.

31. COPPERS ON THE TAKE (1877)

The Metropolitan Police force was founded in 1829 with the primary responsibilities of maintaining public order and preventing crime. The investigation of crime and the detection and prosecution of offenders did not fit into this remit; these tasks were left to the forerunners of the force, the Bow Street Runners.

The need for a coordinated approach in crime detection was highlighted by the case of Daniel Good. In 1842, Good murdered his common-law wife, Jane Jones, in Putney, London; over the next few days he dismembered her body and began to burn the evidence in stables at Putney Park, where he was employed. During this period he was seen to steal a pair of trousers from a local pawnbroker's shop and was questioned by a police constable at the stables; whilst searching for the stolen property, the officer came across the dismembered and partially burnt remains of Jane Jones. Good managed to escape by locking the constable in the stables; the subsequent search for him was a disorganised comedy of errors, highlighting the ineptitude within the force in regards to crime detection, and this was pounced on by the media, who were very critical of the Metropolitan Police's failings. Good was arrested on a building site in Tonbridge, Kent, a week after his disappearance, when recognised by a former policeman. With the disbandment of the Bow Street Runners three years earlier, there was a demand from the public and media for a standalone reactive detective branch to investigate the most serious of crimes. Just three months after Daniel Good was executed, the Detective Branch of Scotland Yard was established.

This branch of detectives developed a formidable reputation for themselves – their techniques in the investigation of murder were world-renowned until 1877, when four detective inspectors were charged with criminal offences, leading to a trial that would destroy the reputation of Scotland Yard for many years to come.

In October 1877, Detective Inspectors George Clarke, John Meiklejohn, Nathaniel Druscovich and William Palmer stood in the dock of the Old Bailey together with solicitor Edward Froggatt, charged with 'having conspired to defeat the ends of justice in connection with the recent turf frauds on Madame de Goncourt'. The trial would be recorded in history as 'The Trial of the Detectives', but was also known as 'the Turf Club Frauds' or the 'Madame de Goncourt Case'. The sequence of events that led to the downfall of four of Scotland Yard's finest started with a horseracing scam involving two shrewd young confidence tricksters, William Kerr and Harry Benson.

In early 1877, a gullible Parisian resident called Madame de Goncourt contacted her bank manager asking him to release £30,000 which she wished to be placed on a racehorse in England. The bank manager was extremely concerned, and indeed correctly suspicious, knowing this behaviour to be totally out of character for his customer; he contacted Madame de Goncourt's London-based solicitor, who in turn reported their concerns to detectives at Scotland Yard. When detectives uncovered the circumstances of what had taken place it was quickly established that the whole setup was part of a criminal scam involving William Kerr and Harry Benson.

The scam involved the creation of a fictitious betting periodical called *The Sporting and Racing Chronicle*. Contained in the publication was a fictitious account of a man named Mr Montgomery who had been so successful in betting on horseraces in the United Kingdom that he had been blacklisted by bookmakers the length and breadth of the country; he was therefore looking for individuals to place bets on his behalf. The susceptible punters would unwittingly place bets on horses endorsed by him, writing cheques in their own name and sending him the winnings; in return, he would repay them a fee for their trouble, again by cheque. While the money sent by the victims of the scam was real, the cheques sent back to them would bounce. Kerr and Benson were identified as the scammers (Benson had previous convictions for similar offences), but they disappeared before they could be arrested. Eventually Benson was tracked down to Amsterdam and Kerr to Edinburgh, but until then they had always been one step ahead of the authorities.

Inspector Nathaniel Druscovich was sent to Holland to bring Benson back to face justice, but it was noted by Superintendent

Adolphus Williamson (who later attained the rank of Chief Constable of the CID) that Druscovich was a little unenthusiastic about the prospect and made it into a rather long-winded affair. On 9 April 1877, Kerr, Benson and two lesser associates were convicted at the Old Bailey; Benson received fifteen years' penal servitude, Kerr ten years.

Following their convictions, Kerr and Benson accused several Scotland Yard detectives of being involved in corrupt practices. Inspector John Meiklejohn appeared to be the most corrupt, having accepted bribes from bookmakers and the criminal underworld for much of his detective career; he had first taken money from William Kerr for inside information about possible arrests as early as 1873. The other three – Druscovich, Clarke and Palmer – either displayed a level of naivety or were influenced by peer pressure. The trial at the Old Bailey took place in November 1877 amid tremendous media and public scrutiny. George Clarke was acquitted following a character reference from Superintendent Williamson and immediately resigned from the force; the other three were found guilty and given two-year custodial sentences. Druscovich died prematurely shortly after being released, Meiklejohn became a private detective and Palmer became a publican.

Lessons had to be learnt following such a high-profile court case, in which the integrity of Scotland Yard's detective branch had been savagely damaged. On 8 April 1878 the newly appointed Director of Criminal Intelligence, Howard Vincent, shook up the detective branch by creating the Criminal Investigation Department (CID), which has lasted to the present day. Vincent and Commissioner Edmund Henderson implemented wide-ranging reforms to the investigation of serious crime, increasing the number of detectives to 280 and devolving them to divisions around the force – within six years the number of detectives had increased to 800.

32. MURDER ON THE BRIGHTON LINE (1881)

The murder of retired corn merchant Isaac Gold aboard a train on the London to Brighton line in June 1881 made British criminal history when, during the investigation, a portrait of the murder suspect was circulated in a British newspaper for the first time.

On Monday 27 June 1881 the 2 p.m. train from London Bridge to Brighton stopped at Preston Park, minutes from its final destination. A railway ticket collector observed a man alight from a first-class compartment; he seemed to be unsteady on his feet as he walked toward the exit. On closer inspection, his clothing was dishevelled and he was covered in blood. He informed the collector that he had been attacked on the train by two assailants just before it entered the Merstham Tunnel; he gave descriptions of his attackers, but complained that following a blow to the head he could remember nothing more of the incident. The victim, who gave his name as Percy Lefroy, was escorted to the local police station while the ticket collector went to advise the railway police. Lefroy was interviewed by police officers and made an official criminal complaint of robbery before being conveyed to hospital for treatment. He refused to be admitted, stating that he had to return to London for an urgent meeting, but agreed to return to the police station before his departure.

Lefroy was later interviewed, with one of his interviewers being the chief constable of the Sussex force. During the interview Lefroy reaffirmed the descriptions of his attackers and the circumstances leading to his injuries before offering a reward for the capture of the two men responsible. In the meantime, the carriage from which Lefroy had alighted at Preston Road was located at Brighton and secured as a crime scene; police discovered three bullet holes together with a substantial amount of blood on the carriage's upholstery, footboard, mat and door handle, as well as a bloodied handkerchief and newspaper.

By now the interviewing officers were putting a picture together of what Lefroy was claiming – it was full of ambiguities, as if he were making it up as he went along. Even so, he was allowed to return to London by train, albeit with a detective called George Holmes in tow.

While Lefroy and his escort travelled north to London, railway police officers discovered the body of sixty-four-year-old Brighton resident Isaac Gold trackside in the Balcombe Tunnel. He had been shot and stabbed, and a bloodied knife lay nearby. It would later be established that a watch, chain and a large amount of money had been stolen. A telegram was sent along the line ahead of the train on which Lefroy and Holmes were travelling, and a message was passed to Holmes by the stationmaster at Three Bridges station with instructions not to let Lefroy out of his sight. Lefroy must have realized from Holmes's demeanour that the game was up; he persuaded Holmes to allow him to change his blood-covered clothes and led him to an address in Wallington, Surrey – a boarding house that he claimed was run by a relative. Holmes allowed Lefroy into the address unescorted; he escaped out of the back window.

A nationwide hunt was launched to find Percy Lefroy, whose real name was Mapleton. Wanted notices were published in all the main newspapers around the country with a detailed description. The *Daily Telegraph* went one step further and published an artist's impression based on witness descriptions – the first time this had ever been seen in the British press. However, the suspect had vanished.

An inquest recorded a verdict of wilful murder, and the railway company offered the large reward of £200 for information leading to the arrest and conviction of Percy Mapleton aka Lefroy. He was eventually arrested in lodgings he rented at 32 Smith Street, Stepney. The landlady was suspicious of her new tenant's habit of keeping his curtains drawn all day and only going out at night, and contacted the police. Detectives built a solid case; as well as bloodstained clothing in the lodgings, it was proved Percy had pawned a revolver – the murder weapon – days before. He was tried at the Maidstone Assizes and found guilty following just ten minutes of deliberation by the jury. He was sentenced to death and executed by William Marwood on 29 November 1881.

33. WHAT WOULD YOU HAVE DONE? (1884)

A case that appeared before the High Court of Justice (Queen's Bench Division), London, in 1884 stirred profound emotions in the seafaring communities of south-west England. Four men had drifted many miles from land in rough seas aboard a rickety lifeboat with no food or water. The actions of three of the crew raised the same question for everybody who took an interest in the case: 'What would *I* have done?' *The Crown* vs *Dudley and Stephens* would set the precedent in law that necessity is *not* a defence in a charge of murder.

Australian lawyer John Want purchased a yacht named the *Mignonette*, which he required to sail the 15,000 miles from England to Sydney, Australia. The 52-foot cruiser *Mignonette* was twenty years old, and not designed for long, challenging sea voyages. Want had difficulty finding a crew willing to take on this arduous journey, but eventually hired Captain Tom Dudley, Edwin Stephens, Edmund Brookes and a young seventeen-year-old cabin boy named Richard Parker. The crew set sail for Australia on 19 May 1884 from Southampton. On 5 July the yacht ran into a storm north-west of the Cape of Good Hope. It was struck by a huge wave and capsized; the crew fled in the rickety lifeboat, not having time to collect any fresh water or provisions apart from two tins of turnips. Dudley estimated that they were about 700 miles from land. The crew managed to go two days before the first tin of turnips was shared, but they were unable to catch rainwater to drink. Their plight was eased when they managed to catch a turtle, which they devoured raw.

By mid-July, their supply of food was exhausted. They had begun drinking their own urine. Young Parker became seriously ill – probably from drinking seawater – and fell into a coma. By 23 July, having been adrift at sea for eighteen days, desperately hungry and with little likelihood of being picked up, Captain Tom Dudley suggested to the other two that it was better one of their number die in order for the other three to survive and that they should draw lots; Edmund Brookes refused to take part and the idea was abandoned. It became abundantly clear that Richard Parker was at death's door, and Dudley again raised the idea – this time only with Edwin Stephens – that Parker should be sacrificed to enable their survival. Stephens helped pinion the unconscious Parker whilst Dudley slid his penknife into the young lad's jugular vein – Brookes later claimed that he had taken no part in the event, neither assenting to the act or raising an objection.

The three desperate men fed on Parker's body and drank his blood. Dudley later described the terrible scene: 'I can assure you I shall never forget the sight of my two unfortunate companions over that ghastly meal. We all was like mad wolfs who should get the most and for men, fathers of children, to commit such a deed we could not have our right reason.' The body of Richard Parker sustained the three remaining men until they sighted a German sailing boat – the *Montezuma* – on the morning of 29 July 1884, which transported them and the remains of Richard Parker to the port of Falmouth in Cornwall.

On their arrival the survivors were summoned to the customs house, where they were required by law to make statements in the event of a shipping loss. Present during the depositions by all three was customs officer and police sergeant James Laverty, who questioned them about the circumstances surrounding Parker's death and in particular what method Dudley had used to kill him. Dudley and Stephens were frank about their actions, believing they had done no wrong and were protected by a custom of the sea (a custom practised by the officers and crew of ships and boats whilst in the open sea, as distinguished from maritime law).

Laverty seized the knife as evidence and telegraphed the depositions to the Registrar General of Shipping in London, who advised Sergeant Laverty that the men should be detained. Laverty obtained warrants for the men's arrest from the Mayor of Falmouth and detained Dudley, Brookes and Stephens in the borough police station. All three appeared before the town magistrates on Monday 8 September. Dudley in particular seemed confident that they would be exonerated, but things didn't go to plan as the justices had been instructed to seek the advice of a Treasury solicitor in all cases of murder, and the three men were remanded in custody. In the meantime Home Secretary Sir William Harcourt conferred with Attorney General Sir Henry James and took the decision to prosecute Dudley, Brooks and Stephens for the murder of Richard Parker.

This story of human survival in the most distressing of circumstances was big news, spreading from the community of Falmouth nationally and internationally. When the three accused appeared again in front of the courts, public opinion was very much behind them; this was buoyed by the fact that Richard Parker's brother attended the court and shook hands with the three men in an apparent show of solidarity, as he was also a seaman and had probably asked himself what he would have done. Immense pressure was funnelled towards Harcourt, who gave his blessing that all three should be released on bail and reunited with their families. But Harcourt felt a profound disgust at the public's attitude to the taking of a young man's life, even under the circumstances in which the three desperately hungry men had found themselves; this made him more determined that they should face trial.

German-born prosecutor William Otto Adolph Julius Danckwerts was briefed for the Crown; although relatively inexperienced at this stage of his career, he had an in-depth knowledge of maritime law. It would appear he was handed a poisoned chalice, as he soon realised that public opinion was very much against him. The only witnesses to the crime were the defendants themselves; any confession was only admissible against the individual making it, and not his co-defendants. As the prosecution had to prove to a jury the defendant's guilt beyond reasonable doubt, he was up against it, and probably thinking of the effect the case may have on his future career. All three men appeared at the magistrates' court on 18 September 1884, when Danckwerts played his ace card by asking that Brookes be discharged with a view to calling him as a prosecution witness against Dudley and Stephens – the magistrates agreed. He called Brookes and other witnesses who had heard the survivors' stories to prove a *prima facie* case; Dudley and Stephens were committed for trial at the winter Cornwall and Devon assizes in Exeter.

The trial opened on 3 November 1884; the prosecution was led by Arthur Charles QC, with Arthur Collins defending in front of presiding judge Baron Huddleston, a late substitute for Sir William Grove.

It would appear Huddleston had been hand-picked along with a 'hanging jury' who had delivered a guilty verdict in Huddleston's previous case, which had ended with a death sentence. Dudley and Stephens pleaded not guilty to the charge. It seemed to both barristers that Huddleston had an agenda, possibly at the direction of the Home Office, to settle the law on *necessity* in relation to murder charges. Charles opened the case to the jury by referring to the depositions initially made by the defendants, which indicated they were fully aware of what they were doing. He introduced several witnesses who had spoken to the defendants when they first came ashore, and then he called Brooks. Brooks informed the court that he had had no involvement in the death of Parker, and then provided a vivid account of the desperate conditions on the boat, the circumstances that led to Parker's demise and indeed his own act of cannibalism. Each witness was cross-examined by Collins, who concluded the case for the defence with a heartfelt closing speech outlining the stark choice facing the defendants in that lifeboat.

Probably even before the case, Huddleston had made up his mind on the law and planned to ensure a guilty verdict to determine the law on the question of necessity once and for all. He offered the jury a blunt choice: find the men guilty of murder (going very much against public opinion) or return a 'special verdict', once common in English law but not used for nearly a century. The special verdict is a verdict by a jury that makes specific factual conclusions rather than (or in addition to) a declaration of guilt or liability. Huddleston produced a pre-prepared special verdict which he read out to the jury, inviting them to indicate their assent to each paragraph by keeping their silence. His final paragraph stated: 'But whether upon the whole matter, the prisoners were and are guilty of murder the jury are ignorant and refer to the court [to make the decision for them].' Huddleston adjourned the case to the Royal Courts of Justice in London, allowing the defendants bail.

On Tuesday 9 December 1884, a panel of judges led by Lord Coleridge delivered its judgement. Coleridge announced that the judges found there could be no common law defence of necessity in a charge of murder, either on the basis of legal precedent or ethics and morality. He went on to say:

To preserve one's life is generally speaking a duty, but it may be the plainest and the highest duty to sacrifice it. War is full of instances in which it is a man's duty not to live, but to die. The duty, in the case of shipwreck, of a captain to his crew, of the crew to the passengers, of soldiers to women and children, as in the noble case of the *Birkenhead* [a troopship that hit an uncharted rock just off Cape Town in January 1852 and sunk; the seven women and thirteen children were evacuated first]; these duties impose on men the moral necessity, not of the preservation, but of the sacrifice of their lives for others, from which in no country, least of all, it is hoped, in England, will men ever shrink, as indeed, they have not shrunk.

Dudley and Stephens were convicted of murder and sentenced to the mandatory penalty of death, but with the added plea for compassion that the 'Crown may wish to consider the possibility of a pardon in such extraordinary circumstances'. Home Secretary William Harcourt commuted the death sentence to one of six months' imprisonment; Dudley and Stephens were released on 20 May 1885.

34. HE COULD HAVE BEEN SAVED BY THE SKIN OF HIS ... (1895)

The identification parade was first introduced in the mid-1890s by the Metropolitan Police as a method of proving, or disproving, the presence of a suspect at or near the scene of a crime. Several men or women, unconnected to the investigation, would stand in line with the accused. A witness or victim would be invited to view the parade and attempt to identify the guilty party. However, the identification parade showed its weaknesses when it played a major part in the wrongful conviction of Norwegian-born Adolf Beck for crimes he did not commit. The result of this case would lead to a change in the law regarding identification, and, most importantly, the creation of a British criminal court of appeal.

Adolf Beck was an educated man, having graduated as a chemist in his country of birth. At the age of twenty-four he decided to see the world and went to sea, eventually settling in England and finding employment as a shipping clerk in 1865. In 1868 he moved to South America, where he made his fortune in the property market before losing much of it investing in a copper mine in Norway. He returned to London short of money and soon got into serious financial difficulties; he stayed at the Covent Garden Hotel until his account went into arrears before taking less salubrious lodgings at 139 Victoria Street. Despite his problems, he had his pride and made the best of a bad situation, always dressing as smartly as his limited budget would allow.

On 16 December 1895 Beck was out walking along Victoria Street when he was approached by a rather irate female named Ottilie Meissonier, a German language teacher, who blocked his way and accused him of stealing several rings and watches from her. Beck attempted to walk around the lady, thinking she must be mixing him up with somebody else or that she was involved in some sort of scam to rob him. Meissonier continued following him, and, to Beck's astonishment, approached a passing police officer – PC 419A Frederick Edwards – and made a formal complaint against Beck, asking the constable to take him into custody.

Meissonier alleged that she had been walking along Victoria Street three weeks earlier when approached by Beck. He had tipped his hat to her and asked her if she was Lady Everton, introducing himself as Lord Wilton de Willoughby. When Meissonier had replied that she was not, the man excused himself, but not before asking where she was off to. Meissonier replied that she was attending a flower show nearby. He advised her not to go, saying the flowers would be of poor quality; he boasted that he was a horticulturist and kept ten gardeners on his Lincolnshire estate, so his flowers were of much better quality.

Meissonier, impressed by his standing and obvious breeding, told him that she had, that very morning, received a box of beautiful Chrysanthemums. The gentleman asked her if he could visit her to see them – Meissonier agreed and gave him her address.

The following day the man arrived at her address and stated that he was extremely wealthy, owning numerous properties in the West Brompton area, and that he was related to Lord Salisbury. The man then suggested that she join him and some friends on a planned trip to the Riviera as she was both musical and multilingual (she spoke English, French and German). After some thought, she agreed that she could come for a fortnight. The man seemed delighted, but commented that her 'toilette' was not good enough and compiled a list of outfits she needed to purchase, writing out a cheque from the Union Bank, St James's Street, for £40 to cover her costs. He also commented on her sub-standard jewellery, which he offered to take and upgrade for her by adding better-quality precious stones; he also took a bracelet and an antique watch. Shortly after he left her house, Meissonier became suspicious. She sent her maid to follow the mysterious stranger, but she lost sight of him. Meissonier took a cab to St James's Street but could find no trace of the 'Union Bank'. She took the cheque to another bank nearby, only to be told it was in fact a fake. Meissonier finished this account to the police officer by confidently identifying Adolf Beck as the thief once more.

Beck was taken to Rochester Row police station and placed on an identification parade with six other local men of similar age, height, hair colouring and dress in the police station's charge room; Meissonier and another victim of the same scam, Daisy Grant, walked along the line and both individually identified Beck as the offender. Detectives looked back at similar offences that had been reported to them over a two-year period and discovered a further twenty or so crimes that matched the *modus operandi*. Beck was picked out in similar identification parades by many victims, and was eventually charged with fourteen offences ranging from fraud to theft and deception.

Several days later, Adolf Beck appeared at the magistrates' court for committal to the Crown Court. At this point the dire circumstances in which he found himself were about to get even worse. Just before he was committed to stand trial at the Central Criminal Court, a police constable called Elliss Spurrell was called to the witness box. PC Spurrell stated that eighteen years previously he had arrested a man who called himself John Smith. He continued:

> In 1877 I was in the Metropolitan Police Reserve. On 7 May I was present at the Central Criminal Court where the prisoner (indicating Adolf Beck) in the name of John Smith was convicted feloniously stealing ear rings and a ring and eleven shillings off Louisa Leonard and was sentenced to five years penal servitude. I produce the certificate of that conviction. The prisoner is the man. There is no doubt whatever ... I know quite well what is at stake on my answer and I say without doubt he is the man.[14]

This was a great shock to Beck, as he was hoping his previous good character would convince a jury that it had all been a terrible mistake. The evidence of PC Spurrell had effectively destroyed his claim to be of good character, and saddled him with a record of previous criminal offending and a prison sentence. However, there was hope for him as he could prove he had been in South America in 1877 and could not possibly be the person convicted and sent to prison under the name of John Smith as claimed by PC Spurrell.

The case of *The Crown* vs *Adolf Beck* commenced on 24 February 1896 at the Old Bailey in front of Common Serjeant Sir Forrest Fulton. Beck was defended by Charles Gill, and the Crown's case was led by Horace Avory. The whole trial was indeed one of errors and missed opportunities to acquit an innocent man. The defence, unsurprisingly, based their case on mistaken identity. PC Spurrell's testimony accusing Beck of being the John Smith previously charged would cause the prosecution more problems than it would solve. All the defence had to do was prove that Beck was in South America in 1877 when these offences were committed; they could then not only prove that Beck had been misidentified in relation to the 1877 conviction by PC Spurrell, but seriously undermine Beck's involvement in relation to the new charges. Avory knew this would

---

14 *Old Bailey Online.*

damage the prosecution case, so decided to simply avoid the problem and not call PC Spurrell at all. This meant that the evidence on which Beck would be tried rested solely on the recent identification by the witnesses and a forensic expert.

A handwriting expert, Thomas Gurrin, gave testimony on behalf of the Crown; he had intended to produce a list of clothing written by the convicted John Smith in 1877 and compare the handwriting to the list of clothing allegedly written by Adolf Beck for Meissonier, and then in turn to Beck's own handwriting on the day. His intention had been to state to the court that the three lists were written, in all probability, by the same person: Adolf Beck, who had cleverly written them with a 'disguised hand'. Again Avory anticipated the problem; if he allowed Gurrin to state that the person who wrote the 1877 list was the same as the person who wrote the recent lists, the defence would be at liberty to introduce the South American witnesses proving Beck was in Argentina in 1877. Cunningly, Avory only asked Gurrin about the more recent lists.

The witnesses pointed to Beck in court; however, a few discrepancies did surface which should have raised serious doubts about the reliability of identification evidence: one witness remembers the offender talking in 'Yankee' slang, while Meissonier remembered that he had a scar on the right side of his neck (Beck had none) and that the offender had a longer waxed moustache. However, none of these inconsistencies were enough to put reasonable doubt in the jurors' minds, and Adolf Beck was found guilty of all charges. Beck was sentenced to seven years' penal servitude; he was to serve his sentence at Portland Prison on the Isle of Portland. Even though it had not been evidentially proved that he and 'John Smith' were the same person, Beck was allocated Smith's previous prison number, 'D523', with the addition of the letter 'W', which labelled him a recidivist.

Beck's solicitor, believing him to be innocent, hit an establishment brick wall. The need for an avenue through which to appeal convictions and sentencing was evident to all in the legal profession, but none yet existed. Between 1896 and 1901, Beck's solicitor presented ten separate petitions requesting that the conviction be re-examined. Bearing in mind the basis of the case was the presumption that Beck and Smith were the same person, nobody other than Beck's solicitor had thought of examining the prison records for a detailed description of Smith to compare with Beck; if they had, they would have discovered an irrefutable physical difference between the two men.

Beck's solicitor was refused access to Smith's prison file, but when it was eventually examined by a Home Office official it was discovered that Smith was Jewish and circumcised – Beck was not. This new evidence was presented to the trial judge, Sir Forrest Fulton, who acknowledged that Smith and Beck could not be one and the same but stubbornly reiterated that Beck had been convicted and sentenced on the basis of the 1894 and 1895 offences. The only benefit received by Beck following this revelation was the removal of the 'W' from his prison number. He was eventually paroled for good behaviour in 1901.

This was not the end of Adolf Beck's horror story. Three years later, in April 1904, Beck left his flat and was again approached by a woman who accused him of the very same offence for which he had languished in prison for five years. The woman was a servant girl called Paulina Scott who had legitimately been swindled out of her jewellery by a grey-haired gentleman after he had approached her on the street and promised her the world. The problem occurred when the investigating officer, Detective Inspector Ward, recognised the *modus operandi* and set up a confrontation between Adolf Beck and Scott in which she accused Beck of the crime. Beck panicked and ran – not the actions of an innocent man according to the detective, who arrested him. Incredibly, Beck faced another jury at the Old Bailey on 27 June 1904, having been identified by a further five female victims of similar scams, and was again convicted. Beck made a statement to the court that 'before God my maker, I am absolutely innocent of every charge brought against me. I have not spoken to or seen any of these women before; they were set against me by the detectives. I can bring many witnesses to prove I have acted honestly in my business in the City from 10 a.m. to 6 p.m. I ask the press to help me to get all evidence in my support from my solicitor.' The presiding judge, Sir William Grantham, less than pleased with the standard of evidence and the quality of the identification, sensibly postponed the sentencing and remanded Beck in custody. Beck and his defence team did not know it, but the delay in sentencing and Beck's incarceration on remand would prove to be the first piece of luck they had received – it would lead to his total exoneration.

On 7 July 1904, just days before Beck was due back in court and facing a substantial prison sentence on the back of his now documented previous criminality, Inspector John Kane, a member of the Criminal Investigation Department, learnt of an arrest on his 'patch' in which a man had attempted to swindle a pair of unemployed actresses of their jewellery. Kane had first-hand knowledge of the Beck case, as he had been present at both of his trials, and also knew him to be in custody awaiting sentence and therefore unable to commit these particular crimes. His curiosity and his 'copper's nose' led him to the custody block, where he entered the cell of a man who had given the name of William Thomas.

Thomas was grey-haired, moustachioed and had a scar on the right side of his neck, as described by Ottilie Meissonier. A number of victims of the crimes for which Beck had been convicted were asked to look at Thomas; nearly all declared this to be the man and admitted that they had been wrong about Beck. The prisoner was identified as an Austrian national called Wilhelm Wyatt. He was widely travelled, having spent time in the United States and Australia before settling in London and choosing his life of crime. When Beck was imprisoned for Wyatt's actions he couldn't believe his luck; he decided to lay low and return to the States, only returning when Beck had completed his sentence, at which point he took up his criminal ways again. Wyatt pleaded guilty to his crimes at the Old Bailey on 15 September 1904 and was given five years' imprisonment (two less than the innocent Beck had received).

Adolf Beck was given a king's pardon in July 1904 and awarded a total of £5,000 in compensation. Beck gave evidence to a Committee of Inquiry that heard from all parties in this awful miscarriage of justice and apportioned blame squarely on the shoulders of the initial prosecution and heavily criticised the trial judge, Common Serjeant Sir Forrest Fulton. As a result of its recommendations, the English Court of Criminal Appeal was created. Beck never recovered from his ordeal, and died of pleurisy and bronchitis in a London hospital on 7 December 1909, aged sixty-eight.

35. HAVE YOU HAD A DRINK, SIR? (1897)

On Saturday 11 September 1897 the *Morning Post* reported a case that appeared before the magistrates at Marlborough Street in London's West End. It is believed to be the first occasion on which a driver was arrested and convicted for being drunk in command of a motor vehicle, in this case a licensed cab. George Smith, aged twenty-five, who lived in Harrow in north-west London, was driving his cab along Bond Street at 12.45 a.m when he was seen by Police Constable 247 'C' Russell to swerve from one side of the road to the other before running across the footway and crashing into 165 Bond Street, breaking the water pipe and the beading of the window. PC Russell went and spoke to Smith; realising he was in fact drunk, he escorted him to Vine Street police station. Smith denied that he was drunk, so a divisional surgeon was summoned.[15] The divisional surgeon certified that George Smith was indeed drunk and shouldn't have been in charge of his cab. Smith asked PC Russell, 'How fast was I going?' Russell answered, 'I should think about eight miles an hour.' The prisoner retorted, 'At the time I was going up an incline, and I could not have been doing six miles an hour. The fastest these cars can travel is eight miles an hour.' The magistrate Mr De Rutzen commented that he had not been charged with driving furiously but driving whilst drunk, and asked Smith what he had to say about that. George Smith replied, 'I have nothing to say to that. I admit to having had two or three glasses of beer. I am very sorry. It is the first time I have been charged with being drunk in charge of a cab.' De Rutzen fined him 20s and pointed out to him that 'you motor-car drivers ought to be very careful, for if anything happens to you – well, the police have a very happy knack of stopping a runaway horse, but to stop a motor is a very different thing'.

---

15 In those days police officers were not yet deemed capable of determining if a person was drunk as they are today. The phrase 'He was unsteady on his feet, his eyes were glazed and his breath smelt of intoxicating liquor' had not yet entered a policeman's evidential vocabulary.

36. DEAF BUT NOT DUMB (1900)

When a crime involves a victim, offender or witness who suffers from a mental health issue or physical disability (including being blind, deaf or mute), there are established procedures contained in British legislation such as the Police and Criminal Evidence Act 1984 to ensure such a person is dealt with equally and with relevant safeguards. Two historical cases demonstrate a certain prejudice against such people, and these were landmark cases to a degree, preparing the way for witnesses with physical disabilities to be heard and taken seriously within the judicial process – something we take for granted in today's society.

The first case dates from 11 January 1786 when a petty thief named William Bartlett appeared at the Old Bailey charged with an offence of grand larceny in that he, on 6 January 1786, did feloniously steal a silver watch, value 20s; a steel chain, value 6d; and a steel seal, value 4d, all the property of John Williamson. Williamson told the court that he was walking along Cheapside in the City when he was jostled by several men, one of whom was the defendant, and his watch and chain were removed from his waistcoat; he saw quite clearly his property in the possession of the defendant.

The prosecution called the only other witness to the theft, a man called John Rasten, who entered the court with his sister, Marta Rasten. The defence barrister stood and exclaimed to the presiding judge, 'My Lord, this is a witness that can neither speak nor hear.' He continued: 'This woman is to be an interpreter to a dumb man, to which I object.' The judge, after establishing that the oath would be explained and taken by the witness who would look up to heaven to show that he understands that he is to answer any questions truthfully, overruled the objection and the evidence was heard via the interpreter. Bartlett was found guilty as charged and transported to Australia for seven years.

The second case was reported in the *Illustrated Police News* of 20 October 1900 with the headline 'Extraordinary Detection of Burglars by a Deaf and Dumb Girl'. The opening sentence read, 'A remarkable case was heard before Mr McConnell QC chairman of the Newington Sessions.' Standing in the dock was a young butcher called Frederick Albert Roberts, accused of breaking and entering into the home of his uncle, contractor Edward Mason of 62 Upper Kennington Lane, and stealing jewellery and money to the value of £350. Mr Mason gave evidence that on the afternoon of 29 July 1900 he had been out enjoying a social engagement with his wife and on their return found their front door ajar. His safe and desk were open, silver watches had been taken from the breakfast room, a bag of gold from a first-floor safe and a quantity of jewellery from the bedroom. Mr Mason also disclosed that the burglars had apparently helped themselves to a drink of rum from a decanter and that rum was the only drink his nephew Frederick would consume. Of course, the fact that the burglar(s) obviously knew where all the valuable items were kept and had access to the safe was circumstantial; what the prosecution needed were witnesses to place Roberts at the scene. A servant in the Mason household left shortly after the departure of the Masons and saw Roberts in the locality, as did a neighbour who identified the defendant as a person she had seen loitering in the area.

The next witness was a young lady called Francis Peck, accompanied to the witness box by a lady who introduced herself as a teacher. It was explained to the court that Francis Peck was 'deaf and dumb' and that her companion would interpret her evidence by means of 'lip language'. What emerged was a fascinating account by Peck, whose actions on the day were extremely courageous.

Peck, through the interpreter, told the court that she had been in the vicinity of the Mason's house and saw the defendant in the company of another male and a woman. Roberts had tried to open the front door with three keys, meeting with success on the last attempt. They had all entered the property; Peck followed them in and hid behind the curtain of a downstairs window. One man produced an iron bar wrapped in paper from his pocket. They went upstairs and returned with an amount of gold and jewellery. Peck then confirmed that all three helped themselves to the Masons' rum before leaving the property by the front door and getting into a horse and trap and driving away. Peck looked to the dock with a steely determination and identified Roberts as one of the two men she saw on the night.

None of the stolen property was recovered, but it was proved by the prosecution that Roberts had previously been a man of minimal wealth and after the commission of the offence had a plentiful supply of gold, with which he made several large purchases of goods. Roberts' pitiful defence was based on being lent the money by an associate, who appeared at court as a prosecution witness denying the existence of such a loan. The court, unsurprisingly given the weight of such strong evidence, in particular that of Francis Peck, found Roberts guilty. Before sentence it was revealed that Roberts had stolen from the Masons on previous occasions but they had declined to press charges. He was sentenced to nine months' imprisonment.

37. 'ALL RIGHT GOVERNOR, I'LL GO QUIET' (1902)

Czech scientist and physicist Johannes Purkinje created the world's first independent physiology department and laboratory. In 1823 he published a paper in which he suggested that an individual's fingerprints were unique, qualifying this with an academically descriptive classification that was deemed to be too complicated for any practical everyday use. Francis Galton, a Victorian anthropologist and sociologist, estimated that the odds of two human beings having an identical set of fingerprints (including identical twins) was 1 in 64 billion. By 1895 he had devised a fingerprint classification system, but again it was deemed too complicated for any practical use.

Developing the system that would revolutionise crime detection and identification required someone with a practical mind to design a workable template – step forward London-born Edward Henry, a member of the Indian Civil Service and Inspector General of the Bengal Police. Henry exchanged ideas with Francis Galton, and on his return to India from home leave he set about devising a workable system of classifying fingerprints; his system of 'arches', 'loops' and 'whorls' has stood the test of time. Henry was appointed Assistant Commissioner of Crime at Scotland Yard in 1901 and established the Fingerprint Bureau in July of the same year; he chose his staff carefully, selecting Detective Inspector Charles Stedman to head the bureau, assisted by Detective Sergeant Charles Stockley Collins and Detective Constable Frederick Hunt. The primary purpose of the recording of fingerprints was to enable identification of offenders with previous criminal records, and it would soon evolve into an effective tool in the fight against crime.

Harry Jackson, a forty-two-year-old habitual thief, specialised in breaking and entering into commercial and residential properties under cover of darkness. He had previous convictions for similar offences under the name Robert Williams dating from 1895. In the summer of 1902, Harry Jackson went on a burglary spree in south-east London. Denmark Hill was a leafy residential area running from Camberwell to Herne Hill. 156 Denmark Hill was home to the Tustin family. At 10.30 p.m. on 26 June 1902, while locking up No. 156, parlour maid Rose Gilder secured the billiard-room windows, the sills of which had been newly painted. The following day, whilst opening the house to a glorious summer's morning, she saw the billiard room had been broken into. The intruder had forced one of the windows and cut a portion of the billiard table's cover, using this to wrap a number of the billiard balls (in those days they were made of ivory and very valuable) before making good his escape. Rose left the scene undisturbed but noticed in the bright sunlight a dirty fingerprint on the newly painted sill, which she pointed out to the police on their arrival. The crime scene was visited by DS Charles Stockley Collins from Scotland Yard's fingerprint bureau, who took a photograph of the print on the windowsill.

On 1 July 1902, cook Beatrice Shergold discovered the pantry at the Hawthorns, Half Moon Lane, Herne Hill, had been broken into; silver and gold medals had been removed from a sideboard, together with silver spoons and serviette rings from the dining table. The stolen property from this burglary was traced to watchmakers Edward Bordelott of Kennington Road and Charles Champion of Walworth Road.

Just after closing time at the Perseverance public house on Vassal Road, Brixton, on 17 August 1902, barman George Heath noticed the shadow of a man on the roof of the billiard room toward the rear of the premises. Heath informed the local beat policeman, PC George Drewitt, who apprehended the offender – Harry Jackson. As Jackson was taken into custody he said to the constable, 'All right governor, I'll go quietly.' Jackson was in possession of a bag that contained his burglary kit: a jemmy[16], a knife and a screwdriver. Jackson was charged with the burglaries at Denmark Hill (of which he denied any knowledge) and Half Moon Lane.

The indictable offences with which Jackson had been charged meant his trial would take place at the Central Criminal Court, Old Bailey. Assistant Commissioner Edward Henry knew this could be a make-or-break case for him and his bureau. Yes, fingerprint evidence had been used in the past to prove the identity and criminal history of offenders, so important when sentencing for a later crime, but Henry's system had never been put to the test in an ongoing criminal investigation in a British court, where the standard and integrity of the evidence could prove the guilt of an offender.

Henry identified the need for a barrister with the mental capacity to understand the new technology and the forthright personality to translate the science to a judge and jury; he chose Richard Muir, widely regarded as the most competent prosecuting barrister of his time. Henry sent DS Collins over to Muir's chambers, and Collins spent four days explaining Henry's classification system and how it related to the hard evidence against Harry Jackson.

Jackson's trial took place at the Old Bailey on 9 September 1902; he admitted that he had handled the stolen goods from the Half Moon Lane burglary – following the evidence of watchmakers Bordelott and Champion he had little choice – stating he had been given two bags of 'good stuff' to sell by a man in Newington Butts, but denied breaking and entering into the Herne Hill premises or 156 Denmark Hill. DS Charles Stockley Collins was called by

---

16 A short crowbar used to force entry.

Richard Muir to give evidence of his examination of the fingerprint left at the Denmark Hill crime scene, allegedly by the perpetrator. DS Collins introduced himself to the court and jury as an officer specially trained in the identification of fingerprints and said that he had been so for several years, having examined many thousands of prints. He went onto explain in layman's terms Edward Henry's classification system, pointing out that he had never found two people sharing identical fingerprints or any change in a person's fingerprint, insisting that the pattern that makes up the mark remains the same on each finger from birth to death. DS Collins was asked by the prosecution counsel to explain what happened on 28 June 1902 (two days after the discovery of the burglary) when he was called to 156 Denmark Hill. The competent detective cleared his throat and related his evidence in a confident manner.

'On June 28th in consequence of information I went to 156 Denmark Hill and took a photograph of a print on the sash of a window in the billiard room.' He produced a negative, an enlargement and some prints from the enlargement for the jury's perusal. 'On August 7th I went to Brixton prison and obtained a print of the prisoner's hand. I compared it with the impression on the window sash, and with a print of the prisoner's hand which we had at Scotland Yard, taken on July 24th 1901, and have no hesitation in saying that they are identical – the print on the window sash is that of the prisoners left thumb.' DS Collins then went on to explain in detail to the court how the lines of the print on the sash window corresponded with those of the prisoner in the dock. Jackson questioned the detective, through his barrister, about the method he used to take the impression of his fingerprints at Brixton prison. Collins explained further:

The reason I placed the steel plate under the paper was to keep it smooth whilst taking the impression – paper with a rough surface would make no difference in getting a good impression, the lines would be the same even if you rubbed your fingers on dirt and put them on the paper, they would still leave the impression of the ridges.

He was also cross-examined about the need for taking seven or eight impressions and answered,

> I took seven or eight impressions until I got one to suit, because the prisoner managed to blur some of them ... The lines were not so plain in some cases, because of your pressing on the paper – that is the reason I took so many impressions – no doubt the man who got in at the window was pressing on his fingers, but he forgot to smudge the impression like you did at Brixton prison – I certainly say that if you put your hand down flat on the dock it would leave an impression which I could take. There is a scar on your thumb hardly visible to the naked eye and there is a faint resemblance of it on the woodwork of the window.

Richard Muir, now convinced of the potential of fingerprint evidence in the future in relation to crime detection, convinced the jury of the utter reliability of the new science presented by DS Collins and they convicted Harry Jackson of the two burglaries and several other similar offences. He was sentenced to seven years' penal servitude. This case truly set a precedent for British courts and the future of crime detection; the only piece of evidence to place Harry Jackson at the scene of the Denmark Hill burglary, his fingerprint, had been deemed admissible evidence at the highest criminal court in the land.

Not all observers were convinced by this new crime-fighting revelation; one wrote to *The Times* commenting that 'Scotland Yard, once known as the world's finest police organisation, will be the laughing stock of Europe if it insists on trying to trace criminals by odd ridges on their skins'. By 1902 burglary was no longer a capital offence; it would be three years before the reliability of fingerprint evidence would receive its severest test to date, during the trial of two brothers facing the hangman's rope for the capital offence of murder.

38. OH BROTHER! (1905)

Shop assistant William Jones was employed at Chapman's Oil and Colour Merchant's, 34 High Street, Deptford, south-east London. He worked six days a week from 8.30 a.m. to as late as 10 p.m. Jones had enjoyed his Sunday off and travelled from home in nearby Greenwich to Deptford on the morning of Monday 27 March 1905. George Chapman owned two shops in the area – the main store on London Street, Greenwich, and the Deptford store, managed by Thomas Farrow, an elderly man in his seventies who lived above the premises with his wife.

Jones arrived punctually for work and was surprised to find the premises secured; Farrow would normally have the shop open by 7 a.m. He had last seen Farrow and his wife on the evening of Saturday 25 March; both were well, looking forward to their day of rest. Jones attempted to get in through the street door but it was fastened; he banged on the door to draw the attention of the Farrows but received no reply. He walked to George Chapman's shop in Greenwich and returned with another employee, Louis Kidman. On their arrival the shop was as Jones had left it; the pair went around the back and gained entry via a rear door to the premises. They were greeted by the disturbing sight of Thomas Farrow's body, which lay bloodied and battered on the floor of the parlour. Shocked by what they had seen, Jones and Kidman didn't venture upstairs, where Mrs Farrow was likely to be, but alerted the police and owner George Chapman.

One of the first police officers to attend the scene was Sergeant Albert Atkinson; he discovered Mrs Farrow lying on the bedroom floor unconscious and immediately summoned medical help. Sergeant Atkinson discovered an empty cash box on the bedroom floor; its inner tray lay nearby with a couple of discarded coins. He picked the box up with his bare hands and placed it to the side for safe keeping; the importance of protecting possible fingerprint evidence at a crime scene hadn't yet filtered out to the far reaches of some police districts. In the downstairs parlour, near to the lifeless form of Thomas Farrow, Atkinson discovered two masks made from stockings with string ties, obviously pointing to two suspects. This element of the crime was sensationalised by the press, who dubbed the crimes 'The Mask Murders'.

The divisional police surgeon, Dr Dudley Burnie, arrived at the scene and sent the unconscious Mrs Farrow off to the Seaman's Hospital. Burnie conducted a post-mortem examination on Thomas Farrow on 28 March, recording the extent of his injuries as a wound above the right eye, another on the right side of his nose and several to the head resulting in fractures to the skull. Mrs Farrow had similar injuries; they had both been bludgeoned with a blunt instrument. The cashbox remained *in situ* until officers of Scotland Yard's fingerprint bureau attended, one of whom was Assistant Commissioner Melville Macnaghten, head of the Criminal Investigation Department. McNaughton supervised the careful packaging and removal of the cashbox to Scotland Yard for examination. Shop owner George Chapman told detectives that he normally called in at the shop mid-morning on Mondays, when he would collect the previous week's takings from Thomas Farrow; they normally totalled about £12 to £13. The takings for the previous week were missing.

A traditional murder investigation commenced to establish the last known movements of the victims. Had they been seen alive since Saturday night? The motive would appear to be burglary, with two suspects involved; urgent enquiries would have to be made with local people regarding sightings of possible suspects in the area. This part of Deptford was bustling, and several witnesses came forward with descriptions of two men leaving the shop at 7.30 a.m. The physical descriptions of each suspect were patchy but the clothing they wore gave detectives something substantial to work on; one dressed in a dark brown suit and cap, the second in a dark blue serge suit and bowler hat.

Two such witness were milk carrier Henry Alfred Jennings and his eleven-year-old assistant Edward Russell, who were travelling down Deptford High Street around 7.15 a.m. when they saw two men leave from the front entrance of Chapman's shop, they were in a rush. Jennings shouted out, 'You have left the door open.' One of the men replied, 'Oh! It is alright, it don't matter.' The descriptions given by Jennings and Russell matched those of earlier witnesses. In the meantime the cashbox had been examined by the Fingerprint Bureau at Scotland Yard. Having already tested the admissibility of fingerprint evidence in a British court with the conviction of burglar Henry Jackson in 1902, they were confident of future success. The unit was now headed by the now promoted DI Charles Stockley Collins. Collins lifted a print from the cashbox and compared it to the 80,000–90,000 fingerprints on the Scotland Yard files but found no match; he would have to wait for a suspect to be arrested.

A break in the investigation occurred in the early afternoon of Monday 27 March 1905 when two separate witnesses contacted police with information that would lead them to a suspect. The first was a professional boxer called Henry (known as Harry) Littlefield, who lived in Vansittart Street, New Cross. At 2.30 a.m. that morning he spent some time at a coffee stall on Deptford Broadway. He left to make his way home, and as he approached the High Street he saw two men running, passing within yards of him. A few minutes later he saw them again, and on this occasion recognised them as Alfred and Albert Stratton. Alfred Stratton said, 'Hullo Harry, out again?' He replied, 'Yes.' Littlefield noticed that while Alfred was talking to him he was looking around him furtively whilst Albert was fumbling with his coat as if he had something underneath it. Littlefield's description of the clothing worn by the two men matched that of other witnesses. As the Strattons walked away, they headed in the direction of the oil shop. The second witness was Ellen Stanton, who commuted to London daily from Deptford station to Charing Cross, normally catching the 7.20 a.m. train; Stanton knew Alfred Stratton through a relationship with her partner. As she rushed to catch her train on that Monday morning she saw two men running from the High Street into New Cross Road; she recognised one of the men as Alfred Stratton.

Alfred Stratton was arrested along with his brother Albert on suspicion of burglary and the murder of Thomas Farrow. The evidence they had against the two men was at this stage very circumstantial; they could only place the brothers in the area at 2.45 a.m. and Alfred at 7.15 a.m. later the same morning. When arrested the brothers were in possession of tools that matched the suggested murder weapon identified by Dr Dudley Burnie. Detectives waited anxiously to see if Mrs Farrow regained consciousness hoping she would be able to assist with a description of her attackers – sadly she died of her injuries on Friday 31 March.

On 3 April, police setup identification parades at Blackheath police station. Littlefield was not asked to attend as he knew both suspects (Alfred for six years and Albert for seven months), and would merely identify them from past knowledge rather than as the two persons he saw that night. Ellen Stanton did attend and participated in the parade, reaffirming the identity of Alfred as he stood in line, but failed to identify Albert. Police were pinning their hopes on milkman Henry Jennings and his young assistant Edward Russell – both failed to identify either of the brothers as being the men they saw leaving the murder scene that morning. Detectives were struggling to prove a *prima facie* case against the two brothers. In the meantime, Charles Stockley Collins and his colleagues were comparing the fingerprints of both prisoners with the print found on the cashbox. Collins claimed that the fingerprint, caused by sweat, was an exact match to Alfred Stratton.

Alfred Stratton lived with girlfriend Hannah Cromarty in Brookmill Road, Deptford; they had been together for about one year. Cromarty was interviewed by detectives and examined by a magistrate; she stated that in the very early hours of Monday 27 March 1905 she lay in bed with Alfred when she heard a tap on their bedroom window, which opens out on to the street at ground-floor level. She watched as Alfred pulled the blind to one side and heard a voice from outside ask, 'Shall we go out tonight or leave it for another night?' She claimed not to hear Alfred's reply, saying she turned over and went to sleep. She stated that she did not hear him leave that night, but when she woke he was standing at the bedroom door fully dressed. He came to bed in his clothes smelling of paraffin. She asked him what the smell was; he told her he had spilt paraffin over his trousers when filling the lamp. She confirmed that Alfred did own a brown jacket and cap, but said the jacket had vanished a few days later; Alfred explained he had given the jacket away. She also revealed that Alfred was almost penniless on the Sunday – they had no money for food or firewood – but on the following Sunday morning she went with him to a waterworks called Ravensbourne.

Alfred started digging, first stating that he was looking for some tools he had buried there for safekeeping before changing his story, saying he was digging up money (£4), which he told Hannah was no longer there. Cromarty was taken back to the waterworks by Detective Sergeant Frederick Cleveland, and pointed out the spot where Alfred Stratton had been digging; Cleveland marked the spot and returned the following day with other officers and dug 3–4 inches down and discovered a piece of black material containing two sovereigns and a half-crown. Alfred and Albert were charged with the murders of Mr and Mrs Thomas Farrow, and their trial was set for 5 May 1905 at the Central Criminal Court, Old Bailey.

The trial would be an uphill struggle for the prosecution – they had no eye-witnesses placing the brothers at the scene, and the money found hidden by DS Cleveland could not be definitively linked to the Farrows. All the evidence was circumstantial. Detectives knew they had the right men but realised that only a seed of doubt needed to be planted in the minds of the jurors for an acquittal. Representing the Crown was leading prosecution barrister Richard Muir, who led the Crown's case three years earlier at the same court when Henry Jackson went down for burglary. But this would be the first occasion where a fingerprint was the *only* tangible piece of evidence, and against defendants who, if found guilty, would hang.

Richard Muir called over forty witnesses for the prosecution in order to paint as credible a picture of the circumstantial evidence as he could, emphasising that the brothers were seen in the vicinity of the crime scene at both 2.45 a.m. and 7.15 a.m. on 27 March 1905. The witness descriptions of the clothing worn by the suspects seen running from the shop were consistent and matched the clothing described as belonging to the brothers. Alfred had no money on the eve of the murder, but evidently buried at least two sovereigns in a nearby waterworks on the pretence of hiding it from his partner, Hannah Cromarty. But the witness on which the case would succeed or fail was DI Charles Stockley Collins.

DI Collins took to the witness box armed with documents and photographs. He explained that he had been a founding member of the Fingerprint Bureau in 1901 and had studied the works of Francis Galton in the field of anthropometry (the scientific study of the measurements and proportions of the human body) and Edward Henry (the founder of the bureau). As in the case of Jackson in 1902, he outlined to the jury, under the expert guidance of Richard Muir, the Edward Henry system, culminating in the crucial declaration that he had never seen two identical sets of fingerprints from different people. DI Collins stated, 'This cashbox was handed to me [producing the exhibit to the court]. I found a fingerprint on the inner tray; it is visible now.'

Collins explained that he examined the fingerprints of the deceased and anybody else who had come into contact with the box, including the first police officers on scene, to identify and eliminate any prints left by them. This process left the one unidentified print; he reiterated to the jury that he had taken the fingerprint impressions of both prisoners himself and 'found that Alfred's right thumb corresponded with the mark on the cashbox'. Collins then produced enlarged images of Alfred Stratton's thumb and the remaining mark on the cashbox to the jury and explained in detail the characteristics present that, in his opinion, proved Alfred Stratton had handled the cashbox and therefore was present at the scene of the murders. Collins, at the request of the jury, demonstrated the procedure for obtaining a suspect's fingerprints and how the application of pressure affected the quality of the print.

Richard Muir produced a number of further witnesses, all offering circumstantial evidence, which, he hoped, created a safety net of understandable truth to support Inspector Collins' scientific revelations. This included evidence from the Home Office pathologist who conducted the post-mortem examinations on Mr and Mrs Farrow; he told court that the injuries received by the victims were consistent with tools discovered in the possession of the Strattons at the time of their arrest. However, much of this evidence was rebutted by the defence, who had plausible explanations for the movements of the defendants during the crucial period of time in which the murders took place. It was now time for the defence case; it was abundantly clear to all those present in the courtroom the case was going to succeed or fail on the crucial evidence of Detective Inspector Collins and the legitimacy and legality of one thumbprint allegedly belonging to Alfred Stratton.

Following the successful rebuttal of much of the prosecution witnesses' evidence, and confident of shooting down the prosecution's reliance on the fingerprint evidence with expert testimonies, the defence presented Alfred Stratton's defence claiming that on the night of 26 March he had an argument with his girlfriend Hannah Cromarty and struck her in the eye before storming out. He returned about 11.45 p.m.; he and Cromarty eventually went to bed about 2.30 a.m. on the 27th. Shortly after Stratton claimed (evidence backed up by Cromarty at an early stage) that he heard a tap on the bedroom window and on investigating saw his brother Albert, who asked him for some lodging money. Alfred explained that he had no cash but told his sibling to 'wait here a minute or two and I'll slip you in here'; when he returned after dressing, Albert was gone.

Alfred informed the court that he went out to find his brother and caught up with him in Regent Street, Deptford, where both men were seen by witnesses Littlefield and Compton. They returned home, and Alfred lay upon the bed fully clothed whilst Albert slept on the floor and left before Hannah Cromarty awoke. The brothers agreed with witness descriptions of the clothing worn by them on the night, and Alfred admitted that he gave his brown jacket away to a man in a lodging house when the murder hit the newspapers. Both men denied being at the scene of the crime, claiming they were indoors asleep at 7 a.m. on 27 March.

The defence called self-proclaimed expert Dr John Garson. Garson was the president of the Anthropometry Society and partly responsible for the introduction of the Anthropometry Department and its register at Scotland Yard between 1895 and 1901, a system used to maintain criminal records for identification purposes using various body measurements. In 1900 a committee chaired by Lord Belper sat to consider the benefits and failings of both anthropometry and the emerging science of fingerprinting; Garson had argued for his established system and made known his profound concerns over the reliability of identification from a person's fingerprints. The newer science was presented by Edward Henry, who practically demonstrated to the Belper Committee the reliability of his system by producing a collection of 7,000 fingerprints. The committee concluded by recommending that fingerprints of prisoners should routinely be taken and added to anthropometric records.

Garson entered the witness box at the Old Bailey with an air of authority; he explained that he had experience of the fingerprint system relied upon by the prosecution and that DI Collins had been a student of his, thereby giving the impression that he had the far greater experience in this field than his previous subordinate Inspector Collins. He then gave evidence to the jury designed to undermine the reliability of Collins' findings. During his cross-examination, Richard Muir asked Carson to inform the court of his last dealings with the fingerprint system; he replied that his services were dispensed with in October 1901 and acknowledged that the number of identifications using fingerprints had exceeded greatly the identifications of his day and the experience of the officers of the Fingerprint Department since he left had greatly exceeded his own in regard to fingerprints. It was pointed out to him that he had vehemently spoken out about the unreliability of Edward Henry's system to the Belper Committee in 1900, and the most damning of all was the emergence of two letters to the court by Muir in which Garson offered his services to testify as an expert to both the Director of Public Prosecutions and the solicitor for the defence – depending on whoever was willing to pay the most. This ruined any credibility attached to Garson's evidence the judge Mr Justice Channell advised the jury during his summing up that Garson was to be treated as an 'absolutely unreliable witness'.

Following the summations by the prosecution and defence, Mr Justice Channell directed the jury to retire to consider the verdict on which they must all be agreed. The jury deliberated for two hours before returning guilty verdicts against both brothers for murder. They were sentenced, as the law directed, to death by hanging. The sentence was carried out by public executioner John Billington, aided by two assistants, Henry Pierrepoint and John Ellis. The *London Daily News* of 24 May 1905 reported that:

At nine o' clock yesterday morning the young brothers Albert and Alfred Stratton, who were convicted of the murder of Mr and

Mrs Thos. Farrow, an aged couple, at 34 High Street, Deptford, on March 27th, paid the extreme penalty at Wandsworth Prison. The executions were carried out by Billington and two assistants. The convicts made no formal statements or confessions; but as they were proceeding to the scaffold Albert muttered a few words, which were understood by those standing round to be: 'Alfred has God forgiven you?' If any reply was made it was not audible to those in the procession.

Albert Stratton, who weighed 172 lb, was given a 6-foot 6-inch drop which cleanly broke his neck; his brother Alfred, who was lighter at 147 lb, was given an extended drop of 7-foot 7-inches but alas it was not enough to break his neck cleanly, and signs of asphyxiation were noted following a post-mortem examination. This was truly a landmark trial for a system of crime detection that has stood the test of time.

39. LET ME HAVE MY SAY (1907)

An experienced wily prosecutor, a theatrically animated 'celebrity' defence counsel, a deceitful yet innocent defendant whose appearance in the witness box would make British criminal history – this trial, which took place at the Old Bailey in December 1907, would resonate for many years within the halls of this most famous of courts.

Robert William Wood stepped briskly into the dock at the New Bailey [the new Central Criminal Court had only been open since February 1907] and in a clear, firm voice announced that he was not guilty of the murder of Emily 'Phyllis' Dimmock at her apartments in St Paul's Road, Camden Town on September 12 [1906]. So begun, a trial that has aroused more public interest than any for a long time.[17]

On the morning of 12 September 1906 a man called Bertram Shaw, a chef on the Midland Railway service between London and Sheffield, was returning home to the apartments he shared with his common law wife, part-time prostitute Emily (aka Phyllis) Dimmock, in St Paul's Road, Camden Town, London. Unable to gain entry and concerned about Dimmock's safety, he broke the door down 'to discover the rooms in confusion'. A burnt letter had been discarded in the fireplace and Emily's naked body was on the bed; her throat had been cut.

The deceased had been having an affair with the aforementioned Robert Wood for over three years, a fact that Wood denied at the time of his arrest, claiming to have known her for only a matter of days before she was murdered. The handwriting on the partially burnt postcard was later matched to Robert Wood. He was identified to the police by a former girlfriend called Ruby Young and arrested and charged with the murder.

The streets outside the Old Bailey were teeming with people jostling for entry into the public gallery. Wood had employed the services of melodramatic 'celebrity barrister' Edward Marshall Hall QC. Witness after witness appeared on behalf of the prosecution, each destroyed by Marshall Hall's intensive cross-examination. The case became a landmark in British criminal history when Hall was persuaded by a junior barrister to put the defendant into the witness box. This was a risky strategy, and had never been seen before in a British court, even though the Criminal Justice Bill of 1905 had empowered a defendant charged with murder to give evidence on his own behalf. The jury, after fifteen minutes' deliberation, returned a not guilty verdict and Wood left the court a free man. The murder of Emily 'Phyllis' Dimmock technically remains unsolved.

---

17 *Aberdeen People's Journal*, 21 December 1907

40. MY SHIP WAS FASTER THAN YOUR SHIP (1910)

The first practical wireless telegraphy transmitters and receivers were developed by Guglielmo Marconi in 1895; this scientific breakthrough would ultimately lead to the arrest and execution of one of Britain's most notorious killers – Hawley Harvey Crippen.

Crippen was born in a small town in Michigan called Coldwater. He was an intelligent youth and studied homeopathic medicine at the University of Michigan, eventually graduating from the Cleveland Homeopathic Medical College in 1884. He had a son with his first wife, Charlotte; unfortunately Charlotte died as a result of a stroke in early 1892. With his son being looked after by his parents, Crippen headed off to the east coast where he started his own homeopathic business in New York. This is where he met his second wife, a classically trained music hall singer called Corrine Turner, who liked to be called Cora but also used the stage name Belle Elmore. They married in 1892. Cora had a wandering eye, and often engaged in short-term sexual relationships which she didn't trouble herself too much in hiding from her hard-working husband.

In 1894 Crippen decided to take a job with a larger pharmaceutical company; he stayed for three years before he and Cora decided to move to England. They moved around London, eventually settling at 39 Hilldrop Crescent in London's Camden Town. Crippen obtained a managerial position at Drouet's Institution for the Deaf at the turn of the century, and this is where he met a young typist called Ethel Le Neve. Cora meanwhile had become an integral part of the London West End social scene and treasurer to the Music Hall Ladies Guild; she had little time for her husband, whose salary was so poor they had had to take in lodgers. Cora had an affair with one of the lodgers, and in turn Crippen started a relationship with Ethel Le Neve in 1908.

One will never know if Crippen planned to murder his wife or if it was just a spur-of-the-moment decision. Crippen and Cora hosted a party at Hilldrop Crescent on the evening of 31 January 1910. Later that night, or early the next morning, Cora disappeared, never to be seen alive again. When Cora's socialite friends began to enquire about her whereabouts Crippen came up with an extraordinary story in which he informed them that she had returned to the United States unwell, had died and been cremated in California. In the meantime Crippen invited his mistress Ethel Le Neve to live with him; Ethel accepted and began to openly wear Cora's clothes and jewellery. Several of Cora's friends – aware of the state of their marriage – began to doubt Cora would leave without a word to any of them.

The first to break ranks and head to the police was a theatre strongwoman called Kate Williams, who reported Cora officially missing. However, this didn't stir up to much interest in the police rank and file. In the meantime, Crippen and Ethel lived like man and wife in Camden Town. The police took a little more interest when Cora's friends John Nash and his wife called in a favour from a senior police officer who instructed Scotland Yard's Chief Inspector Walter Dew to investigate. Dew took on the case, which was being treated as a missing person investigation, and visited Crippen at Hilldrop Crescent. Dew interviewed Crippen, who changed his story, claiming that Cora had run off back to America with another man, a music hall actor called Bruce Miller, and that he had made up the story of her illness and death to avoid heaping anymore embarrassment on himself. Crippen invited Dew to look around the property in order to satisfy himself that nothing was amiss; Dew seemed to accept Crippen's new version of events. Crippen, now troubled that the game maybe up, panicked and fled with Ethel to Brussels before boarding the Canadian Pacific liner the SS *Montrose* at Antwerp destined for Canada. It is a little ironic that if he had held his nerve he may well have got away with murder.

A few days later, it came to the police's attention that Crippen and Le Neve had vanished. This roused the suspicions of Scotland Yard, who returned to the house and carried out deeper searches of the property until they found a human torso cleverly concealed under the brick floor of the basement. Eminent pathologist Bernard Spilsbury was summoned and found traces of the drug hyoscine, a poisonous plant extract. The corpse was identified as that of Cora, by a piece of stomach tissue showing an operation scar corresponding to one shown on Cora's medical records; the head and limbs were never recovered. As the investigation turned into a murder enquiry, Crippen and Ethel Le Neve believed they were safe aboard ship and on their way to a new life in Canada. Crippen had disguised Ethel in male clothing, giving her the appearance of a small boy, but the disguise was seen through by the captain of the ship, Henry George Kendall. Kendall acted quickly before his ship went out of radio range and instructed his telegraph operator to send a wireless telegram back to England notifying them of his suspicions. The message read:

> Have strong suspicions that Crippen London cellar murderer and accomplice are among saloon passengers. Moustache taken off growing beard. Accomplice dressed as boy. Manner and build undoubtedly a girl.

Chief Inspector Dew caught the faster White Star liner the SS *Laurentic* from Liverpool and arrived in Quebec, Canada, ahead of the SS *Montrose*. Dew, in cooperation with the Canadian authorities, boarded the SS *Montrose* dressed as a pilot on 31 July 1910. He approached Crippen and took off his hat and introduced himself: 'Good morning, Dr Crippen,' he said. 'Do you know me? I'm Chief Inspector Dew from Scotland Yard.' Crippen looked shocked, and once he had regained his composure said, 'Thank God it's over. The suspense has been too great. I couldn't stand it any longer.' Crippen and Le Neve were returned to England aboard the SS *Megantic*.

The *Shoreditch Observer* of 22 October 1910 sets the scene for the opening of the trial in Court Number One at the Central Criminal Court, Old Bailey:

> The curtain rose on Tuesday morning at the Old Bailey [18 October 1910] upon the opening scenes in the trial of Dr Crippen, charged before the Lord Chief Justice (Lord Alverstone), with the wilful murder of his wife, who was known to the theatrical world as Belle Elmore. The case against Miss Le Neve, who was indicted as an accessory after the fact, was held over pending the result of the trial of Crippen. Although the arrangements for admission to the court had been completed last week, and there was not the slightest possibility of persons without tickets

obtaining admission, a large crowd gathered outside the entrance on the off-chance of seeing some of the folks concerned in the case. Crippen was brought up early from Brixton Gaol, and was hurried in by a side door without being observed by the crowd. Not more than seventy seats were available in the court for the general public, after all those who were entitled by reason of their association with the trial had been provided for. So that as many as possible could witness the scene, half day tickets, so far as the public were concerned, were issued.

Richard Muir opened the case for the prosecution by outlining the facts to the jury, during which he offered motives for the defendant's murder of his wife – money and love. Crippen and Cora had deposited £600 in the Charing Cross Bank between 1905 and 1909, but by the end of 1909, due to their worsening financial position, they had given notice to the bank that they wished to withdraw the whole amount. Muir stated that: 'the position at this time was that the obstacles to his affection for Ethel Le Neve were the physical presence of his wife, added to the fact that he had no money. If Belle Elmore died both these obstacles to his closer relations with the girl would be removed, and her property could be converted into ready money.'

Further evidence included a piece of pyjama top found with the remains; the bottoms were recovered from Crippen's bedroom, but not the top. The top contained a fragment of the maker's label, 'Jones Bros'. The prosecution called a representative of the company, who informed the jury that the garment was not sold in any of their retail outlets before 1908, thus rebutting Crippen's claim that the remains had been placed under the bricked floor before they had moved in in 1905. It was proved that Crippen –who of course was a fully qualified homeopath – had purchased quantities of hyoscine. Muir questioned why a woman would leave all her jewellery and furs if she were voluntarily going back to America. He made great play on the fact that Crippen had initially, before he changed his story to Chief Inspector Dew, written notes and sent cables purporting to be from Cora stating how ill she was, and a final one concocted by Crippen reporting her death. 'Ask yourselves,' Muir told the jury, 'why Crippen fled. What was it he had to fear if that statement he made [to Chief Inspector Dew] was correct? What he fled for was found on 13 July, when under the brick floor of the cellar at 39 Hilldrop Crescent, the police found human remains. It will be for you to say if those were what Crippen fled for.'

Crippen's defence maintained that Cora had run off with Bruce Miller to America (even though Miller would be called by the prosecution and state that he hadn't seen Cora since 1904) and that he and Cora had been living at Hilldrop Crescent only since 1905 and the remains, which they claimed weren't Cora's, had been deposited by a past tenant.

The trial lasted for four days before the jury took just twenty-seven minutes to return a verdict of guilty. Throughout the trial Crippen's only concern was for Ethel Le Neve's reputation and not that of his wife. Hawley Harvey Crippen was hanged at Pentonville Prison on 23 November 1910 and his body buried in the grounds, where it lays to this day; he made no confession to the prison authorities or upon the scaffold. Several newspapers of the day carried a final report of Crippen's last morning:

A deep gloom pervaded the whole prison at 6 o'clock yesterday morning when the warders who had been on attendance of the condemned man throughout the night were relieved of their duty. Every other inmate of the prison was confined to his cell and there remained until the dread sentence of the law had been carried out. On being awakened, Crippen, who had passed a restless night, readily obeyed the summons to dress. The prison garb that he had worn since his conviction was taken away, and he was supplied with his own wearing apparel, the same that he wore upon his trial. The convict presented a haggard and worn appearance. He seemed to lose all fortitude as his end approached, His breakfast, consisting of bread and butter and a pot of tea, was left practically untouched. At a quarter to nine o'clock Under Sheriff Metcalfe, accompanied by a deputy, drove up to the prison and were received by Major Davies the prison governor. Just on the stroke of the hour Ellis, the executioner, with an assistant, entered the condemned cell. Crippen rose from his seat and submitted quietly to the process of pinioning. A procession, headed by a Roman Catholic priest, was then formed to the scaffold which was only a few paces away from the condemned cell.

Bare-headed and colourless, Crippen was escorted to the gallows by the warders and quickly placed in position on the drop. At this point the unhappy man appeared to be at the point of collapse. The noose and cap were quickly adjusted, and the final preparations expeditiously performed, the bolt was drawn. Crippen, who weighed just over ten stone, was given a drop of over seven feet. The death was stated to be instantaneous and the execution to have been carried out in all respects satisfactorily and without any hitch.[18]

Ethel Le Neve was acquitted of being an accessory to the murder of her love rival and emigrated to the United States on the very morning Crippen was executed. It was reported that he requested a picture of Ethel to be placed in his coffin and buried with him.

41. THE RESPECTABLE SPY (1914)

Carl Hans Lody was a German national who spied in Great Britain and Ireland during the First World War; he became the first spy to be executed in the Tower of London. Lody was a lieutenant in the German Naval Reserve. Before the commencement of the war he married an American woman, whom he divorced prior to the start of hostilities before volunteering for the German Intelligence Service in 1914. Initially he was tasked with the gathering of intelligence in

18 *Aberdeen Press and Journal*, 24 November 1910

the south of France, but as he spoke such good English, albeit with a slight American twang, his potential was quickly recognised and he was re-deployed to spy in Great Britain, particularly in Scotland and Ireland. Lody was provided with false identification documents in the name of Charles A. Inglis, an American citizen, together with a considerable amount of money for expenses. On 14 August 1914 Lody departed from Hamburg, Germany, embarking on a convoluted route via neutral Norway, a ship to Newcastle, and then onto Edinburgh, arriving on 27 August 1914, where he found lodgings.

Lody was tasked to spy on the heavily guarded Firth of Forth, a strategically important Scottish port used by the Royal Navy. Lody's spymasters wanted to know detailed information about any losses or damage suffered by the Royal Navy following their engagement in sea battles. Lody, although academically accomplished, lacked both experience and street craft, often sending un-coded messages to German intelligence via neutral countries, which, unbeknown to him, British security services (MI5) were monitoring.

MI5 had identified Lody as a possible spy from the very first letter he sent, addressed to Adolf Buchard at an address MI5 had previously identified as a cover for German intelligence in Stockholm, Sweden. However they were unaware of his true identity or exact location as he signed his letters 'Charles' or 'Nazi'. The latter is not as daft as it seems as 'Nazi' was used as a short form of the name 'Ignatz'; it was also a nickname for Austro-Hungarian soldiers.[19] Adolf Hitler's Nazi Party was not formed until after the First World War. Eventually MI5 identified 'Charles' as Charles A. Inglis. Lody spent several weeks in Edinburgh sending back many letters to his Stockholm contact, all monitored by MI5 who allowed several of the letters, containing misinformation, to reach the Germans, including details of a large deployment of Russian troops in Scotland which was completely inaccurate.

Lody then moved to Dublin via Liverpool, whence he wrote a letter containing current and accurate information about British ship movements to and from the port, which was extremely useful to German intelligence. MI5 decided that it was too dangerous to let

19 www.mi5.gov.uk/carl-hans-lody

Lody remain at liberty and ordered his arrest. Lody's movements, under his pseudonym 'Charles A. Inglis', were traced from Edinburgh to Dublin; Lody was detained on 2 October 1914. His real identity was discovered when a search revealed a tailor's ticket in his real name – Carl Hans Lody – with a Berlin address.

Lody was transported back to London to stand trial on a rarely used charge of 'war treason', under which the act of espionage was treated as a war crime carrying the death penalty. The act of spying for one's country was a legitimate weapon of war on both sides and took great courage as discovery meant certain death. Lody, although inept, earnt the respect of both his German spymasters and of the British public; his patriotism and bravery in refusing to talk or identify his German contacts was widely reported during his very public trial.

Lody was found guilty and sentenced to die. He was taken to the Tower of London and executed by firing squad on morning of 6 November 1914. He was reported to have said to his prison escort on the way from his prison cell to the execution site, 'I suppose that you will not care to shake hands with a German spy.' The officer replied, 'No, but I will shake hands with a brave man.' Following his execution, it was revealed he had written a very moving letter the previous evening addressed to the Commanding Officer of the 3rd Battalion Grenadier Guards, thanking them for his treatment during his incarceration. It read:

> Sir,
> I feel it my duty as a German officer to express my sincere thanks and appreciation to the guards and sentries being and having been my guardians. Although they never neglected their duty they have shown always the utmost courtesy and consideration towards me.
>   If it is in the frame of reglements I wish this may be made known to them.
> I am, Sir, with profound respect
> Carl Hans Lody
> Senior Lieutenant Imperial German Naval Reserves II.[20]

---

20 www.hrp.org.uk

42. GIRL POWER (1920)

The Sex Disqualification (Removal) Act 1919 abolished the debarring of women from public office, including the roles of judge, lawyer, magistrate – and juror. Since the thirteenth century, women had played a minor role in the jury system; a special jury of 'matrons' would convene in capital cases where a female defendant had been found guilty and sentenced to death. They would be tasked with deciding if the defendant was with child, and thus allowed to escape the noose. The first female jurors sworn in as part of a jury were at the Bristol Quarter Sessions on 29 July 1920, when they heard evidence in the case of William Henry Ayton, standing trial for stealing parcels from Weston-Super-Mare railway station. The barrister, in addressing the jury, took great pride in being the first person in British judicial history to open his address with the words 'Ladies and Gentlemen of the jury'.

An article appeared in the *Derby Daily Telegraph* of 20 December 1920 in which a judge commented that 'women jurors are impartial, careful, unbiased, serious, intelligent, refined, studious, attentive, conscientious, able, just, courageous, reliable, fair and altogether admirable. In fact they are as good as men.' Unfortunately, the quote was from an American judge called Robert H. Day; as far as women were concerned at this point in time 'the jury was still out'. It would take another year before the first woman would be summoned to the Central Criminal Court to sit on a jury. Mrs Taylor Bumpstead not only sat on the jury but was elected jury forewoman.

43. FREE SPEECH – THERE'S A LIMIT (1921)

The last person to be sent to prison for an offence of blasphemy was former tailor, draper and trouser salesman John William Gott. Gott led an anti-Christianity movement called the Freethought Socialist League, which encouraged public attacks on the religion it hated. Following his four-month prison sentence for blasphemy in 1911, public opinion swelled on the side of free speech, fuelled by Members of Parliament and ethical societies such as Conway Hall in Red Lion Square, who demanded a change in the blasphemy laws. Prime Minister Asquith agreed, but the bill never made it on to the statute books. Further periods of imprisonment followed for Gott in 1916 and 1917.

Gott's last conviction – one that ultimately broke his spirit – was at the Old Bailey in 1921. He was found guilty of blasphemy and sentenced to nine months' hard labour; an appeal against the conviction and severity of the sentence was lodged, but the appeal court judge, Lord Trevethin, concluded whilst dismissing the appeal that 'it does not require a person of strong religious feelings to be outraged by a description of Jesus Christ entering Jerusalem "Like a circus clown on the back of two donkeys". There are other pamphlets equally offensive to anyone in sympathy with the Christian religion, whether he be a strong Christian or a lukewarm Christian, or merely a person sympathising with their ideals. Such a person might be provoked to a breach of the peace.'

Gott's health suffered during the relatively long sentence, and he died the following year.

44. JUST SIT DOWN AND BE QUIET (1924)

In April 1924, Mr G. H. Coldwell, a member of the Fellowship of Freedom and Reform, became the first person in Great Britain to be convicted under the 1908 Public Meetings Act. He was summoned to appear in front of the magistrates in Yeovil to answer a charge accusing him of 'unlawfully acting in a disorderly manner for the purposes of preventing the transaction of the business' at a public meeting. Mr Coldwell admitted to the magistrates that he was paid a fee to attend public meetings and represent the Fellowship and that he continued to interrupt the meeting even though the chairman pointed out that he was in fact breaking the law. He was fined £2 with £3 3s costs. The *Dundee Evening Telegraph* of 8 April 1924 recorded that this first prosecution under the legislation 'will be of interest to speakers, chairman and societies across the country'.

45. ONE LAW FOR US ... (1925)

The Honours (Prevention of Abuses) Act 1925 was introduced into British law to make illegal the sale of honours such as knighthoods and peerages following Prime Minister Lloyd George selling such titles (which was legal at the time) for vast amounts of money. Between 1917 and the introduction of the legislation Lloyd George's honours broker was a man called Maundy Gregory. Gregory would actively seek wealthy subjects interested in becoming 'Sir' or 'Lord'. During this period, approximately 1,500 knighthoods (£10,000 each), baronetcies (£25,000) and peerages (£50,000 each) were awarded.

Following the act, this distasteful, immoral practice became illegal. However, Gregory continued selling titles instead of quitting while he was ahead. Thankfully, some people are just incorruptible; one such person was Lieutenant Commander Billyard Lake, who reported the illegal approach, and Maundy Gregory was prosecuted – the only person ever to be prosecuted under the act. He appeared before the magistrates at Bow Street, where he was fined £50 and given a six-month prison sentence, of which he served two months.

In March 2006 the Metropolitan Police conducted an investigation following allegations from various parliamentary parties of alleged breaches of the act that had taken place, namely the awarding of four life peerages following the general election campaign of 2005. Following a lengthy police investigation it was announced by the Crown Prosecution Service that no charges under the act would be made against any individual.

46. THE APPLIANCE OF SCIENCE (1927)

The forensic science of ballistics can be explained in layman's terms as the 'art of matching recovered bullets and/or their casings to the firearm from which they were fired'. This discipline has a long history compared to that of DNA or entomology. Tracing a bullet fired from a firearm back to the person who in turn is proved to be in possession of the firearm often completes the evidential chain. One of the first documented cases proving this point was the murder of Lancastrian Edward Culshaw in 1784; the suspect was John Toms, who denied the killing. A surgeon removed a small wad of paper from the deceased's wound (at the time paper was often used to secure the gunpowder and pellet together in a firearm), which was found to be a small corner torn from the ballad sheet found in John Tom's pocket – a powerful piece of evidence that led to his conviction.

Another similar example was the murder of Lincolnshire police officer Alexander McBrian near Wyberton, Boston, who was shot by a suspected poacher, Thomas Richardson, on 26 October 1860. Wadding found at the crime scene was compared to wadding found in the undischarged barrel of a double-barrelled shotgun belonging to Richardson. It was found that both pieces of wadding had come from the same edition of *The Times* newspaper, dated 27 March 1854. The jury at the Lincoln Assizes found Richardson guilty based on this compelling evidence and he was sentenced to death.

One of the earliest examples recorded in British courts in which a forensic ballistic examination was made of a *bullet* discharged from a firearm was in the murder of Police Constable Cole in Dalston, London, on 1 December 1882. PC Cole, who had only joined the police service ten months before, had apprehended a young burglar attempting to break into a chapel; the officer and suspect fought before the suspect broke away. PC Cole gave chase and four gunshots rang out from the thick fog. The first two evidently missed the chasing officer and the third was found embedded in his truncheon, but the fourth hit its target, striking PC Cole behind his ear. The fatally injured officer was conveyed to the nearby German Hospital but died of his injuries. When the area in the vicinity of the attempted break-in was searched, police found a chisel, presumably dropped by the killer, with the letters 'Rock' scratched into the surface of the handle and a 'billycock hat' but no sign of the killer.

Following the inquest and a verdict of 'unlawful killing', notices were posted offering a reward for information leading to the conviction of PC Cole's killer. It wasn't until early 1884 that detectives had a breakthrough when information was received from two men that the killer was serving time for another offence. The informants, called Miles and Evans, claimed that on the night of the murder they were drinking with a man they named as Thomas Orrock who confided in them that he intended breaking into the Baptist chapel and stealing the sacramental plate; he asked them to go with him. Orrock showed them the chisel he had with him as well as a revolver. The men had agreed to go along and help carry the stolen goods away; Orrock told them he would quickly get rid of the stolen property through his brother-in-law, a local fence. When asked where he bought the gun, he told them he purchased it in Tottenham and had practised firing it on Tottenham Marshes. Miles and Evans claimed they heard the shots and found the murdered policeman on the pavement and called for a doctor.

The area where Orrock stated he had practised shooting the gun was located by Sergeant Cobb, a colleague of Cole's, who retrieved a bullet from the bark of a tree. The bullets from the tree, the truncheon and PC Cole's skull were examined by Whitechapel gunsmith James Squires, who testified at Orrock's trial that they were three-pin bullets matching that in the tree. The hat discarded at the scene also fitted the accused. A closer examination of the chisel inscribed 'Rock' under a powerful microscope revealed the faint words 'Orrock'. He was found guilty of murder and sentenced to death. PC Cole's widow, who was in the court, was heard to shout, 'I'd like to kill the brute.'[21]

The next two cases demonstrating the advance of forensic ballistic examinations also centre on the murder of two policemen. The first was dubbed the 'Hooded Man Case' and took place in 1912. In October of that year, Police Inspector Arthur Walls responded to a call about a suspected burglary taking place at the Eastbourne home of Countess Flora Sztaray. On his arrival, Walls saw the suspected intruder hiding above the front porch of the house; as he tried to coax him down he was shot dead. Scotland Yard detectives were called in to carry out the investigation and approached Robert Churchill, a London gun shop owner who was speedily attaining a reputation as a ballistics expert. His uncle Edwin had assisted in the investigation of the murder of Miss Camille Cecile Holland by Samuel Dougal at Moat House Farm in Clavering, Essex, several years previously, in which he fired bullets into the heads of sheep to judge the distance and trajectory of the fatal shot.

Robert Churchill examined the bullet which killed Walls and a casing found at the scene and concluded that the weapon had been a

---

21 *Worcester Journal*, 27 September 1884

.25 automatic pistol; his knowledge of the rifling of all makes of gun assisted the detectives regarding which weapon they should be looking for. A break in the investigation came when a search of Eastbourne beach uncovered the remains of a broken firearm; Churchill fitted a new hammer and springs to the recovered weapon and fired it under test conditions. He concluded that the bullets fired had the same rifling patterns as the bullet recovered from the body of Inspector Walls, but this only proved that a gun of the same make had been used. To try and convince a jury that this was probably the type of gun used to kill Walls, a police photographer took close-up pictures of the grooves on the bullets and assisted Churchill in making a cast of the rifling inside the gun's barrel using cool dentist's wax, removing it when dried and showing how the marks on the bullets matched exactly the marks in the barrel. This seemed to convince the jury, who found the owner of the gun, John Williams, guilty of murder, and after appeals to the Court of Appeal and the Home Secretary he was executed. The case was dubbed the Hooded Man Case because detectives regularly placed a scarf around the head of Williams at court appearances so as not to compromise any future identification evidence.

Forensic ballistics had yet to reach the holy grail of proving a particular bullet had been fired from a particular firearm; this was achieved with the murder of PC George Gutteridge in September 1927. Early on 27 September, William Alec Ward was driving along the Ongar Road from Stapleford Abbots in rural Essex. As he approached a place called Howe Green he saw a bundle on the roadside; as he got closer, he saw that it was in fact a body of a man in a sitting position, with his legs spread out before him. To his horror, he recognised the man as PC Gutteridge. The alarm was raised, with uniform and CID officers attending, the most senior being Detective Inspector John Crockford from Romford. Crockford noticed, during an initial examination of the body, two bullet holes on the left side of PC Gutteridge's face with exit wounds to the right side of the neck. Shockingly, both eyes were shot through by two further bullets. Crockford concluded that the officer had stopped a car and been in the process of talking to his killer(s), as he held a pencil in one hand and his pocket notebook laid beside him on the road.

Information quickly surfaced that a Morris Cowley motor vehicle belonging to a doctor from Billericay had been stolen during the night. The vehicle was found abandoned in a narrow passage in Brixton, south London. The expertise of Scotland Yard's murder squad was called upon, led by Detective Chief Inspector James Berrett. The crime scene yielded two .45 bullets from the road surface, and two further bullets of the same calibre were recovered from the officer's body during a post-mortem examination. A fingertip search of the stolen vehicle revealed an empty cartridge case and blood on the running board of the vehicle. The cartridge case had a marking, 'RLIV', which indicated that it was an old Mark IV type manufactured at the Royal Laboratory in Woolwich Arsenal during the First World War. The investigation didn't yield any results until information led the police to suspect a Clapham garage owner and serious criminal, Frederick Guy Browne, and an associate named Pat Kennedy, but they had little evidence at this stage.

As detectives kept observations on the home of Browne, the bullet casing found in the stolen vehicle was passed on to Robert Churchill, who noticed that the casing had been scarred by a fault on the discharging weapon's breech block. Churchill was of the opinion that the firearm concerned was a Webley revolver, and that if it could be found he could match the bullet with the weapon. The break came when more information came to light linking Browne to another offence – the theft of a motor vehicle. They went in and arrested Browne; a search of the premises found a loaded Smith & Wesson in his room, and when his car was searched they discovered the real prize: a loaded .45 Webley revolver. Kennedy was nowhere to be found in the capital, but detectives knew he was likely to head towards his home town of Liverpool. When he was eventually accosted he attempted to shoot a police officer, but his gun jammed. Kennedy was returned to London and interviewed by DCI Berrett; he admitted being in the car when Browne shot PC Gutteridge.

Robert Churchill was now in possession of a double microscope that enabled him to prove that the casing found in the car stopped by Gutteridge was fired by the Webley revolver found in Browne's possession on his arrest. Both Browne and Kennedy were charged with the murder of PC Gutteridge. When they appeared at the Old Bailey, both men, who had to be separated in the dock by several burly prison warders, denied the charge. Browne claimed that he had received the gun from Kennedy after the murder, but both were found guilty and sentenced to death. Ultimately, it was the ballistic examination by Robert Churchill and the photographs he produced to the jury that convinced them the two men were guilty. Both men were executed at 9 a.m. on 31 May 1928 at separate prisons – Browne at Pentonville and Kennedy at Wandsworth.

The science of forensic ballistics has moved on rapidly in this country, with intricate methods of examination aided by video-imaging demonstrating trajectory and distance – thanks, in part, to the early work of Robert Churchill. George Gutteridge, a husband and father, was buried in Warley Cemetery with an inscription that reads: 'In proud memory of George William Gutteridge, Police Constable, Essex Constabulary, who met his death in the performance of his duty on September 27 1927.'

47. SHE GAVE IT HER BEST SHOT (1928)

Youth has as much right to protect itself as old age. Would you have said, 'This man is my grandfather, I must let him hit me?' No! The strongest instinct in man is self-protection. This is the most solemn moment in my life, and I leave this young man's life in your hands with a prayer that God may lead you to a right conclusion.[22]

---

22 *Derby Daily Telegraph*, 16 January 1929

These were the heartfelt final words of defence barrister Venetia Stephenson's closing speech to the jury in the murder trial of twenty-four-year-old musician William John Holmyard at the Central Criminal Court, Old Bailey, in January 1929. This trial was remarkable as Miss Stephenson became the first female barrister in British criminal history to lead the defence during a trial for murder.

William John Holmyard was discharged from the army in November 1928. Having served as a bandsman, he left the military with an excellent record. He returned to London and lived with his parents at 39 Tachbrook Street, Pimlico. As with many soldiers leaving the armed forces and returning to Civvy Street, he found that life could be daunting, and he struggled to find employment. Holmyard's seventy-two-year-old grandfather, a wealthy bookmaker who was also called William, lived next door at 37 Tachbrook Street. He lent his grandson £5 to bide him over. Holmyard quickly paid back the initial loan, but borrowed more money in the subsequent weeks.

The fact that grandson was borrowing money from grandfather came to the attention of Holmyard's father; when the younger William discovered what he perceived as a betrayal on 7 December, he stormed next door in a foul mood. A heated argument followed between grandson and grandfather, resulting in William striking his grandfather over the head with a pair of fire-tongs, fracturing his skull and leaving him for dead. The grandfather managed to crawl to his front door and summon help and was taken to hospital. William was arrested by police and charged with wounding – this escalated to a charge of murder when the old man died of his injuries three days later. When questioned by police, Holmyard claimed that his elderly grandfather had attacked him with a chair and he had defended himself.

At his trial at the Central Criminal Court, in front of Mr Justice Humphrey, William Holmyard pleaded not guilty to murder. Very few witnesses appeared for the prosecution, who in their closing speech argued they had heard no evidence to justify an alternative verdict of manslaughter and urged the jury to find Holmyard guilty of the capital offence. Venetia Stephenson stood confidently to her feet to deliver her closing speech. As recorded by the *Derby Daily Telegraph*, she 'was clearly enunciated. She had a photograph of the room where the quarrel took place put before the jury, and submitted that the salient features of a murder charge were absent'.

The reporter went onto describe the hold she had over the jury: 'Miss Stephenson held the court with her dramatic description of the struggle between the two men, raising her hands over her head to illustrate the old man's attack with the chair.' She asked, 'What is the motive for murdering his grandfather? What is the evidence of intent to murder his grandfather? Holmyard's father says that his father was eccentric and bad-tempered, and he lost his temper on this occasion. He was a bookmaker and perhaps he had had a losing week. The statement of Holmyard on which the prosecution relied, was made at eleven o' clock at night, when the man had had no food since half-past-one, and when he did not know the serious condition of his grandfather.' Miss Stephenson sat down, emotionally exhausted, to await the judge's summation, which he prefaced with a tribute to Stephenson's professionalism (some will interpret it as condescending) by stating, 'This case has been defended with conspicuous ability.' The jury retired to consider their verdict and found William Holmyard guilty of the murder of his grandfather. He was sentenced to death by hanging.

On 11 February 1929, Venetia Stephenson, under the leadership of Sir Henry Maddocks KC, appeared at the Court of Criminal Appeal to challenge the conviction of William Holmyard. The appeal was based upon the fact that the jury members were supplied copies of newspapers in their private rooms during the trial, bringing to their notice a legal argument between Miss Stephenson and Mr Justice Humphrey, in the absence of the jury, in relation to the admissibility of certain evidence which may have prejudiced the jury against the defendant. Lord Chief Justice Mr Justice Avery stated that he had read the legal argument referred to during Holmyard's trial and he saw nothing contained in it that could not have been disclosed to the jury, commenting that the practice of asking a jury to retire (a commonplace occurrence in today's courts) whenever there is a legal argument is rather on the increase and quite unnecessary. Sir Henry fought back by arguing that it was for the prosecution to satisfy the court that anything the jury had read in the newspapers was innocuous and could not have hurt the prisoner. The Court of Criminal Appeal ruled in favour of the Crown and the conviction was upheld. On 27 February 1928, William Holmyard was executed at Pentonville Prison by Robert Baxter and Lionel Mann.

48. MURDER OF A VICTIM UNKNOWN (1930)

As fireworks exploded across a dark, clear sky on Bonfire Night 1930, an unidentified corpse burned inside a Morris Minor motor vehicle near the small Northamptonshire village of Hardingstone. The case, imaginatively labelled the 'Burning Car Murder' by the media, would attract worldwide interest for the very reason outlined by the prosecution's opening speech to the jury at the offender's trial:

> In order that I might clear it out of the way right at the outset, you need not be troubled in this matter at all by the fact that the remains [of the victim] are not identified as those of any previously living person. It makes no difference in the law upon this matter, but you may regard it in the special circumstances of this case as a factor very important and most significant.[23]

Just after midnight, two men who had been to a local Guy Fawkes dance turned into Hardingstone Lane and passed a man later identified as Alfred Arthur Rouse; neither party spoke as they crossed paths as the men's focus was on a bright burning blaze up ahead in the direction from which Rouse had come. One said to the other, 'What is

---

23 *Northampton Mercury*, 30 January 1931

that blaze up there?' Rouse shouted back at them, 'It looks as though someone has had a bonfire up there.'

Alfred Rouse was born in Herne Hill, south London. On the outbreak of the First World War he enlisted and was posted to the 24th London Regiment. During his basic training he got married before being sent to France in 1915. He was based in Paris before experiencing active service at the Battle of Festubert on the Western Front; on the last day of the battle he was seriously injured by a high explosive shell, sustaining wounds to his head and leg. Surgery was performed to successfully remove shrapnel from the left temporal region, but his leg injury left him with severe difficulty in walking. He was repatriated back to England for recuperation and eventually appeared in front of an invaliding medical board and was formally discharged from the army in February 1916, receiving a modest pension of 20s a week.

Rouse had annual medical examinations and by 1919 it was declared that he had no further disability from his head wound and that there was no physical reason for any limitation in the use of his leg. In 1920, when a final examination deemed Rouse to be fit with only a slight limitation to the movement of his leg, his pension was stopped, with a final settlement of £41 5s. Rouse had found employment as a commercial travelling salesman with a Leicester-based manufacturing company. His district comprised the south coast, London and as far north as Leicester. He was earning a good wage: £4 a week plus £1 fixed expenses, commission on orders and further expenses for petrol and hotel accommodation. He lived in a nice house in Buxted Road, North Finchley, with his wife and owned a Morris Minor motor vehicle.

Rouse's downfall was his insatiable sexual appetite – on his travels he had many affairs, resulting in two children with different women. With child support orders being served and marriage expected from at least one woman, he looked for a way out and decided to fake his own death, attempting to pass off the body of another as his own.

The two men realised that they were in fact seeing a burning car; they were beaten back by the intensity of the heat but could see the charred, recognisable remains of a human body face down across the passenger and driver seats. The emergency services arrived, and a search of the area surrounding the car turned up a mallet lying in the grass some fourteen yards in front of the car; the head of the mallet had a mixture of blood and human hair attached to it. A petrol can was discovered inside the car, and a fire investigator concluded that the conflagration was started by design rather than accident. The fire was concentrated on the front end of the car, leaving the rear number plate undamaged; a check on police records revealed the registered owner as Alfred Arthur Rouse.

Rouse's trial commenced in February 1931 in Northampton. He was charged with the murder of a person unknown. Pathologist Bernard Spilsbury carried out the post-mortem examination on the charred remains in the garage of a local public house and suggested that the body was of a healthy male aged approximately thirty years, and there were indications from his examination of the victim's lungs that he had been a coalminer or in an occupation that involved working in a dust-ridden atmosphere. He also informed the court that the victim was alive when the fire started and must have lived for a short time while it burned – smoke particles were present in his air passage. Police made intensive enquiries to try and identify the victim but did not succeed.

Following his arrest, Rouse made a statement to detectives at Hammersmith police station that was read out to the jury at his trial. He stated that whilst driving from his home in Finchley up the Great North Road half a mile past Tally Ho Corner he was flagged down by a man requesting a lift. He described him as aged around forty, 5 feet 8 inches tall, medium build with a fresh complexion, dark hair and clean shaven. He was wearing a light-coloured overcoat, fawn trilby hat, and a collar and tie. Rouse believed that he had been drinking. As they approached Hardingstone, Rouse claimed that the engine of his car started to sputter so he stopped to check how much petrol he had. As he got out his passenger asked if he had a smoke. Rouse had a cigar in his pocket, which he tossed to the passenger, and asked if he had a match, to which the man answered that he did. Rouse lifted up the bonnet to discover he only had enough petrol for another twenty miles, so asked the passenger to take the spare petrol can from the back seat and top up the tank while he went to the toilet. As he walked away he saw a bright light reflected on the hedgerow; he turned to see his car in flames.

Rouse claimed that he tried to get the man out but was beaten back. He ran away from the car shouting for assistance, and eventually passed the two men aforementioned, but strangely decided not to ask for their help. He managed to flag down a passing lorry driver, who gave him a lift back to London, and then travelled to a friend's house in Wales for a few days; on his return to London he was arrested. He told police that the mallet found nearby had been used to beat dents out of his bumper following an accident and that he left it in the well of the car. He could not explain the human hair, stating that he may have rubbed it through his own hair at some stage. The jury did not believe the far-fetched story, and found Rouse guilty of murder; he was sentenced to death and executed at Bedford Gaol on Tuesday 10 March 1931.

The victim of this heartless crime still remains unidentified to this day. During the post-mortem on the charred remains of the victim, samples of body tissue and organs were taken and preserved. In light of advances in DNA investigations, the family of a missing man called William Briggs, who disappeared around the time of the murder, asked Northamptonshire police to investigate the possibility that William was the victim – something they had always suspected. A forensic team consisting of academics from the University of Leicester and the University of Northumbria and detectives from Northampton Police were allowed access to some of the stored body tissue, but sadly for the family the results proved William Briggs was *not* the victim burned alive in Alfred Rouse's car. The University of Leicester are hopeful that the victim will one day be identified, as the results from the DNA analysis of the tissue samples represent an uncontaminated profile.

49. A SETBACK FOR FREE SPEECH (1934)

British citizens have not always enjoyed the right to freedom of speech that our tolerant modern laws allow today. 1930s Britain was in a deep depression, with another world war on the horizon only fifteen years after the supposed 'War to end all Wars', and the government of the day were sensitive to public criticism, dealing firmly with citizens who wished to air dissent in public. Katherine Duncan was an active member of the National Unemployed Workers Union, an organisation set up by members of the Communist Party of Great Britain in 1921 to bring attention to the plight of Britain's unemployed following the end of the First World War through the 1926 General Strike and the Great Depression of the early 1930s and to contest the hated Means Test.

On 25 May 1933, Duncan addressed a meeting in Nynehead Street, Deptford, opposite a training centre for the unemployed. The meeting led to a disturbance inside the training centre and the police were called to quell a near-riot. A year later a similar meeting was about to take place in the same location, but this time the police were forewarned and sent units to stop any similar breach of the peace. As Katherine Duncan was about to stand on a box placed in the roadway, she was informed by the police that she would not be able to speak and that the meeting would have to be held in another street a quarter of a mile away. Duncan took no notice and stepped up to address the assembled crowd. She was promptly arrested for unlawfully and wilfully obstructing a police officer in the execution of his duty, and was convicted and fined. However, she appealed against her conviction, stating that there was no obstruction to the highway except the box on which she had stood and the small crowd surrounding her (about thirty) and that neither her nor any other speaker had incited or provoked a breach of the peace.

Duncan's appeal was dismissed, putting the right to freedom of speech back many years. Today freedom of expression is protected by Article 10 of the Human Rights Act 1998, which includes the freedom to hold opinions and to receive and impart information and ideas without state interference. This, of course, can still be overridden by the Public Order Act 1986 if anybody oversteps the mark.

50. IT ALL TURNED ON A LOAF OF BREAD (1934)

The murder of a child in a close-knit community can understandably arouse deep anger, aggression and anxiety, often from fear for one's own family. The murder of little Helen Priestly in Aberdeen in April 1934 was one such crime. It was notable at the time not only for the evil, callous way the killer attempted to deflect responsibility for the crime but for the groundbreaking forensic work involved, including the first use of a bacteriologist in a murder investigation.

On 21 April 1934, eight-year-old Helen was sent on an errand by her mother from her home at 61 Urquhart Street, Aberdeen, to a nearby shop to buy a loaf of bread. She did this chore nearly every day and was known by the shopkeeper and many local people; sadly, this time she did not return home. Her frantic parents reported her missing to the local police, who organised a search with the aid of hundreds of local people. The search, the most extensive ever seen in Aberdeen, continued throughout the night. The police and the family were working on the theory that Helen had been abducted locally and were searching every alleyway, shed, nook and cranny where a young girl could be concealed. Helen's exhausted father was persuaded to go home in the early hours of 22 April and get some rest; he was unwilling to do so until a friend, Alexander Parker, promised he would wake him at 5 a.m.. When Parker returned to the parent's house as promised, he noticed a large blue hessian sack outside the address. Helen's body was inside. The post-mortem examination revealed Helen had been strangled, and she had severe bruising to her thighs and mutilation to her sexual organs. The cause of death and the fact that Aberdeen was harbouring a sexual predator united groups of local people to arm themselves with weapons, intent on hunting the killer down – a most dangerous situation, as such actions are often misguided and lead to violence against the innocent. Police had to act quickly and find the killer before a community tore itself apart.

Door-to-door enquiries by detectives discovered two witnesses who believed they had heard a young girl screaming in the vicinity of the Priestley home at the time Helen would have been expected back after her visit to collect the bread. This concentrated the search for the killer closer to Urquhart Street. Detectives had two main lines of enquiry in the form of forensic details: on Helen's body, and on the hessian sack in which she had been dumped. The sack had previously contained flour imported from Canada; detectives traced a local bakery close to Helen's house that received deliveries of flour in these sacks, and struck lucky; the baker remembered being asked for such a sack by a woman but her description was insufficient in detail to aid identification but again all the evidence was pointing to the killer living nearby and this woman being a possible accomplice.

Local enquiries also revealed a history of friction between the Priestlys and a family living in the same road – the Donalds. Their differences had come from a trivial matter some time before – in fact the Priestlys couldn't even remember what had caused the bad feeling amongst them; in particular between Jeannie Donald who lived with her husband, a local barber, and a daughter of similar age to the victim. Detectives – under extreme pressure from the local community and the vigilante groups – arrested Jeannie Donald, who matched the description of the woman who collected the hessian bag, and her husband. When detectives interviewed Jeannie Donald's daughter she told them that the day Helen had gone missing she had noticed that the bread her mum gave her had a different taste to their normal bread; the local baker confirmed to police that the loaf found in the Donald's kitchen was the same variety of loaf he had given Helen.

By now the police station in which the Donalds were being held was surrounded by a very vocal and aggressive crowd baying for the blood of Mr Donald, whom they assumed to be the killer; in fact if they had reached him before the police he may well have been lynched, such was the anger of the crowd. Detectives quickly established that Mr Donald had been at the barber's shop all day; his alibi was backed up by a number of customers so now the suspicion turned to Jeannie Donald. Jeannie Donald was charged with the murder of Helen Priestley and went on trial at Edinburgh High Court on 16 July 1934.

The reliance on forensic science made this a landmark trial in Scottish criminal history. Professor John Glaister of Glasgow University proved that hair found on the victim's body and inside the hessian sack matched the hair of the defendant. Forensic scientists also found fibres from the hessian sack inside the Donald's home and for the first time a bacteriologist assisted in a murder investigation by discovering bacteria in the sack matched bacteria present in Jeannie's house. The most damning evidence was the discovery during the post mortem that the injuries to Helen's sexual organs had been caused by the handle of a hammer or a broom to make it appear she had been sexually assaulted by a man. The jury took less than twenty minutes to convict her and she was sentenced to death. On 3 August the defence team lodged a successful appeal against Donald's sentence, which was commuted to life imprisonment and incredibly, she was released after serving just ten years. She died in obscurity; she never admitted to her guilt or offered any reason why she had committed this horrible and senseless crime.

51. PROVE IT (1934)

In February 1935 twenty-one-year-old Reginald Woolmington of Castleton, Sherborne, Dorset, appeared at the Bristol Assizes charged with the murder of his seventeen-year-old wife Violet, shooting her through the heart with a sawn-off shotgun. The *Taunton Courier and Western Advertiser* (20 February 1935) records that: 'Woolmington stepped briskly into the dock, dressed in the same smart brown suit and spotted red silk scarf that he had worn at his previous trial.' Having faced a jury that could not decide on his guilt or innocence, a re-trial had been ordered.

Reginald Woolmington, a farm labourer, had become acquainted with Violet when the deceased was fifteen years old; she fell pregnant and the two were married on 24 August 1934 and the baby born in October of the same year. However by the November Violet seemed very depressed and would often be found by her mother in tears in the couple's cottage. On one occasion, when Reginald was present, he accused her of looking at other men and forbade her to leave the cottage in the afternoons. It was agreed that for the time being Violet should go and stay with her mother in Newtown, Milborne Port. This arrangement seemed to have a permanent feel about it and by December Reginald Woolmington decided on drastic action. On 10 December 1934, having had his breakfast and worked during the morning, he went over to the mother-in-law's address on his pushbike armed with a double-barrelled shotgun and cartridges that he had stolen from his employer; he had sawn off the barrels for easier conveyance. When he arrived he found Violet alone, next door was Violet's aunt who heard raised voices and the sound of gunshot. She looked out of her window and saw Woolmington riding away on his pushbike. The aunt hurried next door and found her niece lying on the floor of the front room dead; she had been shot through the heart. Woolmington went to his mother's house proclaiming that 'I have shot Violet.' He went onto Mr Cheeseman his employer and informed him that he would not be coming to work anymore because: 'I have been up and shot my wife – I have done it.'

Following his arrest the gun was found in a shed behind his house. When charged Woolmington replied: 'I have done it and they can do what they like with me. It was jealousy I suppose. Her mother enticed her away from me. I done all I could to get her back. That's all.' An apparent suicide note was discovered in the pocket of the coat Woolmington wore on the day of the shooting it read:

> Goodbye all. It is agonies to carry on any longer. I have kept true hoping she would return. This is the only way out. They ruined me and I will have my revenge. May God forgive me for doing this, but it is the best thing. Her mother is no good on this earth. I have no more cartridges only two, one for her and one for me. I am of sound mind now. Forgive me for all the trouble caused. Goodbye all. I loved Violet with all my heart. Reg.

At his trial Woolmington gave evidence that on the morning of the shooting he had formed a desperate plan to try and get Violet to come home. His plan was to go and see his wife; if she refused to come home he was going to shoot himself in front of her. He sawed the barrels of the gun off so that he could conceal it whilst on his bike. When he arrived Violet let him into the house – he had no intentions of harming her. He asked her to come back but she replied she didn't want to as she was going to go into service, possibly in London. The gun at this point was hanging from his shoulder under his coat; he claimed that he opened his coat, showing her the gun and threatened to shoot himself. As he brought the gun up to waist height it went off accidently. His wife fell to the floor and he left the house in shock as he didn't know what to do. On arrival at his mother's house he told her what he had done and threw the gun into the shed. He then claimed that having changed his clothes he went out to the shed with the intention of shooting himself but was talked out of it by his father. Following a contentious summing up by the trial judge Mr Justice Swift, in which he wrongly directed the jury that the case was so strong against the defendant the burden of proof was on him to show that the shooting was accidental, in order to reduce the severity of the charge to manslaughter. The jury returned a guilty verdict in just over one hour and Woolmington was sentenced to death.

An initial application to the Court of Criminal Appeal failed but the Attorney General Sir Thomas Inskip gave his fiat (his authority) for Woolmington's legal team to appeal the case to the House of Lords and the appeal was upheld. The Lord Chancellor Viscount Sankey ruled that:

> ...it is true that there was apparent authority for the law as laid down by Mr Justice Swift [at the trial] but no matter what the charge or where the trial, the principle that the prosecution must prove the guilt of the prisoner is part of the common law of England, and no attempt to whittle it down can be entertained ... When dealing with a murder case the Crown must prove a) death as a result of a voluntary act of the accused and b) malice of the accused... It was not the law of England to say 'if the Crown satisfies you that this woman died at the prisoner's hands then he has to show that there are circumstances to be found in the evidence which has been given from the witness box in this case, which alleviates the crime so that it is only manslaughter,' or which excused the homicide altogether by showing that it was a pure accident.[24]

Reginald Woolmington's conviction for murder was quashed; he was released just three days before he was due to be executed. This case confirmed the basic fact of English common law that a person is innocent until proven guilty and that it is the prosecution's responsibility to prove a defendant's guilt beyond any reasonable doubt and not the defendant's responsibility to prove his innocence.

---

24 *Nottingham Evening Post*

52. MAGGOTS AND A NEWSPAPER (1935)

A ground-breaking case in which a badly decomposed victim was identified using the science of entomology (the study of insects) and an innovative early form of forensic facial reconstruction occurred in 1935. The case became known as the 'Jigsaw Murders'.

Bukhtyar Chompa Rustomji Ratanji Hakim was born in Bombay, India, in March 1899. He studied medicine at Bombay University and in 1930 took the bold step of moving to Lancaster, England, where he set up his own doctor's practice. He lived at No.2 Dalton Square with his common-law wife Isabella and their three children Elizabeth, William and Diane. He changed his name to Buck Ruxton by deed poll in order, one would imagine, to fit in with the local community. He was a hard-working man who quickly formed a close relationship with the community he served; often foregoing payments of his fees for any patients who could not afford treatment (it was another fifteen years before the creation of the NHS). His domestic life was not so agreeable; he attracted the attention of the ladies but regularly accused his wife of having affairs, often subjecting her to domestic violence; on one occasion this was reported to the police but with no further evidence they took no action. The combustible nature of the relationship was witnessed by maid Mary Rogerson who often listened to the violent arguments between the two. In September 1935 the distrust between husband and wife exploded into a furious argument in which Ruxton strangled Isabella in the front room of the house, witnessed by Mary Rogerson. He had no choice (in his mind), Mary had to die as well and suffered the same fate as her mistress.

Ruxton was now faced with the problem of disposing of the bodies to conceal his crimes. He took both corpses into the bathroom and skilfully dissected each into small enough pieces to be packaged and disposed of easily. There was no panic, Ruxton was thinking logically enough to consider where he was going to dispose of the body parts; he placed the dismembered bodies into his car at night and drove over one hundred miles to the Scottish Borders, a location he knew well. He travelled to an area known as Gardenholme Linn just south of Edinburgh near to the town of Moffat. He drove to a ravine and cast the packages of human flesh down into the River Annan below, confident that nobody would ever find the remains and that he had committed the perfect murders. With adrenalin coursing through his body and planning an alibi he drove at high speed to get back to Lancaster in quick time. This is where his plan started to fragment; as he passed through the town of Kendal in Cumbria he hit a cyclist and failed to stop; the irate cyclist, who was unhurt, had the sense to take down the number plate and reported it to the police immediately. The police acted speedily and set up a road block in Milnthorpe, seven miles south of the incident and waited for the vehicle to arrive. As Ruxton entered the outskirts of the small town he was waved down by a police officer who questioned him about the Kendal incident, he must have been hugely relieved when he was allowed to proceed with an instruction to produce his driving documents at his local police station in Lancaster the following day.

It was not long before the expected knock at his door came – he was prepared. Mary Rogerson's mother had reported her missing to the police; Ruxton told them that she had not turned up for work for the last two days and he was mystified as to her whereabouts. A few days later he was again visited by the police who had received reports from Isabelle's friends that she had not been seen – one would have thought the report of two missing people both connected to the good doctor would have aroused suspicion; apparently not – the police accepted Ruxton's explanation that his wife had gone to Blackpool with her lover. Ruxton sent his children off to boarding school and carried on with his practice. It was difficult to see how Ruxton ever hoped to get away with the disappearance of two women so closely associated with him but seemed confident he could ride the storm – they were never going to find the bodies were they!

On 29 September 1935 a holidaymaker called Susan Haines Johnson was walking along the Carlisle to Edinburgh Road two miles north of Moffat and as she crossed over a bridge she looked down into the five-hundred foot ravine known locally as the Devil's Beef Tub. She spied from a distance what she thought to be a human arm protruding from a parcel. She ran back to her hotel in Moffat and alerted her brother, who returned to the ravine and confirmed what his sister had seen and called the police. Several hours later the Borders police discovered thirty packages containing seventy pieces of rotting flesh wrapped in newspaper, children's clothing and bed-sheets. Detectives initially believed they could be dealing with the body parts of up to five victims. The remains were examined by Professor John Glaister and Professor James Brash both of Edinburgh University in an effort to identify the victims. Glaister and Brash immediately came to the conclusion that there were in fact two victims, and that the murderer was a medically skilled man as normal means of identification – fingers, teeth, and any distinguishing marks – had been removed and separately disposed of. The best that they could do was to identify the victims as female, their approximate age and build.

Scotland Yard's Detective Inspector Lynch was called in to assist the Lancashire police with the investigation. The first break came when a newspaper – wrapped around one of the body parts – was identified as a section of the *Sunday Graphic* dated 15 September 1935. This particular edition was sold only in the Morecombe and Lancaster areas of the country. The date was connected to the period of time when missing person reports of Isabella Ruxton and Mary Rogerson had been filed. Buck Ruxton was again questioned but with a little more zeal. He was asked if he had ever been north of the border, bewildered by how the police had connected him to Scotland he naively claimed that he had not. Detectives were by now convinced of Ruxton's involvement in the disappearance of Isabella and Mary but needed proof. The investigation started to gel when the police officer who had stopped Ruxton in Cumbria on the day in question came forward with his valuable evidence. However, with the body parts discovered in Scotland still not identified as Isabella and Mary, the case was purely circumstantial and not enough to charge Ruxton.

Whilst Glaister and Brash were working on a method to identify the body parts Dr Alexander Mearns – an entomologist from the University of Glasgow – was able to give vital information to the police. By studying the life-cycle of the maggots (bluebottle larvae) discovered munching away at the flesh of the victims he was able to state accurately that the gruesome packages were deposited at the scene some twelve to fourteen days before discovery, which tied in with the Kendal pedal cycle incident; the net was closing in on Dr Ruxton.

Glaister and Brash came up with an innovative idea in order to at least identify one of the corpses. They placed the one skull that had been recovered on a stand and photographed it. They then superimposed the image on to a portrait picture of the missing Isabella Ruxton. The jawline and other facial features matched exactly to the photograph. With this evidence, the evidence of entomologist Dr Mearns, the push bike incident placing Ruxton going south from Scotland to Lancaster and the newspaper which was wrapped around a body part being only delivered to a small area of Lancashire, including Ruxton's house, the police had enough to charge and hopefully convict the evil Doctor.

The trial of Dr Buck Ruxton took place in March 1936; he was indicted on the murder of his wife only, as the prosecution could offer no evidence in the case of Mary Rogerson, who had not yet been identified. When the jury, having heard the compelling evidence from detectives in relation to the newspaper and the collision with the cyclist, and the credible new sciences of basic facial mapping and entomology, convicted Ruxton and he was sentenced to death. Following a failed appeal against his conviction and a petition signed by ten thousand people urging clemency Buck Ruxton was executed at Strangeways Prison, Manchester, on 12 May 1936. The bath that Ruxton had dismembered his victims in, and several other artefacts, were allegedly taken to Lancashire Police Headquarters in Hutton, near Preston, after the trial. After a few years it was rumoured that the bath was in fact used as a horse trough (a copper's sense of humour for you).

53. THE FASCIST NEWSVENDOR (1937)

The Public Order Act 1936 was designed to control extremist political movements within Great Britain (such as the British Union of Fascists) by prohibiting the wearing of uniforms in connection with political causes by private persons or associations and to preserve public order on the occasion of public processions and meetings in public places. It also required police consent for any public demonstrations or marches to take place. The first landmark conviction under this act was of twenty-five-year-old William Henry Wood of Leopold Road, Leeds, on 28 January 1937 at the city's Magistrates Court. Wood openly admitted he was a member of the British Union of Fascists, indeed he was selling the party's newspaper but whilst doing so he wore a peaked cap displaying two badges commonly associated with the British Union of Fascists, a black shirt and a blue tie. The stipendiary magistrate – Mr Horace Marshall – who was acutely aware this would be a test case in relation to the new Public Order Act, went out of his way to, as he put it, 'not lay down any general principles of law'. He was satisfied that each case must be treated on its own merits according to the evidence available. Mr Marshall convicted William Henry Wood explaining, 'I think the average person would have said not "Oh, there's a man representing the Action Press" but "Oh, there is a fascist".' Wood attempted to defend himself by arguing that he was wearing the livery of a newsvendor of the paper titled 'Action' issued to him by the company Action Press Ltd. Wood was fined a nominal forty shillings (*Western Daily Press* 28 January 1937). The Public Order Act 1986 updated the original act and now includes much wider ranging offences and police powers to reflect modern society but keeps many of the principles contained in the original act.

54. 999 EMERGENCY (1937)

An innovative emergency, telephone system where any member of the public could pick up a telephone and dial 999 free of charge was launched in London on 30 June 1937, accompanied by a public education campaign in many of the newspapers of the time to inform Londoners how to use the service; one example featured in the *London Evening News*:

> Only dial 999 if the matter is urgent; if, for instance, the man in the flat next to yours is murdering his wife or you have seen a heavily masked cat burglar peering round the stack pipe of the local bank building... If the matter is less urgent, if you have merely lost little Towser or a lorry has come to rest in your front garden, just call up the local police.

Operators, working for the General Post Office, who originally operated the system, were alerted to an incoming call by the illumination of a red light accompanied by a very loud klaxon. A report in a subsequent issue of the *Post Office Telecommunications Journal* (1951) reported: 'When the raucous buzzer sounded in the quiet disciplined switch rooms a few of the girls found the situation too much for them and had to be carried out. It was even suggested in the press that the buzzers were disturbing other people living in the vicinity of the exchanges.'

The new 999 emergency call system quickly proved to be a success when just a week later the first arrest was made as a result of a 999 call. Early morning on the 7 July 1937 police received a call from architect John Stanley Beard who lived in the well-to-do area of Hampstead in north London. He had been awoken by a noise coming from below his bedroom window. As he peered out he saw what he presumed to be a burglar, later identified as Thomas Duffy. The homeowner shouted at the would-be-intruder who ran off down the garden path heading towards Primrose Hill. John Beard's quick-thinking wife rang the new 999 emergency service with a description and within a short time the police had apprehended Thomas Duffy who they charged with attempted breaking and entering. Following Duffy's conviction at Marylebone Magistrates Court a delighted Mr Beard commented in *The Times*:

> My wife made use of the new signal that we were instructed to use yesterday on the telephone, and as a result of using that signal almost instantaneous connection was made with the police station, and in less than five minutes this man was arrested... It struck me, as a householder and a fairly large taxpayer, that we are getting something for our money, and I was very impressed by it.

Of the 1,336 calls made in the first week following the 999 launch ninety-one were pranks. The service was launched in Glasgow the following year but the rest of Britain's major cities had to wait until after the Second World War. Surprisingly, the nation only enjoyed full 999 emergency coverage after all telephones exchanges were automated in 1976. Today the 999 system handles over thirty-million calls a year.

55. MURDER ON THE TUBE (1939)

If one considers that the London Underground system caters for in the region of two million passenger journeys every weekday it is incredible that violent crimes such as murder, rape and robbery are not more common. Of course there have been many instances of murder on the underground in modern times including the devastating attacks by terrorists in July 2005. There have also been very rare incidents of people intentionally being pushed under a train; one of the first recorded examples of this occurring on London's underground system was in February 1939.

Avril Ray Waters was a few weeks short of her fifteenth birthday when she left her home at No.71 Broadfields Avenue on the newly developed Broadfield estate in an area described in the *Hendon and Finchley Times* (17 February 1939) as 'New Edgware'. Avril, who lived with her parents and ten-year-old brother Alan, travelled daily, with a friend, to attend a business college in Russell Square, catching a tube train from either Burnt Oak or Edgware on the relatively new extension of the Northern Line. She would travel south to Tottenham Court Road station then walk to Russell Square. Late afternoon on 15 February 1939 she entered Tottenham Court Road station, alone as her friend had been unwell, to travel north and home. The northbound Northern line platform was filled with rush hour commuters awaiting an Edgware-bound train. The *Hendon and Finchley Times* takes up the story as the train rattled into the platform between fifteen and twenty miles per hour:

> A moment later there was a scream and the girl [Avril] was seen to fall in the path of an oncoming train. It was said that three coaches passed over her before the train could be stopped. Hundreds of passengers saw railway employees working for half-an-hour to release the girl and she was carried onto the platform, where a doctor came forward and offered his services. Morphia was administered and Avril was carried up the escalator on a stretcher, to be removed to Charing Cross Hospital, but she passed away whilst in the ambulance.

London Transport station and platform staff prevented further passengers from entering the platform and awaited the arrival of the police. Detectives interviewed the stationmaster and the driver and guard of the train involved. The unfortunate driver – Mr B.W Whiting – who witnessed the full horror of the tragic event would later tell a court that Avril had been conscious beneath the second carriage when he managed to get to her and had begun to tell him her name and address before she lost consciousness. Avril's handbag had been retrieved from the track which contained identification details and a police car was despatched to Edgware to deliver the tragic news to the parents, who had become very worried when Avril had not returned home.

The incident was witnessed by several passengers, two of whom chased and detained the man responsible for the death of Avril. His name was Leonard Ward Davies, a twenty-nine-year-old barman of Windsor Road, Holloway. Davies was conveyed to Tottenham Court Road police station where he was charged with the murder of Avril Waters. The following day he appeared at Marlborough Street Magistrates Court:

Leonard Ward Davies, aged 29, a barman, of 48, Windsor Road, Holloway, who was arrested on Wednesday night appeared at Marlborough Street Police Court yesterday, charged with the murder of Avril Waters. The girl was described as a shorthand student at a commercial school. The court was crowded soon after the magistrate, Mr Ivan Snell, took his seat, and the case was first taken. Davies wore a dark blue suit and a white sports shirt. He was allowed to sit whilst the evidence was given. Div. Det. Inspector Peter Beveridge asked to offer evidence to justify a remand. He said: 'At about 10.45pm, on February 15, 1939, I saw the prisoner detained at Tottenham Court Road Police Station. I said to him: I am a police inspector. I have just seen the body' – at this point Waters [mis-reported should read Davies] sat down and lowered his head in his hands – 'of Avril Ray Waters at Charing Cross Hospital, and as a result of the inquiries I have made I am now going to charge you with her wilful murder' I cautioned him, and he said 'Yes sir, She's dead is she?' He was later charged, and when the charge was read over to him he said 'I will say nothing now.' Inspector Beveridge continued: 'This morning, at a quarter to four, he said to me in the presence of Inspector Long "I don't know what made me do it. A sudden impulse came over me and I wanted to push someone under a train. I have been worried because I could not get work."'[25]

25 *Hendon and Finchley Times* 17 February 1939

Several witnesses gave evidence at the subsequent committal hearing. Terence Marne, a cellar-man of Archway Road, Holloway, stated that from March to May the previous year he had worked with Davies. The day before this event Davies had come to see him and they went for a walk; Marne noticed that Davies seemed depressed before he asked Marne if he thought people can have split personalities. Marne stated that Davies asked him in a nervous, sensitive way, what he would 'think of a man who had an uncontrollable impulse to throw someone under a train'. Marne also informed the court that he was aware that Davies had been certified insane at the end of 1937. A second witness – Mr R.E.W Fisher of Antrim Mansions, Hampstead, said that he saw the defendant push Avril Waters under the train before running away. He gave chase but Davies had been held by two other passengers and was repeatedly saying to them 'I couldn't help it.' Davies was committed to the Central Criminal Court to stand trial for murder.

The Waters family were of the Jewish faith and therefore, as is customary, the funeral took place very soon after her death; the body was quickly released by the coroner as there was little ambiguity surrounding the circumstances of her death. The funeral took place at Willesden Jewish Cemetery, Pound Lane, Willesden, following a short service in the chapel. The *Hendon and Finchley Times* (24 February 1939) records that sad day and the terrible toll on the bereaved parents:

> The funeral of Avril Ray Waters took place on Friday. The body of the child was placed in a white wooden coffin and brought from the mortuary to Edgware, where the cortege stopped for a few moments outside the home of her parents while mourners entered the cars. Her father was so overcome that he had to be assisted from the house to the awaiting car by his two brothers. It is the Jewish custom that women are not encouraged to attend a funeral, but Mrs Waters was so ill that she could not have done so if she had desired it. Neighbours had drawn their curtains in sympathy and as the procession moved slowly away there was a deep silence.

Leonard Davies appeared at the Old Bailey toward the end of March 1939 charged on indictment of the murder of Avril Waters. During a hearing that lasted less than ten minutes Mr Justice Hawke, having heard medical evidence, ruled that Davies was unfit to plead and ordered that he be kept in custody during His Majesty's pleasure.

56. FROM ROWING BOAT TO THE GALLOWS (1940)

The Treachery Act 1940 was introduced into British Law by Winston Churchill's government following the Nazi invasion of France in May 1940 in order to update and facilitate the prosecution of enemy spies. The act simplified the offence of treachery with a very clear outcome. The first section read:

> If, with intent to help the enemy, any person does, or attempts or conspires with any other person to do any act which is designed or likely to give assistance to the naval, military or air operations of the enemy, to impede such operations of His Majesty's forces, or to endanger life, he shall be guilty of felony and shall on conviction suffer death.

The first persons to be convicted and executed under this act were a German national Jose Waldberg and Dutchman, of German origin, Karl Heinrich Meier. The two spies had been escorted across the English Channel by boat and completed the last few hundred yards by rowing boat, landing at Dungeness on the coast of Kent on 3 September 1940. At the same time further down the coast two more spies landed by the same method. If apprehended they planned to claim they had escaped from the Nazi-occupied Netherlands and then travelled around England reporting back on military installations and any troop movements and the morale of the British people. They had been supplied with a large amount of cash to sustain their efforts; three carried Dutch passports, the fourth had no identification. They were to remain in the United Kingdom until the anticipated German invasion of England later the same month. They would not have the opportunity to carry out their plan. Meier was approached by an ARP warden; the suspicious warden asked for Meier's identification but he claimed he had only just landed. The warden detained him and after some questioning Meier gave them the location of Waldberg, who was also arrested. The other two spies, Charles Van Kiebaum and Sjoerd Pons, were captured when they asked local people where they were. The four men had in their possession, in addition to the cash, two wireless transmitters and receivers, a loaded revolver, a pocket compass, a jackknife, food and a list of several names and addresses in the United Kingdom.

The men were further questioned by MI5 and admitted the true purpose of their mission; Waldberg allegedly proudly proclaimed that he was a 'student of espionage'. The four were tried at the Central Criminal Court, Old Bailey: Waldberg, Meier and Van Kiebaum were convicted and sentenced to death. Sjoerd Pons was acquitted when he convinced the jury that he had been compelled to take on the mission by the Gestapo when caught smuggling jewellery between Germany and Holland. It would seem Pons' acquittal gave Waldberg a window of opportunity to save himself. Waldberg's execution was briefly postponed when he appealed to the home secretary that he had not been given the chance during the trial to explain fully to the court that his actions were as a result of the Nazis holding his father and the promise if he served Germany in this way he would obtain his release; if he had made this claim during his trial he may well have received the benefit of the doubt. Waldberg and Meier were hanged at Pentonville Prison on 10 December 1940. Kiebaum was executed one week later

57. IT WAS HIM – NO, IT WAS HIM! (1942)

The science behind fingerprinting made its 'mark' in the world of crime detection in the very early part of the twentieth century. Fingertips are indeed unique, as is the palm and the very edge of each hand, known as the 'chop'. It wasn't until 1942 that the first palm-print contributed to the conviction of a murderer. On 30 April 1942 Leonard Moules was about to shut up shop for half-day at 1pm; he had been the proprietor of the pawnbrokers at 299 Hackney Road, Shoreditch, for many years. Two local East End villains: Samuel Dashwood and George Silverosa, burst in just before closing time intent on robbing the seventy-one-year-old shop-owner. Moules attempted to blow a whistle that he kept under the counter for security but was hit over the head with a revolver to silence him and the pair stole £40 in cash and assorted rings from the safe before making their escape.

Later that evening a patrolling police officer responded to information from a member of the public who had reported a light still on in Moules' pawnbrokers – contravening strict blackout laws in place during the war years. On investigating the police officer found Leonard Moules in the basement, he had serious head wounds but was still alive, although only semi-conscious. He was taken to Bethnal Green Hospital; he never recovered consciousness and died of his injuries on 9 May 1942.

A proper examination of the scene was postponed until the morning light due to the blackout but when carried out revealed a pool of blood by the counter and spots of blood around the premises – probably deposited by the victim as he wandered around his shop disorientated by the severity of his head injuries. In the back of the shop police discovered three safes, one of which had a clear palm print on the inside. They established, by a process of elimination, the mark did not belong to Moules or any of his staff. Detectives started their investigation by concentrating on known local violent offenders who used a similar modus operandi; one man stood out from the rest – George Silverosa. Detectives visited all Silverosa's known haunts but couldn't find him, he seemed to have gone to ground. They spoke to his known associates, one of whom informed them he had seen Silverosa in a café on St Peters Street on 28 April 1942 with another man for whom he gave a description. Detectives followed the trail to Pitsea in Essex where they bumped into Samuel Dashwood in the company of George Silverosa's sister; Dashwood matched the description of Silverosa's companion in the St Peters Street café. Eventually, both men were arrested for the murder of Leonard Moules. The palm print found in the safe proved to be Silverosa's, they had little choice but to admit they were responsible for the pawnbrokers raid but blamed each other for the fatal blows that led to the death of the proprietor. Much of the stolen jewellery was recovered – sold on by the two. Both men were tried at the Old Bailey and convicted of the murder. Both were hanged side by side on 10 September 1942 at Pentonville Prison.

58. TWO LOST SOULS (1942)

Opposites do tend to attract; this next case tells the story of two very different people from diverse backgrounds who lost their way through childhood and adolescence only to cross paths in later life with the most tragic and horrific outcome. It also gives the first opportunity in this volume to examine and appreciate the outstanding work of one of Britain's finest forensic pathologists – Professor Keith Simpson. Simpson was an extraordinary man whose ground-breaking advances in forensic science and forensic dentistry qualify him as a major influence on British crime detection and hence he is frequently mentioned in a volume of this nature.

This sickening tale revolves around the somewhat unconventional relationship between a French-Canadian soldier called August Sangret and a difficult teenager – nineteen-year-old Joan Pearl Wolfe. Sangret was born of mixed race, into poverty in the town of Battleford, Saskatchewan, in Canada; his family originating from the Cree Indian population. Blighted with illness, he received little education; although illiterate he was an intelligent boy who spoke both English and the Cree language fluently. During his late teenage years he worked as a labourer in the town of Maidstone, fifty-two miles west of Battleford. As he progressed through his thirties worrying violent trends appeared in his character resulting in several criminal convictions. He served custodial sentences for offences of violence including assault and threatening a woman with a firearm as well as petty crimes such as vagrancy and theft. As an outlet for his aggression he enlisted with the Battleford Light Infantry in 1935 where he remained until 1939 and the beginning of the Second World War. With Canada joining the war effort in 1940 Sangret enlisted as a full-time soldier in the Regina Rifle Regiment where his indiscipline and violent tendencies blighted his record. In March 1942 his regiment was deployed to England and initially posted to Fleet in Hampshire and then onto the army town of Aldershot and finally Godalming, Surrey. It was during his posting in this small town that he met Joan Wolfe.

Joan was born in Tonbridge, Kent; brought up in a strict Catholic household she attended a convent school. In contrast to Sangret she was well-educated and could speak fluent French; however her childhood and education were marred by the suicide of her father who gassed himself whilst she was away at school. She ran away from home at the age of sixteen following the re-marriage of her mother and the birth of a half-sister. She went missing for a month before being found in Aldershot and returned home. She hated life at home with her stepfather and half-sister and decided to head off to London to seek a career; she found employment as a storekeeper in an aircraft factory. During her late teens she became very unstable, her behaviour erratic, she had many sexual encounters, mainly with Canadian soldiers. Her mother attempted to steer her wayward daughter back onto the right path, imploring her to return to the safety and stability of her home but in the end gave up on her.

In the early 1940s Wolfe lived an itinerant existence in cheap lodgings, staying with friends or sleeping rough. In July 1942 Joan Wolfe met August Sangret in a pub in Godalming; on leaving the pub they went to a nearby park and had sex. They arranged to meet again in the near future but Wolfe failed to show. A few days later Sangret and Wolfe again crossed paths outside a fish and chip shop, Wolfe told Sangret that she had nowhere to stay that night. Sangret, remembering his inherent skills from his Cree past, offered to build her a wigwam in the undergrowth on Hankley Common near to his military camp. The structure was made from tree saplings, with birch bark as a roof covering; his only tool was a strangely crooked knife unique to the Cree Indians. On finishing its construction Sangret and Wolf spent the night together before he returned to camp near Hankley Common early the following morning. He later returned bringing with him stolen army issue blankets. Sangret would visit Wolf frequently until the wigwam was discovered and Wolf evicted; Sangret's answer was to simply build another in a different location on the common.

Wolfe was admitted to hospital in late July; she wrote to Sangret intimating that she was pregnant. When she was released they returned to the wigwam arrangement until they were again discovered and this time Sangret was arrested for illegally keeping a girl within the camp precincts. Wolfe was detained by Surrey police and taken to Guildford Hospital for her own safety and remained there until 1 September 1942. Sangret did visit Wolfe at the hospital during this period but was never given a definitive answer as to her 'pregnancy'. On 1 September 1942 Wolfe convinced the hospital matron that she wanted to go into Guildford to shop for some new clothes. She instead spent the day with Sangret and the night sleeping in the waiting room of Guildford railway station. Her next abode was an abandoned cricket pavilion in the town of Thursley where Sangret would visit her bringing food, clothing and blankets from the camp; they would discuss marriage and their future together. Wolfe spent the next two weeks living in the cricket pavilion whilst obtaining short-term part-time work as well as picking blackberries on the common which she would sell to the Canadian soldiers. The last time Joan Wolfe was seen alive was on 13 September 1942 by a lady called Alice Curtis, who saw Wolfe in the company of a 'dark-complexioned' soldier with black hair. Sangret mentioned to a fellow soldier, around the time of Wolfe's disappearance, that he believed she had taken his water bottle and his Cree Indian knife.

On 7 October 1942, nearly four weeks after Wolfe was last seen picking blackberries, two Royal Marines were on exercise on Hankley Common, as they approached an area known locally as Houndown Wood they made a gruesome discovery. Protruding from a freshly dug mound of earth was a human arm; a number of fingers had been gnawed away by vermin. Closer examination revealed a foot. Both men returned to their camp and reported it to their senior officer and the police were called. Detectives from the local Surrey police and Scotland Yard – having attended the scene – decided to summon the Surrey County Coroner and the forensic pathologist Dr Keith Simpson to excavate the remains of the victim. The body had badly decomposed; maggots had eaten away at much of the soft body tissue around the neck and head apart from a small section of the scalp and hair. Simpson described the head, chest and abdominal cavity as a 'seething mass of maggots'. Simpson made an initial assessment that death had been caused by blunt trauma to the skull, which he noted was 'all but collapsed'. The body was fully recovered and transported to the mortuary at London's Guy's hospital for a post mortem examination.

Keith Simpson carried out the post mortem on the yet unidentified victim ascertaining that she was a white female, approximately twenty-years of age, 5 feet 4 inches tall. He meticulously re-constructed the victims shattered skull – piece by piece – allowing him to identify the point of a single fatal blow measuring five inches in length and one-and-three-quarters in breadth which, he concluded, was delivered by a pole or bough from a tree whilst the victim had been lying face down. Simpson also noted numerous knife wounds to the forehead and defensive wounds to the right forearm and right hand, which were inflicted before the victim had died. This knife attack would have been most savage with the victim initially facing her attacker and being stabbed on the head several times, receiving the injuries to her arm and hand as she tried to protect herself. The wounds were on the left side of the skull and forehead, indicative of a right-handed attacker. Simpson also noted that the soft tissue around the stab wounds to the arm and hand of the victim had been pulled outwards on the weapon's extraction therefore indicating the blade had been either curved or had a hooked point like a parrot's beak; this was backed up by the wounds on the re-constructed skull. The post mortem also revealed the victim's jaw had been broken and three front teeth had been knocked out, all these injuries were – Simpson concluded – inflicted while the victim was still alive. Simpson gave the investigating detectives crucial evidence in relation to the time of death. He calculated that the victim had been dead for one month basing this on the extent of saponification of the remaining body fats that hadn't been destroyed by vermin and the continued presence of heat generated by the maggot infestation. The infestation also indicated that the body was exposed to the air (probably lying partially concealed until the killer could return to bury it) for at least twenty-four hours.

Back at the crime scene police teams carried out co-ordinated searches of Houndown Wood, their priority was to find any personal belongings of the yet unidentified victim and the murder weapon. Over sixty officers scoured the area; within 350 metres of the burial site and sixteen metres from a military trip wire officers discovered a blood-stained Birchwood bough on which Simpson matched strands of hair to the victim's skull. A few days later, as the police widened their search area, they located property belonging to the victim: a handbag containing a rosary, a national registration card in the name of Joan Pearl Wolfe, a blank Canadian Army application to marry form and a letter written to August Sangret, a Canadian soldier.

Keith Simpson wrote a detailed report about his findings and how he saw the sequence of events unfolding:

> I thought it had begun in the dell where Joan's papers were found, probably with the stabbing attack on her head... She must have run downhill, screaming with pain and fear, inviting pursuit to silence her. Her crucifix ornament must have been torn or pulled away and the contents of her handbag spilled out as she ran... Dizzy and faint because of her head wounds and with blood running from her head wound into her eyes, she was already stumbling at the rivulet, where a tripwire had been laid

by exercising troops... She fell heavily, knocking out her front teeth and further dazing herself, but was almost certainly still able to cry out for help, still inviting a silencing injury... Lying prone, her right cheek on the ground, she was struck the final blow with the birchwood.[26]

Detective Chief Inspector Edward Greeno from Scotland Yard's murder squad was to lead the initial interview with August Sangret and subsequently the formal interview at Godalming police station. Greeno recorded a written statement given by Sangret between 12 and 16 October 1942 totalling seventeen thousand words until then the longest statement of its kind to be recorded in British criminal history. During the statement Sangret gave a detailed account of his meeting Wolfe and their subsequent relationship. He re-affirmed that he had not seen her since 14 September 1942 admitting that they had argued on this date. When asked what had become of his knife he replied that he had given it to Wolfe. At this stage Greeno did not have enough evidence to charge Sangret and released him on police bail. As he was told he was being released Sangret commented to Greeno: 'I guess you have found her; I guess that I will get the blame.'

Greeno continued the hunt for the murder weapon questioning several Canadian soldiers in Witley Camp before his tenacity paid off when Private Samuel Crowle informed Greeno he had been out blackberry picking when he came across the wigwam Sangret had constructed, he had heard voices from inside, as he walked away he saw a black-handled knife stuck into a tree, he thought it not a service knife and took it; he noted it had a blade with a hooked point. He intended to keep it, but in the end handed it to Corporal Harding explaining where and under what circumstances he had found it, who in turn returned it to Sangret believing it belonged to him. A month or so after his release on bail the knife was found by Private Brown whilst unblocking a drain in the camp, both Crowle and Harding identified it as the knife found on the common and returned to Sangret. The knife was examined for blood and fingerprints but none were found due to it being in the drain for some considerable time.

---

26 *Forty Years of Murder* Keith Simpson 1978, p.66

Greeno took the knife to Simpson who matched the tip of the knife exactly to the stab injuries to the skull. Sangret was arrested and charged with Joan Wolfe's murder.

The trial commenced at the Kingston Assize in February 1943; by this time the media were referring to the case as *'The Wigwam Murder'*. There was little evidence against Sangret, forensic science or witnesses had been unable to place him at the murder/burial site. Crowle and Harding could prove continuity of the knife found in the tree next to the wigwam where Sangret regularly visited Wolfe through to the handing of the knife back to him. Keith Simpson's job was to prove this knife had been the weapon that inflicted the injuries on Wolfe. Simpson stood in the witness box and caused quite a stir when he removed the victim's skull from a container – the first time this had been witnessed in a British court – and demonstrated to the mesmerised jury exactly how the point of the blade fitted into the wounds on the skull. The jury took the knife and the skull into the jury room to consider their verdict; two hours later they convicted Sangret of murder, although accompanied with a recommendation for mercy. August Sangret was executed at Wandsworth Prison at 9am on 29 April 1943 by Albert Pierrepoint.

Keith Simpson went on to a brilliant career in forensic medicine and is recognised as one of the world's most knowledgeable authorities on the subject; he founded and became the first president of the Association of Forensic Medicine.

59. ALL FROTH AND MIRRORS (1944)

It may come as a surprise that the last conviction under the Witchcraft Act of 1735 was as recently as 1944 when Scottish medium Victoria Helen McCrae Duncan was imprisoned for nine months in March of that year.

Duncan was born in Callender, Perthshire in 1897. She believed that she had a talent in the world of the supernatural. She married a First World War veteran at the age of nineteen and by her mid-twenties she was regularly offering séances in which she would claim to summon the dearly departed of those who attended by emitting ectoplasm (a viscous substance that supposedly exudes from the body of a medium during a spiritualistic trance and forms the material for the manifestation of spirit). She was shown to be a fraud – in 1928 a photographer attended several séances at Duncan's house and recorded the supposed materialisation of the spirits, one of which was a spirit guide called 'Peggy'. It was proved from the photographs that the 'spirits' were in fact a fraud, one being a doll draped in an old sheet. Three years later in 1931 the London Spiritualist Alliance that would form the basis of the College of Psychic Studies discovered Duncan's ectoplasm was in fact cheesecloth mixed with egg white which she would regurgitate during her performances.

In 1933 Duncan was prosecuted and convicted of fraudulent mediumship at an Edinburgh court and fined ten pounds following a séance in the city when she introduced 'Peggy' as a physical entity in the séance room, only for it to be revealed by one of the attendees as a knitted fabric doll. Not fazed by her brush with the law she carried on but went a step too far when she revealed the spirit of a lost sailor at a séance in Portsmouth in November 1941 who 'foretold' the sinking of HMS *Barham* (sunk by a U Boat on the 25 November 1941). This attracted the attention of the authorities as the sinking of this particular ship would not be made public knowledge until January 1942, although the next of kin of those who died were informed shortly after its loss. The Royal Navy sent two officers along to one of Duncan's séances in January 1944. One of them was a Lieutenant Worth; Worth was less than impressed with Duncan when a figure in a white sheet appeared in the room claiming to be the spirit of Worth's deceased aunt, which came as a surprise to him as his aunts were alive and well; this was repeated later in the séance, this time it was his sister. Worth reported the fraudulent goings on to the police who sent officers to the next séance to investigate. They were amazed to see a white-sheeted figure emerge, later revealed to be Duncan herself – the game was up and she was arrested. But how did she know of the sinking of the *Barham*? Eight-hundred and sixty-one sailors lost their lives in this terrible incident and each of their next of kin were informed, so in fact this 'closely guarded secret' to presumably protect public morale was in fact common knowledge to several thousand people.

Duncan, now aged forty-six, was initially detained under Section 4 of the 1824 Vagrancy Act which dealt with, in the main, begging and vagrancy offences. But this was a much more serious offence and caused a lot of angst among the population, so prosecutors identified section 4 of the Witchcraft Act of 1735, an offence triable by a jury alleging engagement in fraudulent spiritual activity, an offence the authorities believed would demonstrate the seriousness of her actions. She would stand trial with Ernest and Elizabeth Homer who allowed her the use of their premises in Portsmouth and Duncan's agent, who aided and abetted her at the séances; they faced two charges of conspiracy to contravene the Witchcraft Act 1735, two charges of obtaining money by false pretences and three lesser common law charges of public mischief. At one stage during the trial Duncan offered to demonstrate her powers to the court and thus disprove the allegations of false pretence. The *Liverpool Echo* (27 March 1944) was one newspaper that covered the extraordinary request under the headline 'Spirits for the Old Bailey' followed by 'Demonstration Proffered [in] "Witchcraft" Case'. Duncan's defence barrister Mr C.E. Loseby stated his client was willing to proffer herself to produce the form or voice of the spirit guide: 'It is the acid test' he informed the court: 'If Mrs Duncan has a guide, he will be with her now probably, trying to help her here in the Central Criminal Court.' Loseby informed the Recorder of London – Sir Gerald Dodson – that all Mrs Duncan needed was a bare room with a small proportion curtained off and a red light. The request was turned down but when Dodson suggested to Loseby that maybe his client should consider giving evidence Loseby retorted that: 'Mrs Duncan can give no evidence at all – her case being that she is in a trance – other than this one point of saying – "I proffer myself".' Loseby argued (as reported in the *Liverpool Echo*) that the Witchcraft Act was obsolete referring to the allegation of using a kind of conjuration to bring about the appearance of the spirit of a dead person, Mr Loseby asked if there was any evidence to say that Mrs Duncan had done anything more than be a materialisation medium, a person through whom, with or against her will, certain spirits came from another world. 'Can the Lord's Prayer' he asked 'be called a conjuration? I am going to argue that the Witchcraft Act 1735 is obsolete as far as this type of case is concerned.'

Chemist Ernest Homer who stood in the dock beside Duncan gave evidence during the trial. He introduced himself as a chemist over whose shop the séances were held. He told the jury that thirteen séances had taken place there for which he paid her £8 per appearance. He charged twelve shillings and sixpence entrance fee; for one of the meetings in January 1944 he had eighteen attendees. Homer, in an effort to counteract the charge of fraud, attempted to give a factual account of what he witnessed during several of the séances: 'The voice of Albert' one of the spirit guides he recalled 'was not like Mrs Duncan's, Albert looked like a spirit form, six feet tall with a thin face and a beard. I could see ectoplasm from Mrs Duncan's mouth, and out of it was built up the Great Spirit form of Albert.' On a subsequent occasion another form of a 'little lady came out three feet from the cabinet. I saw her features – pointed chin, very old face, grey hair, very thin, and about five feet two inches tall. She disappeared in front of my eyes through the floor.'

Many well-known public figures gave evidence on behalf of Mrs Duncan; one was English journalist and critic of the day – Mr Hannen Swaffer, who wrote for the *Daily Mail* for seventeen years before moving to the *Daily Express* and *Sunday Express* as a drama critic. He told the court that he had carried out experiments with Mrs Duncan in 1932 in the presence of four magicians. Mrs Duncan had been tied up with forty yards of sash-cord, handcuffed with regulation police handcuffs, her thumbs being tightly tied together with eight feet of thread so tightly that it cut into her flesh. This application took eight minutes but she escaped her restraints in three minutes 'Even Houdini did not do that,' Swaffer exclaimed. He described the ectoplasm seen coming from Duncan's mouth as resembling 'living snow'. Flight Lieutenant Harold Miller informed the court that he had attended no less than sixteen of Mrs Duncan's séances at which he had witnessed fifteen 'recognitions' of materialised forms.

The jury returned a verdict of guilty in contravention of the Witchcraft Act – falsely claiming to procure spirits – against all four defendants; Helen Duncan was sentenced to nine months imprisonment, the agent Brown to four months and the Homers were bound over to keep the peace. The Witchcraft Act was replaced by the Fraudulent Mediums Act of 1951. Duncan died in Edinburgh in 1956 at the age of fifty-nine.

60. A GOOD-TIME GIRL (1948)

A troubled marriage ending in brutal murder resulted in the introduction to the British courtroom of a ground-breaking forensic technique pivotal in the conviction of the offender.

Robert and Phyllis Gorringe were married in October of 1947 and lived with Robert Gorringe's parents at 78 High Brooms Road, Tunbridge Wells, Kent. Robert was a twenty-one-year-old gasworks labourer; his wife a postal telephonist aged twenty-three. The marriage seemed to hit the rocks very early on evidenced by a difficultly worded letter from Robert to Phyllis:

I hope these small gifts will show that I really do love you and always will in years to come. I guess that I have not been such a good husband as you would wish. I am sorry. I only hope you will never leave me. I guess you will go on dancing and I will have to let you go or live by myself, and that will finish me. Happy Christmas, love Bob.[27]

On Boxing Day the couple spent the evening at Phyllis' parent's house which annoyed Robert who wanted to leave early and go home, but Phyllis refused, causing an argument between them. As alluded to in his letter Phyllis loved to dance but Robert was happier down the pub with his mates so when Phyllis arranged to go to a dance at the town's assembly hall on New Year's Eve with her sister, Robert rebelled and went on a pub crawl with a friend called Ernest Cotterell. They visited a number of pubs in the town centre before walking to the assembly hall arriving at 8.50pm and after initial hesitation they decided to go in. When Phyllis, wearing a white dance dress, and her sister arrived shortly after 9pm they were with a man called Alan Hobbs, whose company they kept for most of the evening, on two occasions leaving the hall and going to a local pub for a drink. Robert would chat to his wife on and off and had one dance with her, when he asked her to have a drink with him she refused, which upset him. He complained to Phyllis' sister about the brush-off. About 11.15pm as the New Year approached Robert and Phyllis were seen to leave the hall; Robert returned thirty minutes later on his own asking two women, one called Vera Hicks, if they had seen Phyllis – neither had – he remained in their company until gone midnight, even dancing with one of them. At 12.30am Robert left the venue with Miss Hicks and he walked her as far as his parent's house commenting that Phyllis would probably be home by then.

At 7.30am Phyllis Gorringe's body was discovered between a lorry and a brick wall in Hollybank Yard, a short distance from the hall; her face had been covered by a fur cape, her white dance dress covered in blood, she had been sexually assaulted and murdered. Dr Keith Simpson the home office pathologist and rising star in the world of forensic examination performed the post-mortem on New Year's Day and would later give evidence that Phyllis had bruising to her mouth consistent with a punch, a bruised scalp over her temple

---

27 *Kent & Sussex Courier* 6 February 1948

consistent with her hitting her head on a hard surface, scratches to the neck and a bite mark on her right breast. He also determined that there had been a very heavy blunt injury to the face and the jaw was fractured. He formed the opinion that at the time the facial injury was sustained her head had been resting on the ground. She had bled into her mouth and the cause of death was asphyxia due to partial strangulation and the inhalation of blood from the facial injuries. He believed the sexual assault and bite mark were probably caused when the victim was pinned by the neck but before the fatal blow. The bite mark was made by two upper front teeth and four lower front teeth and Simpson believed they showed some unusual irregularities and spacing.[28]

An hour after the discovery of his Phyllis' body Robert Gorringe walked into Tunbridge Wells police station to report his wife missing. When he gave a physical description of his spouse to the police, together with the fact that she was wearing a white dress, he was detained and when told that his wife had been raped and murdered he made two statements. He claimed that on the night Phyllis had asked to speak to him outside the hall; he followed her out to a yard and they stood by a lorry. Phyllis told Robert that she was fed up with him criticizing her about her dancing and the clothes she wore and that she talked about going to live back home with her parents. At his trial at the Kent Assizes in February 1948 he continued with the same story that he gave to police: 'I told her not to be silly... in the end she told me to go to the devil and that was when she lost her temper and struck me across the face. I lost my temper, that was when I struck her with my fist in her face. The next thing I could see she was at my feet. I turned and left and went to the dance hall.' When it was put to Gorringe that somebody had violently sexually assaulted his wife and asked if he had taken any part in that assault he replied 'I feel sure I did not.'

The prosecution case was in the main circumstantial; as the defence, and the judge in summing up, emphasised, Robert Gorringe had no blood on his clothes after such a violent attack, he had walked back into the dance hall as if nothing had happened (even though he admitted to police and to the court that he had lost his temper and

28 *Forty Years of Murder* Keith Simpson

punched his wife in the face). Gorringe did have scratches on his hands, noticed by the police when he reported his wife missing, but he claimed these were inflicted at work – Vera Hicks didn't recall any blood on his hands when he returned from the hall. The real crux of the defence case was would a man who apparently had a normal sex life with his new bride feel the need to violently rape her after the kind of argument most married couples experienced? The turning point in the trial had been the evidence regarding the bite mark on the victim's breast. Professor Keith Simpson, had made casts of the suspects teeth and explained to the jury that he was all but certain the bite mark, which had been very defined due to the victim dying so quickly after the bite had been administered, was identical to the teeth pattern of her husband Robert Gorringe. The jury returned a verdict of guilty. This was the first time in British criminal history that forensic dentistry/odontology had been used to convict a murderer. The *Kent and Sussex Courier* (27 February 1948) captured the defendant's reaction as he learned of his fate:

Without showing the slightest trace of emotion and maintaining the imperturbable expression which had been a feature of all his appearances in court Robert Holman George Gorringe, 21-year-old gasworks labourer, of Tunbridge Wells, heard the jury declare him guilty of the murder of his wife and sentence of death passed on him at Kent Assizes on Tuesday. Then he turned in the dock half-saluted and half-waved to his mother and father who were sitting in a packed public gallery, and ran down the steps to disappear from public view.

With the support of the public, and to a certain extent the media, Robert's father organised a petition against the implementation of his son's execution, which he forwarded to the home secretary:

Whereas Robert Holman George Gorringe was on the 24th of February 1948 at the Kent Assizes holden at Maidstone convicted of the murder of Phyllis Lucy Kathleen Gorringe, and was sentenced to death. We the undersigned loyal citizens of King George 6th humbly pray that the said Robert Holman

George Gorringe may be reprieved and the sentence of death commuted to imprisonment.

The petition, backed by growing public support, was successful and Robert Gorringe's death sentence was commuted to life imprisonment; he was released on licence on 26 August 1957 – serving just nine years. This is sadly another case in which the media and the judiciary chose to forget the violent death of a young girl and the incalculable suffering of her family.

61. FINGERPRINTS GENTLEMEN PLEASE (1948)

Its every parent's nightmare, you leave your child in a place of safety and return to discover him or her missing. This happened to the parents of three-year-old June Anne Devaney on 15 May 1948; the place of safety – a hospital. June was recovering from a bout of pneumonia in a ward at Queen's Park Hospital in the Lancashire town of Blackburn. In the early hours of the morning the ward nurse heard a cry and went to investigate but everything appeared to be okay. An hour or so later she felt a draught coming from a door leading from the ward out into the hospital grounds which was wide open; as she secured the door she noticed June Devaney's cot was empty. A search of the ward was made and the local police called in. An extended search of the grounds located the body of this young child, a post-mortem revealed she had been raped and died from multiple fractures of the skull; in the pathologist's opinion she had been held by her legs and swung repeatedly against a brick wall. The ward was secured and the area around the cot and exit preserved as a crime scene; it was here under the cot that police found a water bottle and muddy footprints clearly visible on the spotlessly clean, polished ward floor. They led from the door to the cot and back. Fingerprints were found on the bottle – believed to be the killer's.

Detectives were convinced that the killer was a local man due to an obvious knowledge of the hospital grounds and the tracing of a local taxi driver who had picked up a man with a local accent at the material time. A search of the fingerprint database revealed no matches indicating the killer had not come to police notice before. The senior investigating officer, Chief Inspector Capstick, proposed that a mass voluntary finger-printing take place of all men in the Blackburn area aged sixteen and over who had been in the town on the night of 14 to 15 May 1948 – this was the first occasion in British criminal history this massive operation would be undertaken. There was no template for such an operation, a special card was created requiring the volunteer to provide an impression of their left fore-finger, middle finger and little finger which corresponded to the prints found on the bottle as well as their name, address and national identity registration number. The task was a massive undertaking but a dedicated team of police officers, determined to see the killer of June Anne Devaney brought to justice, and armed with an electoral register, set about their task. Forty thousand sets of prints were taken; frustratingly no match was found. Capstick decided to widen the search to those men who had not made themselves available and eventually matched the prints on the bottle to a twenty-two-year-old former serviceman called Peter Griffiths who lived in Birley Street, Blackburn, and worked at a local flour mill.

The trial commenced at the Lancaster Assizes in October 1948, Griffiths pleaded not guilty. His defence counsel sought to prove that Griffiths was suffering from schizophrenia and therefore, as the *Lancaster Guardian* (22 October 1948) recorded it, 'suffering from a split mind – and that he was mad at the time the murder was committed'. With this admission the case was going to rest on past history supplied by the family and medical evidence as to the defendant's mental state. Griffiths' mother Alice was called and she told the court that Peter was the youngest of three children. She informed the court that her husband – whom she married in 1923 – had been a patient in the Prestwich Mental Hospital before they had married. She recited an incident when Griffiths was six years of age when he fell from a milk-float landing on his head and was sent home from school. At the age of seventeen he would play with match boxes and toys that her grandchildren had left out and he was always a loner before joining the Welsh Guards Regiment in 1944 and serving overseas.

A doctor from the Whittingham Mental Hospital near Preston examined Griffiths and was of the opinion that he was schizophrenic: 'I think he knew what he was doing but do not think he fully appreciated what he was doing was wrong.' The doctor believed that the cause was sixty per cent hereditary, an unhappy or frustrated love affair and excessive consumption of alcohol had been contributory factors. There were contradictory medical opinions from D Brisby, principal medical officer at Liverpool Walton Prison where Griffiths had been held on remand, who appeared for the prosecution. He stated to the court that he had found no evidence of any disease of the mind. Griffiths' defence barrister Mr Basi Nield submitted to the court that the evidence had built a complete picture of a typical schizophrenic and asked the jury to return a verdict of guilty but insane. Mr Nield addressed the jury further: 'The manner in which this young child's life ended had caused widespread horror and anger. Mothers clasped their children and went in fear and you may think also there are those who feel a desire for revenge. It would be gravely unjust and inequitable to let those things override the evidence.' The prosecution barrister Mr Gorman on the other hand dismissed the medical evidence and asked the jury to say this man was not insane, but guilty of this dastardly crime. Mr Justice Oliver asked the jury to consider the vital question – did Griffiths know that what he was doing was wrong or did he not?

The jury took twenty-three minutes to convict Griffiths of this terrible crime. Before sentencing Griffiths to death Mr Justice Oliver told him that: 'This jury have found you guilty of a crime of the most brutal ferocity and I entirely agree with the verdict.' Griffiths was returned to Liverpool Prison where he was hanged on 19 November 1948. The Chief Constable of the Lancashire force kept his promise to the people of Blackburn when he announced that the fingerprint cards could be collected by any individual on application or they would be destroyed. The destruction of the cards not collected at a local paper mill was witnessed by members of the local press.

62. MURDER! WHERE'S THE BODY? (1949)

'Acid Bath Murderer' John George Haigh infamously threw down a challenge to Detective Inspector Webb of the Metropolitan Police when interviewed about the disappearance of a woman with whom he had been acquainted: 'How can you prove murder if there is no body?' The rule in English Common Law stating that a body is necessary to prove the charge of murder arose from the 'Campden Wonder' case in the 1660s (see page 15). This law survived for nearly three hundred years, only practically abolished in 1954 following several high-profile cases where the advances in forensic science had provided such a convincing circumstantial case against the accused they were convicted despite the absence of the victim's body. The three cases below were instrumental in reaching an understanding in law that the prosecution have to prove a crime of murder was committed but not necessarily produce a dead body to do so.

The *Durban Castle* was a passenger carrying ship belonging to the Union Castle Line sailing regularly between South Africa and England. The ship set sail from Cape Town, its destination was Southampton, England. One of the passengers on board was an attractive twenty-one-year-old actress and performer: Eileen Isabella Ronnie Gibson, who used the stage name of Gay Gibson. Gibson was travelling back to London after performing several roles in stage productions in accordance with her duties as a member of the Women's Auxiliary Territorial Service. She travelled first class occupying Cabin 126.

The key characters in the Great Detective Case of 1877. (*Illustrated Police News*, 17 November 1877)

Adolf Beck giving evidence to the enquiry into his wrongful conviction. (*The Graphic*, 29 October 1904)

Above: A feature on the murder of Isaac Gold on the Brighton Line. (*Illustrated Police News*, 9 July 1881)

Below: Wanted notice for Percy Lefroy Mapleton for the murder of Isaac Gold. (www.btp.police.uk)

MURDER.

£200 REWARD

WHEREAS on Monday, June 27th, ISAAC FREDERICK GOLD was murdered on the London Brighton and South Railway between Three Bridges and Balcombe in Kent Sussex.

AND WHEREAS a Verdict of WILFUL MURDER has been returned by a Coroner's Jury against

PERCY LEFROY MAPLETON,

A sketch of John Tawell during his trial at Aylesbury in 1845. (*Leicestershire Mercury*, 5 April 1845)

Sarah Hart's cottage in Salt Hill, Slough. (*Railway Bell*, 1845)

Calthorpe Arms Public House, Gray's Inn Road, London. This is where the fatally injured PC Robert Culley died on 13 May 1833. (Author's collection)

Morgan, the dog whose nose led to the conviction of a child murderer in 1876. (*Lancashire Daily Post*, 30 May 1933)

Above: No. 4 Burgh Street, Islington, where businessman James Cameron was murdered on 14 October 1970. (Author's collection)

Right: Cecil Court, Charing Cross Road, where Elsie Batten was stabbed to death in 1961. (Author's collection)

Above: West End Central police station, where Edwin Bush confessed to the murder of Elsie Batten. (Author's collection)

Below left: Dr William Palmer, the 'Rugeley Poisoner'. (Unknown court artist)

Below right: Daniel M'Naghten, who mistakenly murdered Edward Drummond in Whitehall in 1843.

Drummonds Bank, Charing Cross, from where Edward Drummond emerged moments before his murder. (Author's collection)

Norwich Castle, where James Blomfield Rush was tried and executed in 1849. (Author's collection)

Left: Charles Wheatstone, inventor of the electric telegraph. (Courtesy of BT Heritage and Archives)

Below: The former Marlborough Street Magistrates Court, which witnessed the first recorded trial for the offence of drink-driving in 1897. (Author's collection)

THE ILLUSTRATED
POLICE NEWS.
LAW-COURTS AND WEEKLY RECORD.

No. 201.] LONDON, SATURDAY, DECEMBER 21, 1867. [PRICE ONE PENNY.

HOUSE OF DETENTION, CLERKENWELL—SCENE AFTER THE EXPLOSION.

Devastation after the Clerkenwell prison explosion, 1867. (*Illustrated Police News*, 21 December 1867)

Fenchurch Street station, where Mr Briggs began his fatal last journey in 1864. (Author's collection)

St James's Palace, where Charles I spent his final night before his execution on 30 January 1649. (Author's Collection)

Edward Marshall Hall, a 'celebrity barrister'. (*The Bath Chronicle and Herald*, 18 April 1925)

Cuttings regarding the 'Cannibalism at Sea' case; the accused, from left to right, are Capt. Dudley, Edwin Stephens and Edmund Brookes. (*Aberdeen Weekly Journal*, 20 December 1884)

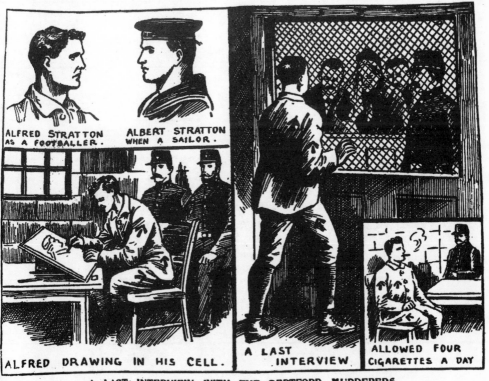

A feature on Albert and Alfred Stratton, the first murderers to be convicted on fingerprint evidence. (*Illustrated Police News*, 27 May 1905)

Robert Wood, the 'Camden Town Murderer', 1907. (*Illustrated Police News*, 19 February 1914)

Bow Street Magistrates Court, where Daniel M'Naghten appeared after shooting Edward Drummond. (Author's collection)

William Calcraft, public executioner from 1829 to 1874. (*Illustrated Police News*)

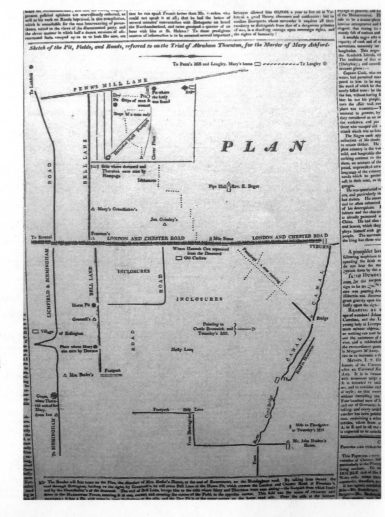

Sketch of the pit, fields and roads used in the trial of Abraham Thornton, 1817. (*Chester, Cheshire and North Wales Advertiser*)

Left: The 'Dark Angel of the North', Mary Ann Cotton. (*The Northern Star*, 19 July 1872)

Below: Insurance policy signed by Mary Ann Cotton. (*The Northern Star*)

Industrial Branch.—*Policy Department.* | Not to be filled in by the Agent. } No. 16995

INFANTILE.

Mr. Wilson Agent at Blaydon on Tyne

PRUDENTIAL ASSURANCE COMPANY,
CHIEF OFFICE:—LUDGATE HILL, LONDON.

DECLARATION TO BE SIGNED BY THE PROPOSER.

I declare that the following answers are strictly correct, and that I have withheld no material information. I agree that the following statements shall be the basis of the contract between me and the said Company, for effecting the Assurance herein proposed, on the terms to be contained in such Policy as shall be granted in pursuance of this Proposal. And when such shall be effected, I agree to conform to the Deed of Settlement, the Bye-Laws and Rules of the said Company.

Witness. *Mr. Wilson* — Father's or Mother's Signature. *Mary Ann Cotton*

Dated this 3 — day of *Oct.* 1871

CERTIFICATE OF AGENT.

I have personally seen the Child mentioned on the other side, and am of opinion that he is in good health, and that his appearance indicates that he is of the age which is stated, and I recommend the Directors to accept the Proposal at full 1 class rates.

(Signature of Agent.) *Mr. Wilson*

SHOT CONSTABLE—William Kennedy (left) and Frederick Browne who were sentenced to death at the Old Bailey yesterday for the murder of P.c. Gutteridge last September. (See Page Seven).

William Kennedy and Frederick Browne, murderers of PC George Gutteridge in 1927. (*The Sheffield Daily Independent*, 28 April 1928)

Rochester Row police station, where Adolf Beck was wrongly identified by many witnesses. (Author's collection)

DIAL 999

Above: Burglar Thomas Duffy was the first to be apprehended and convicted through the new emergency hotline introduced in 1937.

Left: Spy Jose Waldberg was one of the first to be executed under the Treachery Act 1940. The pathetic efforts many German spies made to conceal themselves on entry to the UK has led some to believe they were not sent with any real intent to gather information or commit sabotage.

It wasn't long before she attracted the wandering eye of a womanising ship's steward – James Camb. On 18 March 1947, with the ship only a couple of hundred miles off the West Coast of Africa, Gay Gibson was reported missing; with the whole ship thoroughly searched the ship's skipper – Captain Patey – came to the obvious conclusion that the missing woman had fallen overboard. The ship retraced her path searching shark-infested waters but to no avail, Miss Gibson had completely vanished. Captain Patey conducted an investigation into Gibson's disappearance; he questioned the crew in the relevant part of the ship to which the missing actress had access. Watchman Frederick Steer remembered that the service bell for Cabin 126 had been pushed several times in the early hours of the morning. He had attended but got no answer, when he knocked he noticed that the two lights outside the cabin – one green and one red depending on whether a steward or stewardess had been summoned were both illuminated. The door was slightly ajar and when Steer sneaked a look he saw James Camb; the steward informed him everything was okay and told him to return to his duties. Captain Patey – now concerned that foul play maybe involved – informed his head office, who in turn contacted Scotland Yard. The captain received instructions to lock the cabin door and preserve what could be a crime scene.

When the ship arrived in the waters near Southampton it was boarded by officers of the Criminal Investigation Department. Detectives soon established Camb as a possible suspect in the disappearance of Gibson; many of the crew told the police that he was always boasting of his conquests and had been heard to remark that 'I have half a mind to take a drink to her cabin tonight.' One of the investigators –Detective Sergeant Quinlan – interrogated Camb. Having initially denied being in Gibson's cabin to the captain, he changed his story to the police. Yes he had been in the cabin, he had been invited in by Gay Gibson; she had removed her nightgown revealing nothing underneath, they had got into bed and during sex Camb claimed that Gibson's body stiffened, she was foaming from the mouth before going limp. 'I tried artificial respiration on her.' He claimed that while he was trying to revive her the night-watchman Frederick Steer knocked and tried to enter; he shut the door in his face not wanting to be found in such a compromising position. He then informed DS Quinlan that he panicked seeing that Gibson was clearly dead and worried that he may be blamed he opened the porthole and squeezed her body through and out into the open sea.

Camb was charged with the murder of Gay Gibson and appeared at Winchester Assizes on 29 March 1948. He stuck to the story he had given to DS Quinlan that Gibson had died during sex and he panicked and disposed of her body through the cabin's porthole. The body of Gay Gibson was never found so the prosecution had to rely, in the main, on circumstantial evidence formed on the basis of forensic and medical evidence. When Camb was suspected of some involvement in the disappearance Captain Patey had him examined by the ship's physician Dr Phillips who found scratch marks on Camb's arms, wrists and shoulders and Phillips gave evidence that in his opinion they were made by the victim defending herself, not of a woman having a heart attack. Blood was found on the pillow case, which proved to be type 'O'; Camb's blood group was Type 'A'. Urine also stained the bed sheets, a normal reaction during strangulation. Although Camb tried to suggest that Gibson was provocatively naked when he arrived at the cabin detectives discovered that her favourite blue pyjamas were missing, suggesting her state of dress at the time of her death. The defence called witnesses from around the globe in order to paint a picture of Gibson as a devious, sex-mad neurotic in order to give more credence to Camb's version of events. The jury were not to be hood-winked. Following four days of evidence they took just forty-five minutes to convict him of murder. Although sentenced to death, a debate in the House of Commons regarding the abolition of the death sentence was in progress (the bill was eventually defeated); the home secretary decreed during this period all death sentences would be commuted to life imprisonment. Camb was one of the lucky few to escape the hangman's rope.

The second trial is that of callous serial killer John George Haigh. Haigh had been raised by deeply religious parents who belonged to the Plymouth Brethren, a non-conformist Evangelical Christian group; music, newspapers and any other form of entertainment were deemed sinful and forbidden. He rebelled against his parents and his strict religious upbringing; his rebellion started with pushing social boundaries, testing the rules. He jumped from one job to another; on one occasion being sacked on suspicion of theft. In 1934 he received his first custodial sentence for an offence of fraud. In 1936 he moved to London finding employment as a chauffeur to a businessman called William McSwan who owned an amusement parlour empire. It wasn't long before his dishonest tendencies re-surfaced. A fraudster at heart, a man with the 'gift of the gab', unfortunately for him he was careless and impatient – traits that would ultimately lead to his downfall. He spent a great deal of the next eight years in prison for various fraudulent offences from impersonating a solicitor to petty scams. It was whilst in prison that he formed a plan to murder. He studied the intricacies of the law around proving murder and the use of acid to dissolve and destroy all traces of the human body in order to commit the perfect crime.

Following his release from prison he reacquainted himself with the McSwan family telling them that he had invented a range of products which he made in a rented basement workshop in Gloucester Road, Kensington. On 9 September 1944 he invited the McSwan's son Donald to view his work; as he looked around the premises Haigh clubbed Donald to death. He then placed the corpse in a forty-gallon barrel which he then filled with sulphuric acid and left overnight returning the next day to find the corpse had dissolved into a sludge, which he disposed of down a nearby drain. Thinking he had got away with the perfect murder he forged documents in Donald's name obtaining control of all of his assets. He told the anxious parents that Donald had travelled to Scotland to avoid conscription to the armed forces and cleverly sent postcards to the McSwans purporting to be from their son. In the meantime he – through forgery – gained access to property and cash from the McSwans. It wasn't long before he had bled them dry and decided they served no further use; on 2 July 1945 the McSwans disappeared, both murdered by Haigh and their remains disposed of in a similar way to their son Donald.

In August 1947 he met his next victims: Dr Archibald Henderson and his wife Rosalie. He befriended the couple; using his charming and personable nature he gained their confidence. He had moved from the Gloucester Road workshop to other premises – Leopold

Road, Crawley. He again used the façade of being an inventor and persuaded Dr Henderson to visit the Leopold Road premises to see his latest innovation. Haigh drove him to Crawley and when inside the premises shot Dr Henderson through the head with a revolver he had stolen from the victim's house. Haigh then summoned Rosalie on the pretext that her husband had fallen ill; on her arrival she met the same fate as husband Archibald. He again disposed of the bodies in sulphuric acid and forged letters giving him access to their possessions, which he sold for £8,000.

By 1949 Haigh had moved into the Onslow Court Hotel in Kensington where he would meet his last victim, a wealthy widower – Olivia Durand-Deacon – and her close friend Constance Lane. Haigh's cover story on this occasion was that he was an engineer; Durand-Deacon was taken in by his charm; Haigh interested her in a venture he was starting in which he was allegedly producing false fingernails for the more fashionable women of London. On 18 February 1949 Haigh invited Durand-Deacon to his premises in Crawley where he shot her through the head; he relieved her of all her valuables including a Persian lamb coat and placed her, fully clothed, into the vat of sulphuric acid. The jewellery and the coat produced a disappointing return, only just enough to cover an ever-increasing hotel bill. His next victim would probably have been Constance Lane but he had met his match in this feisty, suspicious widower. She questioned him about the disappearance of her close friend and wasn't taken in by the web of deceit Haigh spun. Haigh was shocked to hear that Durand-Deacon had confided to her friend about her planned excursion with him to his 'factory'. Haigh informed Constance that she didn't turn up at the arranged meeting point at the Army and Navy store even though he waited for over an hour for her. She informed Haigh at breakfast the following day that she was going to report her missing; to avoid any suspicion being directed his way, Haigh, with the bravado of a man confident that he would never be caught, escorted Lane to the nearest police station.

Police Sergeant Lambourne listened closely to Constance Lane's concerns about her missing friend who provided a physical description of her friend and a description of the clothing she last saw her wearing, in particular the Persian lamb coat, whilst keeping one eye on her rather laid-back companion to whom she had taken an instant dislike. Lambourne contacted the manager at the Onslow Court hotel and discovered that Haigh was slow at paying his bills and was in debt. She passed her suspicions onto Detective Inspector Shelley Symes in the CID who ran a criminal records search revealing Haigh's chequered past. Symes interviewed Haigh at the Onslow Court Hotel and learned of his premises in Leopold Road, Crawley. Symes asked the local force in Sussex to search the premises; the evidence quickly accumulated against Haigh. The searching officers found a .38 Enfield revolver and eight rounds of ammunition, three carboys of concentrated sulphuric acid with rubber gloves and protective clothing and crucially, a dry-cleaning receipt for a Persian lamb coat dated 19 February, the day on which she had last been seen alive. This was followed up by a report from a local jeweller who informed police that he had purchased Durand-Deacon's jewellery for £100.

Detectives invited George Haigh to return to Chelsea police station on 28 February and he was interviewed under caution by Detective Inspector Webb. Professor Keith Simpson the home office pathologist, who would play a crucial part in the prosecution's case, records in his autobiography *Forty Years of Murder* a snippet of the interview between Webb and Haigh. Following a series of questions that were answered with contradictions and lies, a short break was taken during which Haigh – probably realising the game was up and thinking along the lines of escaping the noose – asked Webb:

Tell me frankly, what are the chances of anyone being released from Broadmoor? Webb chose not to answer. Haigh continued: 'Well if I told you the truth, you wouldn't believe me. It sounds too fantastic for belief.' At the recommencement of the interview Haigh was again cautioned by Webb to which he replied: 'I understand all that' he barked impatiently. 'I will tell you about it. Mrs Durand-Deacon no longer exists. She has disappeared completely, and no trace of her can be found again'. Following a prompt from Webb he continued. 'I have destroyed her with acid. You will find the sludge which remains in Leopold

Road. Every trace has gone'. He looked at Webb inquisitively and said: 'How can you prove murder if there is no body?'

Following this startling admission he gave a full voluntary statement and an indication of a future defence to murder – insanity. He admitted the murders of the McSwan family, the Hendersons and reiterated his guilt of the murder of Durand-Deacon and added that after each murder he would drink a glass of each of the victim's blood. He clarified that he had taken Durand-Deacon to the Leopold Road address and shot her whilst she examined some plastic fingernails. He made an incision in the side of her throat with a penknife, collected her blood and drank it. After placing her into a steel tank he went to a nearby café and had poached eggs on toast and a cup of tea before returning and administering the acid. He returned three days later and having lost patience, he drained off the acid and disposed of the remains – his impatience was his downfall as the body hadn't completely dissolved, as Professor Keith Simpson was about to discover.

As Simpson was driven to Leopold Road he considered what parts of the body, if any, would survive such treatment. Simpson recalled that: 'The ground outside the storeroom was rough, with many small pebbles lying on the earth. Almost immediately…I picked one up and examined it…' He turned to Chief Inspector Mahon who was leading the investigation and said: 'I think this is a gallstone.' This was the start of a remarkable recovery of evidence including a significant part of a foot bone and a hairpin. Blood splashing was present – consistent with a person standing looking downwards whilst being shot in the back of the head; the blood proved to be human. Further examination of the remaining sludge revealed two more human gallstones, eighteen fragments of bone, one, a fragment of pelvic bone, displaying a groove proving that it had belonged to a female, together with a red plastic handle of a woman's handbag and the metal cap of a lipstick case. But most importantly the recovery of upper and lower dentures that would later be identified as Durand-Deacon's from dental records. Professor Simpson was of the opinion that if Haigh had shown more patience and left the remains in situ for longer, the resin, which the dentures were made of, would have dissolved making the identification less conclusive.

Haigh tried desperately to convince doctors and eventually the jury that he was insane but the jury took just eighteen minutes to find this evil man guilty and sane. He was executed in Wandsworth Prison on 10 August 1949 by Albert Pierrepoint.

The final case is that of the Crown *v* Michail Onufrejczyk; a case that categorically confirmed a charge of murder, where no body or body parts are ever recovered, could be proven by circumstantial evidence. Onufrejczyk was a decorated Polish war hero and following the end of World War Two he settled in Britain enlisting in the Polish Resettlement Corps in South Wales and purchasing a farm in 1949 – Cefn Hendre, Llandilo in Carmarthenshire. In 1953 Onufrejczyk took on a business partner, fellow Polish war veteran Stanislaw Sykut, who invested £600 in the farm. Onufrejczyk was a loner who had never tried to integrate with his Welsh neighbours so it wasn't long before he fell out with Sykut. It was in fact more than just disagreements, Sykut reported his business partner to the police for assault. The men's relationship became irreconcilable resulting in Sykut visiting a solicitor to legally end their business partnership either by Onufrejczyk buying him out or selling the property and splitting the equity. By the end of the year Sykut had disappeared. When questioned by police Onufrejczyk explained his business partner had taken a two-week trip to London and not returned. Local police, obviously aware of the complaint of violence made against the Pole by Sykut were suspicious of the circumstances in which Sykut had apparently vanished. Several rumours (all started by Onufrejczyk) circulated around the small community that his business partner had gone to London, returned to Poland or even been kidnapped by the Polish secret police. A search by the police of forty square miles around the farm revealed nothing suspicious, certainly not a body. It wasn't until detectives uncovered an attempt by Onufrejczyk to transfer the deeds of the farm fully into his name did a serious investigation commence.

Detectives returned to the farm with a forensics team and conducted a deep search of the farm house. They found over two thousand tiny spots of human blood near to a kitchen dresser, a partial bloody handprint, one spot of blood containing a minute fragment of bone and one bloodspot on the ceiling which could only have travelled that far as a consequence of extreme violence. A Polish woman, Mrs Pawelec, came forward and told police that Onufrejczyk had spoken to her in Polish just before Sykut's disappearance stating that: 'Sykut will rot in the hedges even if I go to prison and his daughter will die as a dog in the depths of Russia by my making.' *Northern Whig* (15 September 1954). When asked about the bloodstains Onufrejczyk claimed they were from rabbits he had cut up and hung in the kitchen. The police had built up a case based purely on circumstantial evidence – although the body of Stanislaw Sykut had not been found Onufrejczyk was charged with the murder on or about 14 December 1953. He faced trial at Glamorgan Assizes in November 1954. The forensic evidence and witness testimonies, although circumstantial in relation to the charge of murder, were compelling; several witnesses gave evidence of conflicting accounts given by the defendant as to where Sykut had gone switching from a visit to London from which he failed to return, going home to Poland and the most bizarre – that Sykut had been abducted from the farm in a car by three men whom he believed were Polish secret police. The jury decided that the circumstantial case presented by the prosecution was enough to prove the charge of murder and Onufrejczyk was sentenced to death. Following a failed appeal he was due to hang on 26 January 1955 but received a reprieve two days before his execution from the home secretary. He was released from prison in 1965 but died in a traffic accident the following year. This final case in particular set a precedent for future criminal trials in which a defendant faced a charge of murder without the presence of a body.

63. LIFE SHOULD MEAN LIFE (1952)

John Thomas Straffen, aged seventy-seven, died in Frankland prison, County Durham, on 19 November 2007 having served more than fifty-five years, making him the longest serving prisoner in British judicial history.

Straffen was born on 27 February 1930 on a British army camp in Borden, Hampshire and spent the first few years of his life in India where his father was posted. The family returned to the United Kingdom in 1938; Straffen's father took a discharge from the British army and they settled in Bath in the county of Somerset. The young Straffen was in constant trouble both at school and with the law – mainly for petty crime including the theft of a purse from a fellow student in 1939 for which he received a two-year probation order. Mainstream education gave up on him and he was sent to special behavioural schools. Straffen was one of three children; his elder sister was certified as a high grade mental defective under the Mental Deficiency Act 1927 and died in 1952. Mental illness ran through the family with John now aged ten being similarly certified under the same legislation, classifying him as having the mental age of six. He was sent to a residential school for the mentally deficient in 1940. At the age of fourteen he was attending a senior school called Besford Court. His behaviour did not improve and he was strongly suspected of being involved in an incident where several geese were strangled, but nothing was ever proved. At the age of sixteen an I.Q. test concluded that he had a mental age of nine and a half years and he was discharged from the school and returned home to Bath with few prospects.

He did find employment but went from job to job and was still deemed to be mentally deficient following an assessment by the local medical officer for health. At the age of seventeen the seriousness of his criminality increased – breaking into unoccupied homes and stealing items of little value or use to him. He was suspected of a frightening attack on a thirteen-year-old schoolgirl in 1947 during which, it was alleged, he placed his hand over her mouth and asked her the nonsensical question: what would she do if he killed her? Shortly after this incident he was arrested for strangling five chickens that belonged to the father of a girl with whom he had a disagreement. When being interviewed for this offence he admitted to a number of burglaries that he had committed. He was charged and remanded in custody where he was examined by the prison medical officer who certified him mentally retarded; he was committed to Hortham Colony, which treated mentally deficient offenders in Almondsbury, north of Bristol. Following his release back into society in 1951 Straffen was examined at Bristol Hospital where electroencephalograph readings (a record of the electrical activity of the brain) revealed that Straffen had suffered 'wide and severe damage to the cerebral cortex, probably from an attack of encephalitis [an inflammation of the brain] in India before the age of six'.[29]

Straffen underwent a further assessment of his mental health in 1951 and was found to have the mental age of a ten-year-old; he gained employment at a market garden. Now aged twenty-one Straffen had developed a hatred of the police whom he blamed for all his woes. In July of 1951 he committed the first of three murders that would see him spend virtually the rest of his life in prison. On 15 July Straffen was going to the cinema and as he walked along Camden Crescent in Bath. He saw five-year-old Brenda Goddard playing with some flowers in the front garden of her foster parent's house. Straffen got talking to the child and offered to show her where to pick nicer flowers. He claimed later when admitting to the killing that he lifted Brenda over the fence and took her to a nearby wood where she fell over and hit her head rendering her unconscious; he then strangled her leaving her body where it lay. Making no attempt to cover up his actions he strolled off to his original destination – the cinema – and later returned home. The police were initially baffled, there were no witnesses, but included Straffen in a list of likely suspects. He was interviewed but stated that he was at work on the day in question; their suspicions rose when they checked his claims out with his employees who disproved his alibi and immediately sacked him; but detectives

---

29 *Trial of John Thomas Straffen* 1954 L.Fairfield/E.Fullbrook

had insufficient evidence to charge him. He later confided to a prison psychiatrist that although he knew he was under suspicion he enjoyed wasting the police's time because he 'hated them shadowing him'. Three weeks after the murder of Brenda Goddard a second murder took place in very similar circumstances. Straffen met a nine-year-old girl called Cicely Batstone at the cinema; he persuaded Cicely to go to another cinema where they watched a film before taking a bus trip to a meadow known locally as 'Tumps' on the outskirts of Bath, where he strangled her. The area was frequently used by local people and a number of witnesses came forward when Cicely failed to return home. The bus conductor remembered Cicely on the bus with a man whom he recognised as Straffen from a former employment, a courting couple came forward having seen the two in the meadow and most importantly, a police officer's wife told her husband that she had seen the two together again in the meadow. When she directed police to the spot where she had seen them they discovered Cicely Batstone's body. She provided detectives with a very good description, on which they arrested Straffen on suspicion of murder. Following his arrest for Cicely Batstone's killing he readily admitted to the murder of Brenda Goddard. He was charged and committed in custody to stand trial for the two killings.

Straffen appeared at the Taunton Assizes on 17 October 1951. Only one witness testimony would be heard by the jury – prison doctor Peter Parkes. Parkes testified as to the state of Straffen's mental health and his fitness to enter a plea to the charges he faced. Following details of his examination Parkes concluded that Straffen was insane and therefore unfit to plead. The trial judge Mr Justice Oliver addressed the jury informing them that: 'In this country we do not try people who are insane. You might as well try a baby in arms. If a man cannot understand what is going on he cannot be tried.' He directed the jury to return a verdict of not guilty of murder due to insanity. Straffen was sent to Broadmoor, a high security psychiatric hospital, in Berkshire, where he was given a job as a prison cleaner.

On 29 April the following year, 1952, Straffen became one of the first patients to escape from Broadmoor. In a pre-planned operation Straffen – wearing civilian clothes under his hospital work uniform – scaled a ten-foot outer perimeter wall to freedom. Straffen was next seen by an elderly resident of the small village of Crowthorne. Doris Spencer was busy in her garden when Straffen approached her and asked for a drink of water, which she provided. During their ten-minute conversation they discussed nearby Broadmoor, even how improbable an escape from the hospital was, before he left. He moved on to the village of Farley Hill where he saw a young five-year-old girl called Linda Bowyer who was riding her bike. Straffen murdered her and dumped her body in a bluebell copse nearby.

Straffen again approached a local resident – Mrs Kenyon – and asked for a cup of tea, which she provided before giving the killer a lift to the nearest bus stop. Just before she dropped him off Straffen saw two uniformed men and asked them if they were police officers before dashing from the car and running. The two men were in fact Broadmoor nurses who were unaware of the escape; they raised the alert and Straffen was captured soon after and returned to the hospital; at this time nobody else was aware of the terrible crime he had committed within the previous hour. During the drive back to Broadmoor Straffen commented that he had 'finished with crime'. A search for the now reported missing Linda Bowyer discovered her body early the following morning. Police officers visited the hospital to question Straffen about his movements after escaping the previous day, they were unaware that about the same time little Linda Bowyer's body had been found. They questioned Straffen about his activities for the four hours or so that he was at liberty, Straffen replied that he had not killed *her*. When it was pointed out that he wasn't being accused of any such crime Straffen replied that he knew what police officers were like and although he was guilty of murdering two children he did not kill the little girl on the bike. Straffen, after making a long statement, was charged with the murder of Linda Bowyer, to which he replied: 'I did not kill her. That is a frame-up that is.'[30] He appeared at Reading Magistrates Court where he was remanded in custody to Brixton Prison. Straffen appeared at Winchester Crown Court on 21 July 1952 to stand trial before Mr Justice Cassels. The trial judge allowed, on application

---

30 *Aberdeen Evening Express* 2 May 1952

of the prosecution, the evidence from the two previous murders, for which Straffen was incarcerated in Broadmoor, admissible in the trial. The prosecution case was opened by Solicitor General Sir Reginald Manningham-Buller who told the jury that 'Under the law of our land, every man is presumed to be sane until the contrary is proved, and that presumption, in my submission, applies even though the accused prisoner has escaped from Broadmoor.' He continued that he was not in a position to call any witnesses that saw Straffen in the company of Linda Bowyer 'But it is clear that she was murdered by strangulation and evidence establishes beyond any reasonable doubt that Straffen's were the hands which strangled her.'

Controversy hit the case when following the completion of the second day of the trial Mr Justice Cassels discharged the jury as it had been brought to his attention that one of its members had offered an opinion in a Southsea club that one of the witnesses who had given evidence was responsible for the murder and not the defendant. A second jury were empanelled with a stern warning from His Honour that any member of the jury who decided to give their opinion regarding the case outside the confines of the jury room would be 'perilously close to committing an offence'.

Evidence was given by two psychiatrists, the first, Dr Alexander Leitch a consultant psychiatrist and former prison doctor at Bristol prison, who told the court that John Straffen was not insane from the medical point of view and that if he had killed Linda Bowyer he would have known what he was doing. Sir Reginald asked Leitch if Straffen had killed Linda would he have known what he was doing when he put his hands on her throat. 'Yes,' replied Dr Leitch. Dr James Hunter Murdoch of Wandsworth Prison gave evidence that Straffen had told him that he had planned his escape from Broadmoor and that in his opinion Straffen was sane on the day he escaped. Straffen was convicted by the jury in less than one hour and sentenced to death. Straffen lodged an appeal against his conviction on the basis that the evidence from the Bristol murders should not have been presented to the jury and that any comments he made on the morning of his arrest to the police who visited him were inadmissible as he had not been cautioned. The appeal was dismissed on both grounds; permission for a further appeal to the

House of Lords was rejected by the Attorney General. Straffen's execution was set for 4 September 1952 but he received a reprieve on 29 August following a recommendation by the Home Secretary David Maxwell Fyfe to Her Majesty Queen Elizabeth II; his sentence was commuted to life imprisonment.

Following a review of security in the wake of Straffen's escape Broadmoor introduced an alarm system to alert local people resident in Sandhurst, Wokingham, Bracknell and Bagshot, in the event of an escaped patient. It was based on a Second World War siren which was tested every week and special procedures were introduced in local schools should such an event occur.

64. IT REALLY WASN'T ME (1952)

The Criminal Cases Review Commission (CCRC) was established by Section 8 of the Criminal Appeal Act 1995. The statutory board with a responsibility for investigating alleged miscarriages of justices started its work in 1997; it has the power to refer a case to the Court of Appeal when, through its investigations, concludes the court may well overturn the original conviction or reduce the severity of the charge or reduce the sentence. The first ever case referred by the CCRC in such a way was the historical case of Mahmood Hussein Mattan.

Mattan was born in 1923 in British Somaliland, a British protectorate situated in what is today the north-west of Somalia. Mattan was a merchant seaman who travelled the world before settling in Cardiff in the late 1940s. He found employment in a steel foundry in Tiger Bay – a local name for an area that covered Butetown and Cardiff Docks and now known as Cardiff Bay. He met Laura Williams, who worked at a local paper factory, and they married and started a family of three boys. Their multi-racial marriage was probably doomed from the start as the two had to deal with intolerance and racial bigotry; they separated in 1950 but still lived in the same street. An event that would blight the family's future for generations to come occurred on 6 March 1952. Lily Volpert owned her own outfitters shop on Bute Street, Cardiff Docks, she was found murdered, her throat cut with what police believed to be a razor and the store-takings, amounting to about £100, had been taken.

Mattan was identified as a likely suspect by the investigating Cardiff City Police and he was detained and questioned regarding his movements on the night of the murder. As part of the investigation detectives searched his address in Davies Street and found what they believed was incriminating evidence – a pair of second-hand shoes speckled with blood and a broken shaving razor – but no sign of any blood-stained clothing, which they presumed would have been disposed of or any of the stolen cash. Mattan told his interviewers that he had not been in the shop or indeed in the street on the day of the murder. He claimed to have been at the cinema until 7.30pm before making his way home. The police did have a witness who claimed to have seen Mattan leave the crime scene at 8.15pm. His name was Harold Cover, a Jamaican with a violent criminal history. A second witness was a twelve-year-old girl who informed investigators that she had seen a black man near the store at the relevant time. She was in fact confronted with the suspect Mattan by the police in what seems to be a hastily arranged attempt at identification but told the police Mattan was not the man she had seen. This evidence was not used during Mattan's trial and the girl never called as a witness – a fact unknown to the jury. He was charged with the murder of forty-one-year-old Lily Volpert and appeared at Cardiff Magistrates Court without legal representation. Mattan was asked if he wished to be granted legal aid and have a solicitor defend him. Mattan replied: 'Defend me for what? I don't want anything and I don't care anything. You can't get me for what I have not done.'[31]

---

31 *Sunderland Daily Echo and Shipping Gazette* 17 March 1952

Mattan's trial commenced in July 1952 at the Glamorgan Assizes in Swansea, he was represented by a barrister provided on legal aid. The main prosecution witness was Harold Cover who confirmed to the jury that the man he had seen on the night of the murder was the defendant (even though he had firstly identified another Somali male called Taher Gass as the man he had seen but again, the jury were never informed of this fact). During the investigation four other witnesses came forward, all failing to identify Mattan on a police line-up and this evidence was also withheld from the jury. No forensic evidence linking the blood on Mattan's shoes to the victim was ever introduced (presumably because there was none). Mattan was not an educated man and had difficulty following the trial having refused the services of an interpreter. Mattan's barrister certainly did his client no favours when he described him as a 'half-child of nature, half, semi-civilised savage'. Mattan was convicted of the murder on 24 July 1952 and sentenced to death. Mattan became the last man to be executed at Cardiff Prison on 3 September 1952 at the age of twenty-nine following a failed appeal.

A series of bizarre events followed in later years; the main prosecution witness Harold Cover, who had claimed the substantial award offered by the Volpert family for his evidence, was convicted in 1969 for the attempted murder of his daughter by cutting her throat with a razor blade. The Somali first identified by Cover – Taher Gass – was convicted in 1954 of the murder of a wages clerk; he was found to be insane and incarcerated in Broadmoor before being deported back to Somalia.

Following a number of failed attempts by Mattan's family to appeal against the conviction the CCRC referred the case to the Court of Appeal in February 1998. Following examination of the evidence in the case and a significant doubt as to the reliability of Harold Cover's identification evidence the Court of Appeal ruled the conviction to be unsafe the appeal was allowed and the conviction quashed. Following their decision the Court of Appeal added:

It is, of course, a matter for very profound regret that in 1952 Mahmoud Mattan was convicted and hanged and it has taken 46 years for that conviction to be shown to be unsafe. The court can only hope that its decision today will provide some crumb of comfort for his surviving relatives. The case has a wider significance in that it clearly demonstrates five matters. Firstly: capital punishment was not perhaps a prudent culmination for a criminal justice system which is human and therefore fallible. Secondly: in important areas, to some of which we have alluded, criminal law and practice have, since Mattan was tried, undergone major changes for the better. Thirdly: the Criminal Cases Review Commission is a necessary and welcome body, without whose work the injustice in this case might never have been identified. Fourthly: no one associated with the criminal justice system can afford to be complacent and lastly injustices of this kind can only be avoided if all concerned in the investigation of crime, and the preparation and presentation of criminal prosecutions, observe the very highest standards of integrity, conscientiousness and professional skill.[32]

65. THE CASE OF THE GREAT TOE PRINT (1952)

The use of plantar evidence (the anatomy relating to the sole of the foot) in British courts can be traced back to three cases. The first of these occurred in March 1952 dubbed 'The Case of the Great Toe Print'. William Gourley was a safe-cracker who, whilst entering a baker's property on 29 June 1952, left behind an impression of his big left toe on the edge of a safe he had gained entry to. At his trial

---

32 R. v. Mahmood Mattan. Court of Appeal 1998

Lord Birnam told the jury that as far as he was concerned this was the first occasion upon which the Crown had sought to prove the guilt of an accused on the evidence of a toe print alone; he was duly convicted.

The second case refers to a burglary in Aberdeenshire in early 1953. Serial burglar James Walker Adams had already been arrested and convicted of burglary at the very same warehouse, first on the evidence of fingerprints and secondly on footwear impressions. So on the third occasion he wore gloves and took his shoes off not realising that he had a large hole in the sock which left plantar evidence wherever he trod. These marks were matched with James Walker Adams' foot and he was again convicted of burglary.

The final example again involves a burglary. Sydney Malkin, a forty-seven-year-old chef, had a penchant for ladies underwear. He broke into the flat of Mrs Edith Bowles in Hastings in 1956 and stole her nylon panties and a silk slip valued at £2. Mrs Bowles had left the underwear out to dry but as her flat was situated well above ground level she left her windows unlocked. Mrs Bowles reported the burglary and a local police constable – Ernest Parker – on examining the point of entry found several bare footprints: one on the top of the television, one on a loudspeaker cabinet and finally a footprint on the floor. The unusual *modus operandi* of stealing women's underwear from high-rise flats matched Sydney Malkin. He was arrested and comparisons were made between the bare foot prints discovered at the scene and impression taken from the soles of his feet. Fingerprint expert from Scotland Yard's fingerprint bureau Detective Superintendent Holten presented his findings to magistrates at Hastings, stating that this was the first time footprint evidence had been used in England. Malkin was bound over for three years to keep the peace.

66. WAS HE BRITAIN'S MOST PROLIFIC SERIAL KILLER? (1957)

Suspected mass-murderer Dr John Bodkin Adams appeared at the Old Baily facing one charge of murder but suspected of over one hundred and sixty. The events leading up to his arrest and trial (much of which is presented in Pamela Cullen's *A Stranger in Blood: The Story of Dr Bodkin Adams* 2004) would go down in the annals of this famous court as one of the most notable, shocking and sensational in its history.

Adams was born in Randalstown, County Antrim, Ireland, on 21 January 1899. His parents were profoundly religious belonging to the Plymouth Brethren, whose origins can be traced back to Ireland in the 1820s. Rather disturbingly, the parents of another serial killer, 'Acid Bath Murderer' John George Haigh (see page 194), were also members. Adams was of average academic ability, graduating from Queen's University in Belfast without honours in 1921. The same year he was offered a position of assistant houseman at Bristol Royal Infirmary by surgeon Arthur Rendle Short, who progressed to Professor of Surgery before he retired in 1948. *The Times* referred to Short (probably in relation to his professional relationship with Adams) as a 'simple-minded man, in the sense that he never saw evil in anyone'. Adams didn't make the grade and was advised by Short to apply for a general practitioner's post in the coastal town of Eastbourne. Adams was successful in his application and arrived in Eastbourne to take up his position in 1922.

He established himself in the community to such an extent he was able to 'borrow' £2,000 from an elderly patient –William Mawhood – in order to purchase a grand eighteen-room house called Kent Lodge where he lived with his mother and cousin. Adams seems to have got his feet well and truly under their table, often inviting himself to the Mawhood's house for dinner accompanied by his mother and cousin; he would regularly charge material items purchased for himself to the

Mawhood's accounts and when Mr Mawhood died in 1949 Adams helped himself to a 22-carat gold pen telling his widow that he wanted a keepsake of her husband's.

Suspicion gradually arose about Adams' relationship with his patients – especially those of a mature age – and his medical competence and methods. In 1935 Adams inherited a huge sum (£7,385) of money from a former patient called Matilda Whitton; his inheritance was challenged by the family but the will was upheld in a court of law. However, this disturbing trend of doctor benefitting from patient continued and by 1956 Adams had featured in no less than one hundred and thirty two of his former patients' final will and testaments. During the Second World War Adams continued his practice in Eastbourne, his reputation for the use of unprincipled methods grew and he was deemed undesirable amongst fellow doctors to form part of a pool system where doctors would treat the patients of colleagues who had been called up to serve their country. By 1956 Adams was extremely wealthy, with many of Eastbourne's rich and famous among his list of patients including a local MP and sports personalities, and had become an important member of Eastbourne's social elite. The *Eastbourne Gazette* (17 January 1945) records a visit to the town of the national president of the YMCA, Lady Helen Graham, and that special invitations were sent to the area's most important people. Guests included 'Her Grace the Duchess of Devonshire and Dr Bodkin Adams'.

In July 1956 suspicion and innuendo turned into an investigation when the local Eastbourne police received information regarding the death of Gertrude Hullett, who had died following treatment by Adams. The deeper the enquiry went the more disturbing it became, until two detectives – Detective Superintendent Herbert Hannam and Detective Sergeant Charles Hewett – from the Metropolitan Police's murder squad took the lead in the investigation.

Sensibly Hannam focussed his investigation on a specific timeframe, a ten-year period going back a decade to 1946 through to the present – 1956. During this period the detectives looked at three hundred and ten deaths; they employed the services of Home Office pathologist Francis Camps to examine each death certificate;

Camps identified one hundred and sixty-three that he deemed to be suspicious. A pattern emerged of Adams administering special injections of which he failed to record any details on any patient's medical record, or to inform the nurses caring for the patient; he would often ask the nurse to leave the room before the injection was administered and would never discuss the treatment with relatives, often isolating the patient from his or her next of kin. On 24 August 1956 Hannam's investigation hit a brick wall when the British Medical Association (BMA), in a bizarre move bearing in mind the seriousness of the investigation, sent a letter to all the doctors in the Eastbourne area reminding them of the need for 'professional secrecy' if they were approached and questioned by the police investigating Dr John Bodkin Adams. Det Supt Hannam was furious with the BMA and considered it tantamount to obstructing the police in the execution of their duty. Hannam and Attorney-General Sir Reginald Manningham-Buller attempted to get the BMA directive lifted and gain some level of co-operation but this initially failed. The BMA stuck to its guns losing the police valuable time in their efforts to unearth the truth behind the mounting allegations against Adams. The police were still in limbo as far as evidence to arrest and charge.

On 1 October 1956 Hannam rather conveniently bumped into Adams (a meeting the defence would allege, at Adams trial, was engineered by the detective). According to Pamela Cullen's research Adams commented to the detective 'You are finding all these rumours untrue, aren't you?' Hannam mentioned a forged prescription. Adams replied 'That was very wrong.' Hannam also brought up the subject of Adams benefitting from the wills of many of his patients, Adams allegedly replied: 'A lot of those were instead of fees, I don't want money. What use is it? I paid £100 super tax last year.' When Hannam put to Adams that he had stated untruthfully on cremation forms that he was not to inherit from the deceased Adams replied: 'Oh that wasn't done wickedly, God knows it wasn't. We always want cremations to go off smoothly for the dear relatives. If I said I was getting money under the will they might get suspicious and I like cremations and burials to go smoothly. There was nothing suspicious really. It was not deceitful.'

On 24 November Hannam decided to search Adams' house and at the same time apply more pressure on the doctor. A search warrant under the Dangerous Drugs Act 1951 was applied for by the head of the Eastbourne CID – Detective Inspector Pugh. Hannam, Pugh and Hewett carried out the search looking in particular for morphine, heroin and pethidine (an analgesic). During the search Adams admitted to the officers that he had never kept a 'dangerous drugs register' as he was required to do by law. During the search Adams was seen to place two bottles into his jacket pocket. The detectives challenged him and he removed them; both bottles contained morphine. Adams told the officers that one was for Annie Sharpe, a patient who had died nine days earlier under Adams' care. The second had the name 'Mr Soden' written on it: Soden had died on 17 September but further enquiries revealed that the patient, according to his records, had never been prescribed morphine. When interviewed formally at a police station later that same day Adams told police: 'Easing the passing of a dying person isn't all that wicked. She [Morrell] wanted to die. That can't be murder. It is impossible to accuse a doctor.' A further search of his house revealed an array of consumer goods, mostly unused and still in original packaging including cameras and other photographic equipment as well as bottles of wine and spirits.

There was no breakthrough with the BMA until November 1956 when the Attorney-General forced the issue by meeting with the BMA Secretary Dr Angus Macrae and showed him a confidential report compiled by Hannam outlining the allegations made against Adams and the evidence they had collected. Macrae rescinded his advice to his colleagues and Hannam and his team received the much needed assistance they had sought, with two doctors giving evidence at Adams' future trial.

By mid-December Hannam felt he had enough evidence to arrest Adams (and to protect any other vulnerable patients in Adams' care). He was arrested on suspicion of murdering four patients: Clara Neil Miller, Julia Bradnum, Edith Alice Morrell and Gertrude Hullett; the strongest of the four cases appeared to be Edith Morrell, with which he was charged. The committal hearing at Lewes Magistrates Court in January 1957 demonstrated the influence

Adam's had nurtured over the Eastbourne community. The chairman of the bench – Sir Roland Gwynne, a former mayor of Eastbourne – had to step down from the proceedings after declaring his close friendship with the defendant. Another twist was the 'misplacing' of an important exhibit in the prosecution case – a cheque for £1000 – which prompted another investigation. Detectives believed it likely that local senior police officer Deputy Chief Constable Alexander Seekings, another close friend of Adams, may have been responsible for its disappearance in an effort to undermine the case – this however was never proved. Adams was committed to stand trial at the Central Criminal Court.

The trial of John Bodkin Adams commenced at the Old Bailey on 18 March 1957, a trial that would be to date the longest in British criminal history. The indictment featured one charge of murder in relation to Edith Morrell, the prosecution had decided to hold back on the case of Gertrude Hullett as a safety net, should Adams fail to be convicted in the first instance. The trial date was significant as three days after its commencement the law changed with the introduction of the Homicide Act 1957 creating a new offence of 'capital murder'. Under the previous law the mandatory sentence for any person found guilty of murder was death by hanging. The new act limited the circumstances when a murderer could be executed; a person was guilty of the new offence of capital murder (for which they could be executed) if the murder was committed in the course or furtherance of theft or by shooting or causing an explosion or resisting a lawful arrest, or the murder of a police officer or prison officer in the lawful execution of their duty. This change in law meant that should Adams be convicted he was still liable to hang; but if acquitted on the Morrell murder charge, he would probably not be hanged if he were tried and convicted of murdering Gertrude Hullett.

Edith Alice Morrell was an Eastbourne resident who fell ill having suffered a stroke whilst visiting her son in Cheshire on 24 June 1948. She was admitted to hospital and prescribed morphine to ease the pain; she remained here until the arrival of Adams, her GP, on 26 June. Adams arranged for Morrell to be transferred back to Eastbourne where he could supervise her care; he prescribed ever-increasing amounts of morphine mixed with heroin (normally administered by nurses) until she became addicted. During this period she made several wills in which Adams would be a beneficiary of large sums of money, a Rolls-Royce Silver Ghost and items of expensive furniture. Edith Morrell died on 15 November 1951 aged eighty-one years. Adams issued a death certificate recording death due to a stroke. He received his inheritance and invoiced the Morrell's estate for £1,674 in medical bills. On her cremation form he declared no pecuniary interest in her death thus avoiding the necessity for a formal post-mortem examination.

The case revolved around the contradictory evidence of the nurses who administered the drugs under the supervision of Adams and medical experts who again couldn't agree if in the first instance a murder had taken place and secondly, if it had, whether Adams guilty of it. The case was also notable for what would be known as the 'Doctrine of Double Effect'. The principle is used to justify the actions of a doctor who gives drugs to a patient to relieve distressing symptoms even though he knows doing this is likely to shorten the patient's life.

The prosecution's best weapon was cross-examining Adams in front of the jury in the hope he would convict himself; so their case took a turn for the worse when the defendant decided not to give evidence. The jury would later be directed by the judge, during his summation, for the first time in a British court, that although the defendant had not given evidence, no prejudice against the defendant should be attached to that fact. On 9 April 1957 after seventeen days of evidence and cross-examination the jury retired and returned a not guilty verdict after just forty-four minutes. The Attorney-General decided against proceeding with a second murder trial.

After his acquittal for murder Adams was tried at Lewes Crown Court in July 1957 and convicted of eight counts of forging prescriptions, four counts of making a false statement on cremation forms and three offences under the Dangerous Drugs Act and fined £2,400 with costs of £457. His licence to prescribe dangerous drugs was revoked and he was struck off the Medical Register in November. He returned to Eastbourne and practised privately until he was reinstated as a general practitioner in 1961. Adams died at the age of eighty-four on 4 July 1983 in Eastbourne Hospital having developed a chest infection following a fall in which he fractured his hip. He left an estate of £402,970.

67. TURN UP THE RADIO AND I WILL GO QUIETLY (1958)

A quite extraordinary trial took place at Glasgow High Court in 1958. The defendant Peter Thomas Anthony Manuel, the first person to be placed on trial for the murder of eight people simultaneously, sacked his legal team and defended himself to such a high standard the trial judge – Lord Cameron –commented that the defence case was conducted 'with a skill that is quite remarkable'.

Peter Manuel was born in Manhattan, New York City to Scottish parents – Samuel and Bridget – in March 1927. They moved to Detroit, Michigan looking for a better life – the 'American dream'; unfortunately the dream never materialised due to the Great Depression. With little money and Samuel suffering from ill health they returned to Birkenshaw, North Lanarkshire, Scotland in 1932; Peter was aged five. He had great difficulty settling in; his thick American accent didn't help. He started his life of crime at the tender age of nine when he broke into a school building. By the age of ten Peter had been caught stealing on several occasions and became a thorn in the side of the Lanarkshire Constabulary, eventually being placed on probation. His probation officer noted that Manuel had the worst criminal record he had ever encountered. To try and combat Peter's terrible behavioural issues the family moved south of the border to Coventry in 1938. He was now eleven years of age.

A year later he was arrested for breaking and entering, shoplifting and larceny, this time he was placed on supervised probation which again had little effect on his behaviour. A disturbing escalation in violence occurred in January 1942 when, aged fifteen and whilst still on probation, Manuel broke into his teacher's house intending to steal. He found the teacher's wife alone in bed asleep and severely beat her with a candle holder. By the age of nineteen with the family moving back to Scotland the seriousness of his offending had escalated again: a violent motiveless attack on a mother witnessed by her young child, numerous thefts, assaults and rape. He was imprisoned for several years following a string of sexual attacks and thirty-plus burglaries. Upon his release from Barlinnie Prison, Glasgow, in 1953 he was soon offending again. Charged with the rape of a local girl he successfully defended himself and walked from court a free man. This was to be the start of a terrifying orgy of violent offences that would shock not only Scotland but the whole of the United Kingdom.

On 2 January 1956 Peter Manuel started his killing spree. His first victim – although he was never convicted of her murder – was seventeen-year-old Anne Kneilands murdered in the grounds of the East Kilbride golf club. She was raped and then beaten to death with an iron bar. Manuel was arrested on suspicion of the murder but released after being given an alibi by his father; he would confess to the murder two years later but was never convicted due to lack of evidence. Now, probably feeling untouchable, he murdered again. On the night of 17 September 1956 Manuel, armed with a handgun, broke into the Burnside, Glasgow, home of master baker William Watt, his wife Marion and their seventeen–year-old daughter Vivienne. William was in fact ninety miles away on a fishing trip to Ardrishaig located on the shores of Loch Fyne in Argyll. Whilst searching cupboards and drawers for items of value he went into one of the bedrooms and discovered Marion Watt fast asleep; Manuel removed his gun and shot Marion twice in the head at close range. Realising the possibility of other people being in the house he entered a second bedroom and found Vivienne and Marion's sister Margaret, who was staying with them while William was away. Both had been awoken by the gunshots. Manuel, now filled with a blood-lust, shot both women at point-blank range. The killer then got into bed next to the body of Vivienne and sexually assaulted her before continuing his search for property to steal. Once finished he drove away leaving a scene of utter carnage behind, disposing of the murder weapon in a river. The following morning the bodies were discovered by housekeeper Helen Collison. She became concerned when approaching the house, noticing that the curtains were still drawn and that a window pane had been broken in the kitchen door. She entered, discovered the shocking scene and raised the alarm.

Peter Manuel was immediately considered one among a number of possible suspects as he was in fact on bail for a burglary in the local area but the police focused their suspicions in completely the wrong direction – husband William. An unfortunate string of events together with two unconvincing identifications led to William being charged with the murders of his wife, daughter and sister-in-law. Detectives suspected that William was an unfaithful husband providing a motive for murder – rather than the more obvious motive of burglary. They believed that William had gone to great lengths in order to convince the police a burglary had taken place by driving through the night, faking the break-in and murdering the women before driving the ninety miles back to Ardrishaig. Two witnesses came forward to add weight to the theory – a ferryman on the Renfrew ferry claimed to have seen William crossing that night and a motorist who believed she had passed him on Loch Lomandside. Both witnesses picked William out on an identification parade. He was charged and remanded in custody for two months in Barlinnie Gaol until the case slowly began to disintegrate. The ferryman appeared confused about the make and colour of the car William was driving and had probably identified William from his photograph published in the media and the motorist admitted only getting a brief glance and identifying William from the way he held his cigarette. Searches of William's car and areas around the guest house in which he had stayed uncovered no evidence in relation to blood-stained clothing or a weapon or any other item that could link him to the crime scene. In the meantime Peter Manuel was convicted of the burglary for which he had been on bail and sentenced to eighteen months imprisonment. Although released from prison and with the charges dropped, William remained a suspect for the murders and was even accused by the defence of the killings during Manuel's eventual murder trial.

In the early hours of 8 December 1957 in the northern city of Newcastle upon Tyne thirty-six-year-old taxi driver Sydney Dunn was looking for a fare. Allegedly (Manuel was never charged or convicted of this murder) Dunn saw the recently released Peter Manuel walking along the pavement and was hailed. Manuel was said to have jumped into the car and shot Sydney Dunn at point-blank range before slitting Dunn's throat after death. The vehicle was driven twenty miles out of Newcastle to Edmundbyers in County Durham where the car was abandoned with the body of Sydney Dunn dumped nearby. It was proved that Peter Manuel was in Newcastle at the time of the murder and returned to Lanarkshire later on 8 December. Two years later a button found inside the abandoned car was forensically linked to a jacket that Manuel owned. He was never tried for this murder.

Manuel next killed three weeks after the Sydney Dunn murder, his victim seventeen-year-old Isabelle Cooke. The young woman went missing on 28 December 1957 after she left her family home in Mount Vernon to the east of the City of Glasgow; she intended to meet her boyfriend at his house and then they were to on to a dance at Uddingston Grammar School. As she walked to her boyfriend's Peter Manuel followed in his car at a distance. When adjacent to a secluded wooded area Manuel rushed from his car and pulled Isabelle into the woods where he strangled her before sexually assaulting the young victim. He dragged her body to a nearby field where he buried the corpse in a shallow grave. Following his later arrest he identified the burial site to detectives. In a bizarre twist, Manuel gave a Glasgow police constable a lift a few days later in a car he took from his next crime when the search operation for missing Isabelle was escalated, an event that demonstrated the evil confidence and manipulative mind of Peter Manuel.

He would kill again just four days later. In the very early hours of 1 January 1958 the Smart family – Peter, his wife Doris and their ten-year-old son Michael – retired to bed having just celebrated Hogmanay. The family lived in a house in Uddingston on the outskirts of Glasgow. Peter Manuel, armed with a Beretta pistol, searched the district for an unoccupied house to break in to. He forced his way into the Smart's home believing the occupants to be out celebrating. He searched for items of value before discovering the house was in fact occupied. The Smarts were fast asleep and if Manuel had wanted he could have stolen any items he found and left without waking them but he choose simply to execute the family in their beds.

Completely oblivious to the carnage he had fashioned Manuel stayed in the house for up to a week. He lived on the leftovers of the Smart's Hogmanay meal; he slept in the beds of his victims rolling their bodies onto the floor, used their toilet facilities and watched their television, even feeding their cat. It was quite extraordinary that he wasn't discovered; this was mainly due to the indifference of the Smart's neighbours who, not seeing any member of the Smart family leave the house over this period, failed to inform the police. Eventually the killer got bored and on a final search of the premises for items to steal Manuel discovered a cache of new bank notes that Smart had withdrawn from his bank for a family holiday later in the year; Manuel made a fatal mistake when he pocketed the cash. The killer waited for darkness and then got into Peter Smart's vehicle and drove from the scene; it was in this vehicle that he gave the constable, involved in the search for his previous victim Isabelle Cooke, a lift before abandoning the car. It would be after the long Hogmanay weekend, on 6 January, when Peter Smart failed to turn up for work, that the alarm was raised. Lanarkshire police responded to the call and were on their way to the Smart's house when they located his car parked only a few hundred metres from the family home. The officers broke into the house and discovered the remains of the Smart family. Detectives now knew they were looking for a serial killer and suspicion fell on Peter Manuel, although unaccompanied by any evidence. They had to wait for the killer to make a mistake – he obliged in mid-January 1958.

A very blasé Peter Manuel, with pockets full of money following the slaughter of the Smart family several days earlier, was flashing his wealth around the pubs and bars of Glasgow's east end. Several members of Glasgow's bar staff knew Manuel well and that he was nearly always skint and cadging drinks and cigarettes from other drinkers. A barman contacted the police reporting that not only was Manuel throwing his money around but he was using brand new bank notes, of which he had retained two. Detectives discovered, when making enquiries with Peter Smart's bank, that he had recently cashed a cheque for a large amount of cash, which he intended to use as a deposit for the family's holiday and received a batch of new bank notes all with sequential numbers (which included the two notes retained by the barman) recorded by the bank. Detectives were also able to trace sequential notes from other pubs and bars Manuel had frequented that night. This was the evidence they needed to place Manuel at the scene of the crime. On 13 January 1958 Lanarkshire police officers knocked on the Manuel family home armed with a search warrant and arrested Peter Manuel. Property linking to the murder scene was recovered including further sequentially numbered bank notes. Manuel was taken to Hamilton police station and proudly confessed to all the killings in which he had been involved, apart from the murder in Newcastle of taxi-driver Sydney Dunn.

Peter Manuel's trial commenced at the Glasgow High Court in May 1958; after several days of evidence Manuel dismissed his defence team in order to defend himself. The presiding judge Lord Cameron, although advising Manuel against the move, had to admit that the defendant had conducted his defence with skill. However, he was found guilty of eight murders and some lesser offences and sentenced to death. On the 11 July 1958 Peter Manuel was to pay for the dozens of lives he had destroyed, the living as well as the dead, during his murderous spree. The gallows were prepared in Glasgow's Barlinnie gaol by executioner Harry Allan. When Manuel was brought to the gallows Allan asked the killer if he had any final words. Manuel turned to him and calmly requested, 'Turn up the radio and I will go quietly.' The noose was placed around his neck; a short prayer from the Reverend Russell Anderson was uttered for the killer and his victims. At 8.01am the life of this most reviled of killers came to an end as he dropped to his death. The 'Beast of Birkenshaw', as he had been dubbed by the Scottish media, was buried in a grave within the walls of the prison.

68. PUTTING A FACE TO THE SUSPECT (1961)

Television detectives frequently refer to a 'mugshot', but what is a mugshot? The *Oxford English Dictionary* describes it as 'a photograph of a person's face made for an official purpose, especially police records'. When police use a 'mugshot' during an investigation the identity of the person is, obviously, known and the circulation of the wanted person's face is usually coupled with a request for the public's help in tracing the whereabouts of the suspect or indeed to warn them that he or she may be dangerous. When a crime has been committed and the police have no idea who is responsible – what then? In the early days of crime detection investigating officers would have relied on simple descriptions (to a degree they still do today) which can significantly differ between one witness and another; this progressed onto artist impressions which still proved problematic. This all changed with the introduction of hi-tec advances in identification: firstly, from America, in 1961, a system called *Identikit*; this was followed by a more refined system called *Photofit* invented by British board-game inventor Jacques Penry and first used in Great Britain in 1970. Both of these methods were deployed to assist the police in identifying suspects who had committed the most serious of crimes.

Cecil Court is a quaint pedestrianised thoroughfare running between Lower St Martins Lane and Charing Cross Road. In 1961 it was, as it is today, a collection of quirky shops selling antiques, books, theatre scripts and musical scores as well as military collections such as medals, weapons and other curiosities. The small shops that exist today may have changed in name but not in purpose. In 1961 antique dealer Louis Meier owned No. 23 Cecil Court. On the morning of 3 March Meier and his shop manager Marie Gray were at an auction to consolidate their stock; the shop was opened by a trusted part-time employee – fifty-nine- year-old Elsie May Batten. Elsie's husband was renowned sculptor Mark Batten who spent most of the working week away from home in his Sussex studio; the job helped Elsie pass the time. Elsie opened the shop on time and was seen by neighbouring shop-owners arranging a display outside. When Louis Meier returned to Cecil Court at midday he was surprised to find the premises insecure with no sign of Elsie. Now very concerned he went into the stockroom at the back of the shop and discovered Elsie's body. She had an 18-inch ornamental dagger jutting from her chest, another from her neck, both blows delivered with immense force; it would later be determined that Elsie had initially been incapacitated from a blow with a vase that lay near her body. A careful forensic examination of the scene yielded one clue – a bloody footprint from a man's shoe stained the carpet nearby. Louis Meier informed detectives that the previous day, 2 March 1961, he had been in the shop when a young man had enquired about a curved dress sword costing £15 and several other daggers. He had explained that his father was Indian and that it was common for people of his faith to carry a dagger. Detectives interviewed other shop-owners who had seen the suspect in the area during the morning including Paul Roberts the son of a local gun dealer; all described a young Indian-looking male of a similar age.

Detectives turned to an innovative idea being developed in the United States of America it was called an *Identikit* originating from an invention by an officer of the Los Angeles Police Department called Hugh C. Macdonald who had worked as an investigator in war-torn Europe in 1940. Macdonald had identified a need for the recording of a suspect's facial features, firstly sketching descriptions himself before hitting on a time-saving system of drawing various facial features onto transparent plastic sheets which could be selected, by a witness, and overlaid on each other resulting in a composite likeness of the suspect. Macdonald returned to the States and approached a Californian company with his prototype identification system. The company – under the guidance of Macdonald – produced a kit of five hundred and twenty-five coded and numbered transparencies featuring one hundred and two pairs of eyes, thirty-two noses, thirty-three sets of lips, fifty-two chins and twenty-five moustaches and different styles of beards.

An *Identikit* image was compiled from the witnesses Meier and Roberts independently and the investigating officers were so amazed at the similarities between the two composite images they released them to the local media and all the beat officers of 'C' division, who covered London's West End, in the hope someone could identify the murderer. On 8 March detectives received the break they needed when an astute beat officer – PC Arthur Cole attached to West End Central police station – was on duty in Old Compton Street. He saw a man and a woman walking toward him, he noticed that the male closely resembled the *Identikit* image of a suspect wanted for questioning in relation to the murder of Elsie Batten. PC Cole arrested the male and his female companion on suspicion of murder. The man's name was Edwin Bush.

Edwin Bush had had a troubled childhood, one of six children who had lived with his parents in just three rooms. He was sent to a children's home in 1955 and then onto a training farm for children suffering with behavioural difficulties in rural Sussex. Following a series of petty theft offences which progressed to more serious crimes such as burglary he spent a period of time in borstal. When interviewed, he denied that he had anything to do with the murder of Elsie Batten stating that he had been at home with his mother at the time of the murder; he admitted that the *Identikit* images in the newspapers resembled him. When detectives spoke to Bush's mother she stated that he had left the house on the morning in question at 7.30am to go to work and was out all day, thus destroying his alibi. Detectives knew they were on the right track but needed more solid evidence than they had and organised identification parades. Louis Meier was the first to attend but disappointingly failed to pick out Bush as the man he had spoken to in his shop on the morning before the murder. Paul Roberts then viewed the parade and confidently identified Bush as the man he had seen that morning. Following the parades Bush was again interviewed and admitted the murder. He insisted that his girlfriend Janet Wheeler had no part in the attack (she had already been released). He told detectives that 'I am sorry I done it I don't know what came over me, speaking personally the world is better off without me.' He was charged with Elsie Batten's murder.

Of course the identification evidence provided by Roberts placed Edwin Bush in the vicinity of the crime and any admission of guilt in a police interview can always be retracted, so detectives reverted to more traditional methods of crime detection by matching the blood-stained footprint to Bush's footwear placing him in the shop where the murder took place; traces of Elsie's blood was also discovered on Bush's shoes. During the trial at the Old Bailey between the 10 and 12 of May Bush tried to defend his actions by suggesting Elsie Batten had made inappropriate racial remarks to which he had angrily and violently reacted. Bush was found guilty of murder and sentenced to death. After a failed appeal he became the last man ever to be hanged at Pentonville Prison.

The *Identikit* was eventually replaced by *Photofit*. The latter had been devised by Jacques Penry as early as 1938. The difference between the two systems was that Penry's used photographs of facial features, giving a more realistic image of a human face than the line drawings of *Identikit*.

Photofit was first used in relation to a murder investigation in Islington in October 1970. On 14 October neighbours became concerned for the safety and wellbeing of wealthy businessman James Cameron, who lived in an expensive Georgian terraced house – No. 4 Burgh Street, Islington – as he hadn't been seen for several days. Cameron was a bachelor who lived alone and was a popular resident of this affluent street. He was known to collect fine arts and antiques and was always immaculately dressed when he left for work as head of the Beecham Group's market research department. The local police made a call and when they received no answer they broke into the house and found the body of James Cameron in his bedroom; he had been bound and shot through the head. There were signs of a disturbance with heavy blood-staining to the carpets. The only lead detectives had to follow was the sighting of a male loitering in the vicinity of Cameron's house, described as wearing glasses and carrying an umbrella. It was established by investigators that Cameron had been forced to sign several cheques before being shot. One of these cheques had been used to book a flight from London to Edinburgh. The witness was asked to compile an image of the person he saw near Cameron's house using the new *Photofit* system for the first time in a British murder investigation. This image was circulated in national newspapers and featured on the ITV *Police 5* television programme (a forerunner of BBC's *Crimewatch*) hosted by Shaw Taylor on the evening of 22 November 1970.

A very important call came into the police as a result of the ITV broadcast from a shop assistant in Victoria, central London, who was sure he had sold an umbrella to a man who very-much resembled the *Photofit*; he had asked the customer for proof of identification when presented with a cheque for payment. The witness recalled that the customer produced a shotgun certificate, the number of which the shop assistant had diligently recorded on the back of the cheque. Detectives traced the shotgun certificate to an address in Nottingham, the home of John Ernest Bennett. On searching the house they discovered what they believed to be the murder weapon and property stolen from Cameron's house.

When interviewed Bennett told police that he had met James Cameron in a gay bar in London's West End and returned to the Burgh Street property with him. Once inside the address Cameron made clear his intention to have sex with him but Bennett had second thoughts and left. He returned ten days later and claimed that when he entered the house Cameron, thinking Bennett had changed his mind, made sexual advances toward him again. Bennett overpowered him and tied him up and threatened him with the gun, which then accidently went off killing Cameron. Following a guilty verdict at the Central Criminal Court John Bennett was sentenced to life imprisonment. Mr Justice Eveleigh commented during his sentencing of Bennett: 'You have not displayed the slightest concern for the death of this man. It was a cold and deliberate murder for money.' He was sentenced to life imprisonment.

Technology has of course progressed rapidly since the introduction of these two systems to aid identification. In October 1988 an electronic version of the *Photofit* was introduced called *E-Fit*, to this day utilised by police forces throughout the country.

69. CRUELTY BEYOND BELIEF (1963)

December 1963 witnessed the first conviction in a British court for a category of offending Professor Keith Simpson dubbed: 'The Battered Baby Syndrome', which he described as 'a relatively modern phenomenon... the brutal bashing, beating and sometimes killing of infants by parents or guardians who lose their tempers'. The sequence of events leading to the case in question started with eighteen-year-old father Laurence Michael Dean calling a doctor to examine his four-month old daughter Susan Moon, whom he claimed to have found dead in her cot. He told the doctor that she had been unwell for the past few days. The doctor examined Susan's body and found evidence of bruising; when he asked the father how she received the injuries he claimed Susan had hit her head on the cot a few days earlier. The doctor correctly reported his suspicions to the Coroner, who in turn ordered a post mortem. The autopsy revealed a catalogue of horrendous injuries including a fractured skull, several fractured ribs, a ruptured liver, and numerous bruises to the abdomen, the jaw and the scalp. Dean explained that when he found Susan in her cot, not breathing, he attempted resuscitation and the 'kiss of life' during which she received the injuries. Sadly – maybe due to the belief that a father would be incapable of inflicting such savage injuries on his infant daughter – the inquest jury returned an 'open verdict' rather than one of unlawful killing.

Laurence Dean moved to Wadhurst in Sussex and married his deceased daughter's mother who bore him another child – a son whom they named Michael. Michael only survived for five weeks; Dean claimed that Michael had been fed and returned to his cot when he started to whimper, he picked him up to comfort him and then placed him back but noticed that Michael's breathing was irregular. He then took him to a doctor. The young infant's body was taken to Guy's Hospital, London to be examined by Keith Simpson. Simpson recorded nineteen separate bruises in six different areas of the body and a ruptured liver. Dean explained to the police that whilst nursing

Michael on his knee he started to roll off. In an effort to prevent him falling, his knee came up and hit the child in the abdomen. Keith Simpson doubted Dean's account. The police produced a case around the deaths of both Susan and Michael, which they passed onto the Director of Public Prosecutions who authorised the arrest and prosecution of Laurence Dean. Dean was convicted of murder at the Old Bailey on 19 January 1965. He was sentenced to death but this was commuted to life imprisonment.

70. A KILLER'S NEW LIFE (1968)

The killers of two-year-old Jamie Bulger, Robert Thompson and Jon Venables, followed by Maxine Carr (jailed for her role in the abduction and murder of two young schoolgirls by Ian Huntley in the village of Soham in 2002) were afforded new identities for life on their release from prison. The precedent for such orders came from the case of child-killer Mary Bell in 1968.

The most serious of criminal acts are often connected with a violent, loveless childhood. Such a claim can be a convenient defence to explain away the violent actions of a defendant. In the case of Mary Bell, her deplorable upbringing, although never excusing her behaviour, must have had a profound effect on her view of this world. Mary Bell's mother, Betty, was a prostitute and an alcoholic who plied her trade on the rough streets of Glasgow, leaving the young Mary at home alone in Scotswood, an inner-city suburb of Newcastle upon Tyne. Betty gave birth to Mary in May 1957 aged just seventeen; Mary never knew her biological father and adopted the surname Bell when Betty married local criminal Billy Bell. Mary gave an insight into her early years when she collaborated with journalist Gitta Sereny in publishing *Cries Unheard: The Story of Mary Bell* (London: Macmillan 1998). The disturbing story reveals several attempts on

Mary's life by her mother; including Mary falling out of a window and 'accidently' swallowing sleeping pills, all treated with suspicion but not acted upon. Mary herself claims in the book that from the age of four she was subjected to sexual abuse and made to perform sexual acts on men by her mother. Unsurprisingly Mary suffered from behavioural difficulties as she grew; she was undoubtedly intelligent and would manipulate those around her including her peers and teachers; she was adept at lying and prone to fits of temper.

She had come to the notice of the local authorities including the police before she was eleven years of age. On 11 May 1968 Mary and a friend, Norma Bell aged thirteen (no relation), were playing with a young boy on top of a disused air raid shelter when the young lad fell, it was believed at the time to be as a result of an accident. The following day the mothers of three of Mary's school friends reported the two girls to police for attacking and choking their children. Mary was questioned by police but no charges were brought; this was a chance missed as the next time she would kill.

On 25 May 1968 Mary Bell, just short of her eleventh birthday, strangled to death four-year-old Martin Brown in a deserted, derelict house in St Margaret's Road, in Scotswood; a subsequent investigation by police concluded that she was probably alone when she took the young boy's life. Four days after the killing Mary Bell turned up at the grieving parent's house and asked to see Martin. When she was reminded of what had happened to Martin she answered 'Oh. I know he's dead. I wanted to see him in his coffin.' Following the murder Mary and Norma broke into a Scotswood nursery which they vandalised but before leaving Mary left a note claiming responsibility for the murder of Martin Brown; these claims were dismissed by the police as a sick prank. Little progress was made with the investigation, Martin Brown's killer was still at large and unfortunately, it would take the death of another small child to provide the breakthrough. Brian Howe, aged just three years, was found dead on a piece of waste-ground off Scotswood Road on 31 July 1968; he had been strangled and his body mutilated with small cuts including to his penis and his torso on which the letter 'M' had been crudely carved. The pathologist, who carried out the post-mortem, suggested to police that the killer may well be a child due to the insignificant force used. Detectives sent out questionnaires to local children including Mary and Norma regarding their movements on the day in question. Suspicion fell on these two when inconsistencies appeared in their stories. Both girls were brought in for questioning and when backed up against the wall they blamed each other for squeezing the throat of their victim, Mary accused Norma of cutting him with a razor blade. Both girls were formally arrested and charged with the murders of Martin Brown and Brian Howe.

Following a trial at the Newcastle Assizes in December 1968 Norma Bell was acquitted of all charges whilst Mary Bell was found guilty of manslaughter on the grounds of diminished responsibility. The trial judge Mr Justice Cusack described Mary Bell as dangerous and a 'very grave risk to other children'. She was sentenced to be detained at Her Majesty's pleasure and sent to a secure unit in St Helens, Lancashire. Bell served twelve years imprisonment before being released from Askham Grange open prison with a new identity in 1980 allowing her to start a new life. She gave birth to a daughter in May 1984, both mother and daughter (who at this stage had no idea of her mother's past) lived in anonymity until reporters discovered their whereabouts in 1998. Both Bell and her daughter's anonymity were protected by the courts although her daughter's protection would only extend to her eighteenth birthday. Bell returned to court and was successful in her battle to extend the anonymity for her and her daughter for life. This case would often be referred to in future similar cases as the 'Mary Bell Order'.

71. TURNBULL (1976)

The case of Adolf Beck in 1895 highlighted the dangers and unreliability of identification evidence alone. Several witnesses describing a suspect they had all seen at the same time will inevitably result in varying degrees of accuracy. One landmark case that laid the specific guidelines in future cases of identification that are still adhered to today is Regina *v* Turnbull 1976.

Turnbull and an associate called Camelo were a couple of local villains who devised a clever scheme where they would induce local shopkeepers and customers of the Gosforth Branch of Lloyds Bank in Newcastle upon Tyne to deposit their Saturday takings through the front door letterbox of their bank rather than use the night safe. They intended to break into the bank later that night (in those days banks did not open on a Saturday) through a window not covered by the alarm system and collect the money. To prepare for the scam they firstly put the night safe out of action by simply hammering a nail into the lock. They then typed a message onto headed bank notepaper. purportedly from the bank manager, advising his customers of the non-availability of the night safe facility due to vandalism and asking them to deposit their cash instead through the branch's front-door letterbox; they pinned this note over the night safe with a similarly headed note over the letterbox with the words 'Night Safe here'. This seemed an innovative idea, no violence or firearms, just a cunning plan. The plot – for a while – worked perfectly. Between 5.30 and 6.30pm on Saturday 21 December 1974 several unsuspecting shopkeepers deposited their bumper pre-Christmas takings totalling £5,000 into what was just an unguarded letterbox. However, one sensible shopkeeper saved the day when he became suspicious of the scam and contacted the local police. At 7.10pm the bank manager Mr Salkeld and his assistant Mr Alderson together with two constables arrived at the bank. They waited for the arrival of a CID officer – Detective Sergeant Wakenshaw – who entered the bank with the officials. Wakenshaw made preparations to ensnare the thieves by having Alderson replace the full cash wallets that lay at the foot of the door below the letterbox with empty ones. As the assistant was doing this he heard a rustling outside the door. He opened the door and saw that the notice had been removed. Alerting the other two he went outside and saw a man standing near to the night safe whom he described as 5'8" tall, with dark hair and wearing a three-quarter length coat. The bank manager

Mr Salkeld hearing his assistant's shouts quickly walked clockwise around the bank, as he did so he saw a van driving from the main road into a side road behind the bank; he took its registration number. The van moved off in the direction of Newcastle. Sergeant Wakenshaw, who by now had come out of the front entrance saw the driver and later identified him as Camelo. As luck would have it, a local Detective Constable called Smith was passing the bank in his car at the material time – DC Smith had finished his duty at Gosforth Police Station only a short distance from the bank. He got into his vehicle and drove up the main road. He stated that as he approached the bank he saw a man in the doorway removing something before quickly moving to the night safe and doing the same again. As DC Smith passed within ten yards the man turned towards his vehicle and DC Smith instantly recognised him as a man he knew as Turnbull, someone he had dealt with before. Smith would later give evidence at the trial of Camelo and Turnbull regarding the distance between him and the defendant when he made the identification, the amount of time he had him under observation, the fact that the street was well lit and how he had come to know the defendant.

At the point Smith recognised Turnbull he saw the door of the bank open, a bank official followed by DS Wakenshaw came rushing out. DC Smith saw Turnbull run. He quickly manoeuvred his car to turn back but couldn't locate Turnbull. Five minutes later, following the vehicle registration number being circulated to all local police officers by radio, the van was spotted with two passengers driving at high-speed by PCs Thompson and Sewell. They gave chase and the van eventually pulled over but not before Turnbull jumped out and moved behind a bush before getting back into the vehicle; PC Thompson searched the bushes and recovered a number of house-breaking tools.

The two men were charged and appeared at Newcastle upon Tyne Crown Court. The identification evidence of DC Smith was strongly tested by the defence counsel for Turnbull and the judge did warn the jury that it was only a fleeting glance from a moving car, albeit in a well-lit street. His evidence was strengthened by the fact that he actually knew Turnbull from previous dealings with him, which made it more recognition than just a simple identification. There was also the descriptions given by the two bank officials that roughly matched the defendants, the coat described by Alderson matched the coat Turnbull was wearing when arrested ten minutes later. The registration, colour and make of the van noted by Salkeld was the same vehicle the two defendants were arrested in following the ditching of house-breaking implements. The identification by DS Wakenshaw of Camelo as the driver in the vicinity of the bank, strongly supported DC Smith's identification as being correct. Both men were convicted and sentenced to three years imprisonment. The case was taken to the Court of Appeal on the basis of the convictions being unsafe due to the identification evidence. The Court of Appeal dismissed the appeals, and Turnbull's application to appeal the length of sentence.

Lord Widgery, on dismissing the appeals, made recommendations on how such cases should be dealt with by future trial judge's, he firstly stated that:

> Each of these appeals raises problems relating to evidence of visual identification in criminal cases. Such evidence can bring about miscarriages of justice and has done so in a few cases in recent years. The number of such cases, although small compared with the number in which evidence of visual identification is known to be satisfactory, necessitates steps being taken by the courts, including this court, to reduce that number as far as is possible. In our judgment the danger of miscarriages of justice occurring can be much reduced if trial judges' sum up to juries in the way indicated in this judgment...

First, whenever the case against an accused depends wholly or substantially on the correctness of one or more identifications of the accused which the defence alleges to be mistaken, the judge should warn the jury of the special need for caution before convicting the accused in reliance on the correctness of the identification or identifications. In addition he should instruct them as to the reason for the need for such a warning and should make some reference to the possibility that a mistaken witness can be a convincing one and that a number of such witnesses can all be mistaken. Provided this is done in clear terms the judge need not use any particular form of words.

In addition he stated that a trial judge should outline the circumstances in which the identification had taken place asking the jury to consider several questions about such identification: the amount of time the witness had the suspect under observation; what the distance had been between the witness and suspect at the time of the incident; the visibility and/or lighting at the time, for example, was it raining or dark? Were there any obstructions between them such as buildings or traffic? Was the suspect known to the witness before the incident? Was there any special reason for remembering the suspect such as hairstyle, tattoos, scars, or an unusual gait? How long was the time lapse between the incident and the identification? Were there any material discrepancies between the description of the accused given to the police by the witness when first seen by them and his actual appearance? These guidelines have been a part of basic police training since this ruling and are normally taught by using the mnemonic ADVOKATE: Amount of time, Distance, Visibility, Obstructions, Known or seen before, Any special reason for remembering, Time lapse and Error or discrepancy between initial description and the actual physical appearance of the suspect. Finally the Court of Appeal directed that the trial judge should always remind the jury of any discrepancies or weaknesses in any such evidence. Lord Widgery pointed out that these were guidelines and not law but a failure to follow these guidelines would likely result in a conviction being quashed. This case is at the forefront of every police officer's mind when recording a witness statement and these guidelines are implemented every day in British courts.

72. IS THAT A HAMMER IN YOUR POCKET? (1976)

The criminal offence of 'going equipped' is a powerful piece of preventative legislation for the police in tackling, in particular, offences of burglary. Section 25 of the Theft Act 1968 simply states that 'a person shall be guilty of an offence if, when *not* at his place of abode, he has with him any article for use in the course of or in connection with any burglary, theft or cheat'. One of the important points to prove in such an offence is that the person in possession of such items (e.g. wire-cutters, a jemmy or implements to facilitate entry into a vehicle) was *not* – as the act states – 'at his place of abode'.

Dennis Bundy was stopped by police officers in his car in 1976. He had articles in his possession that the officers claimed were to be used in the commission of an offence of theft or burglary, they were: a piece of lead piping, a hammer and three pieces of stocking. It was alleged by the police that Bundy was following a woman who was emptying vending machines from various pubs in London. He was convicted of 'going equipped to steal'. Bundy disputed the conviction at the Court of Appeal on 12 March 1977 when he cleverly suggested (or so he thought) that he actually lived rough in his car so therefore when stopped by the police in possession of the articles he was in fact *at* his place of abode and therefore not guilty of the offence. But the Court of Appeal dismissed the challenge to his conviction simply stating that his vehicle could only be classed as his place of abode when he had found himself a location to park at night and not when the vehicle was in motion, as it had been when he was stopped.

Another case challenging the 'going equipped' offence was heard just nine months later in December 1977 and related to the 'cheat' element of the act. A hotel wine waiter called Joseph Doukas took six bottles of his own cheap wine to work with him. The 'cheat' would entail him serving the customer his own cheap wine, making out a separate bill for the wine and pocketing the money whilst the hotel management would be unaware of the deception as their wine was not being consumed and therefore no discrepancy in the takings would be evident. Doukas was charged under S.25 of the Theft Act and convicted. He took his case to appeal that a customer could not be deceived if they had paid for wine and received wine. The Court of Appeal decided that customers were in fact deceived because if they had known that the wine was not the hotel's but in fact the waiter's they would not have paid for it. Joseph Doukas' appeal was dismissed.

73. A DECADE OF PAIN (1981)

Welsh schoolgirl Karen Price disappeared from a children's home in South Wales in July 1981. It was thought she had run away as she had done several times previously but on this occasion she never returned, resulting in nearly a decade of torment for her parents. Several years later two construction workers found the skeletal remains of a young girl in a rolled up carpet at the rear of a house on Fitzhammon Embankment in Cardiff. Detectives made extensive enquiries to identify the remains through local residents and the media, but were unsuccessful. Entomologists assisted the investigation by determining the remains were approximately ten years old. Having exhausted all traditional methods investigators turned to Richard Neave of Manchester University, a British expert in the art of forensic facial reconstruction. Neave reconstructed the victim's face in clay from the recovered skull; the first example of this procedure in relation to a murder victim (it was about this time that a similar technique was used by the British Transport Police in order to identify an unidentified victim of the King's Cross fire on London's underground system in 1987). This was the breakthrough detectives needed, the cast was a likeness of missing Karen Price; her identification was verified through DNA comparisons made between the remains found and Karen's family. Detectives believed that Karen had become entwined in a life of prostitution shortly before she had died; enquiries revealed that the basement flat of the property where Karen's remains were discovered was occupied at the time of her disappearance by local bouncer Alan Charlton and friend Idris Ali; it was alleged that both men had acted as pimps.

Charlton and Ali were arrested on suspicion of murder and charged. They stood trial in 1991 and were convicted. Both men appealed against their convictions in 1994, Charlton's appeal was dismissed but Ali's was successful; a re-trial was ordered at which he pleaded guilty to the lesser charge of manslaughter and released on the basis of time served. In February 2014 Charlton's case was referred to the Court of Criminal Appeal by the Criminal Cases Review Commission (CCRC), responsible for investigating possible miscarriages of justice, based on alleged breaches of integrity during previous investigations by officers involved in this investigation, together with alleged breaches of the Codes of Practice of the Police and Criminal Evidence Act 1984 in relation to the detention and interviewing of suspects in police custody.

In March 2016 the appeals against convictions of both Charlton and Ali were heard at the Court of Appeal; Lady Justice Hallett concluded:

> ...the only way in which an appeal could succeed is if we were to find that the prosecution offended the court's sense of justice and propriety to the extent that it amounted to an abuse of process. As we have indicated, we do not. The police misconduct in the case proven or alleged was not such as to offend our sense of justice or amount to an abuse of process. For those reasons, whilst sharing the concerns of the CCRC about the conduct of some officers in the South Wales Police in the late 1980s early 1990s, we dismiss both appeals against conviction.

74. AN INSPIRATIONAL WOMAN (1986)

Murder is considered to be the most serious of crimes, however serious sexual assault has a profound effect on the victims often resulting in a lifetime of suffering and differing emotional challenges; unlike the offender, who will serve some period of time in custody (not always the case) whilst rarely demonstrating any remorse before moving on with their lives. The following case involved such violence administered to three completely innocent law-abiding victims it shocked a nation and made everybody feel a little less safe in their homes. Out of this evil came one of Great Britain's most inspirational women, who bravely faced the world to tell her story and spent the rest of her life campaigning for the victims of sexual violence.

On 6 March 1986 the vicar of St Mary's Church, Ealing, west London, the Rev Michael Saward, opened the door of the vicarage to three hooded knifemen who burst into the house and commenced a savage attack on the three occupants: Saward, his twenty-one-year-old daughter Jill and her boyfriend at the time David Kerr. Rev Saward and Kerr were beaten with cricket bats and suffered horrific injuries including fractured skulls. Meanwhile two of the men took Jill upstairs where she was repeatedly raped. The media of the day, having identified the location of the aggravated burglary and rape dubbed the case the 'Ealing Vicarage Rape'. Jill Saward was effectively identified as the victim of the rape when days after the offence, pictures of her, only partially disguised, were published in the media. Following the 1987 Old Bailey trial and conviction of the three men involved, the trial judge, Mr Justice Leonard, caused a public outcry when sentencing the offenders. He addressed the court in a most pompous manner with little or no consideration for the victims and family present: 'Because I have been told the trauma suffered by the victim [Jill Saward] was not so great, I shall take a lenient course with you.' He sentenced the leader of the gang Robert Horscroft, who was not involved in the rape to fourteen years for burglary and assault. Martin McCall was given five years for rape and five years for aggravated burglary and Christopher Byrne was sentenced to three years for the rape and five years for burglary and assault. The message clearly sent out by this judge was offences against property are clearly more serious than offences against the person. Politicians, including Prime Minister Margaret Thatcher, and other public figures led the demands for Mr Justice Leonard to be sacked – of course this was never going to happen but it did lead to a change in the law, with the Crown Prosecution Service being given the power to apply for an increase in sentences deemed to be too lenient. Robert Horscroft appealed the length of his sentence at the Court of Appeal but it was dismissed; Lord Lane the Lord Chief Justice commenting that the case was 'about as bad as one could imagine'. On the day Mr Justice Leonard retired he expressed his regret at his comments.

The conviction and sentencing of the perpetrators was never going to be the end of the story for Jill Saward. In 1990 she became the first rape victim to waive her right to anonymity when she published a book called *Rape: My Story*. Its release coincided with an interview she gave in a documentary for the BBC's *Everyman* programme. The documentary was later utilised in the training and education of police officers and the judiciary in relation to rape victims. Saward now had a focus, having been freed from anonymity she spent the rest of her life campaigning for the rights of victims of sexual attack and abuse. She relied heavily on her faith and the support of her family, once commenting to the *Daily Telegraph* (8 March 2006):

Of course, sometimes I thought it might be quite nice to be full of hatred and revenge. But I think it creates a barrier and you're the one who gets damaged in the end. So, although it makes you vulnerable, forgiving is actually a release. I don't think I would be here today without my Christian faith. That's what got me through.

Jill Saward died aged just fifty-one on 5 January 2017 at New Cross Hospital, Wolverhampton, leaving behind a husband and two sons.

75. REMEMBER LEICESTER FOR DNA, NOT CRISPS (1987)

Deoxyribonucleic Acid or (to 99.9% of the population) DNA is the complex chemical that carries genetic information. Its introduction into the world of forensic science in the 1980s was the most important step in crime detection since the fingerprint at the beginning of the twentieth century. DNA testing can be carried out on blood, semen, saliva, skin tissue and hair, many of which are transferred from an offender to a victim and vice versa during a violent criminal offence, or are left at a crime scene. The first conviction in a British court using DNA profiling is generally thought to be that of murderer Colin Pitchfork; Pitchfork was indeed the first murderer to be convicted on the basis of such evidence but the first criminal conviction was that of rapist Robert Melias in 1987.

Melias broke into a flat in Avonmouth, Bristol, belonging to a forty-three-year-old woman crippled by polio; he subjected her to a violent sexual assault before fleeing the scene. A DNA profile was compiled from semen he had deposited on the victim's clothes. The profile matched DNA samples taken from Melias when he was arrested in connection with several other burglaries. He pleaded guilty to rape and five offences of burglary at Bristol Crown Court in June 1987 and sentenced to eight years imprisonment.

The criminal circumstances that lead to the first murder conviction using DNA profiling and just as importantly the first exoneration for such a serious crime, using the same method, began with the disappearance of fifteen-year-old Lynda Mann on 21 November 1983. Lynda left her home in Narborough, Leicestershire, to visit a friend; she was raped and murdered in the grounds of Carlton Hayes Psychiatric Hospital. There were no eyewitnesses to the murder or any information that could lead detectives to a suspect. The only evidence as to the identity of the killer was semen recovered from the scene belonging to a person with the rare blood group 'A' matching only ten per cent of males in the United Kingdom. Following an exhaustive murder investigation, detectives from the Leicestershire police force left the case open but unsolved.

Nearly three years later another young fifteen-year-old girl disappeared in the village of Enderby only a few miles from the 1983 murder of Lynda Mann. Her name was Dawn Ashworth. On 31 July 1986 Dawn took a short-cut and was found two days later in a wooded area; she had been raped and strangled. Semen samples retrieved from Dawn's body showed the same blood type as the first murder. At this stage all detectives had to work on was the fact that the two murders may well be connected as the *modus operandi* was the same and the attacker in both incidents had the rare blood group but they could not definitively state that it was the same man responsible for both crimes. The police had a break in the investigation when witnesses reported seeing a local seventeen-year-old lad called Richard Buckland in the vicinity of the second crime scene. He also worked at the Carlton Hayes Psychiatric Hospital close to the scene of the first murder of Lynda Mann. Buckland, who had learning difficulties, was arrested and interviewed; he allegedly told detectives details of the second crime that had not been released to the press. Buckland admitted to the murder of Dawn Ashworth but denied the murder three years earlier of Lynda Mann.

DNA profiling was developed by British scientist, Sir Alec Jeffreys in the early 1980s. Leicestershire police approached Jeffreys at Leicester University seeking his assistance. Jeffreys and his team compared the two semen samples recovered from the crime scenes in 1983 and 1986 and concluded that the DNA profile was the same, therefore – at last – detectives knew the same man *had* been responsible for both murders. Their joy was short-lived when comparisons were made between the killer's DNA and that of Richard Buckland – already charged with one of the murders – revealing that he was not their man; detectives were back to square one. This was an important step for the future of DNA profiling, convincing politicians and the general public that this new wonder science would not only detect and convict offenders guilty of a crime but also clear the innocent.

Leicestershire police and Sir Alec Jeffreys' department at Leicester University co-operated in a mass screening of all males in Narborough and Enderby between the ages of seventeen and thirty-four who could not prove their whereabouts on the days in question. Blood and saliva samples were taken from over four thousand men, the turnout was 98 per cent and took six months to conclude but no match was found; the screening was expanded to include those men who could prove an alibi – but still no match. The conclusions detectives came to were that either the man responsible had not given a sample or simply lived outside the designated screening area. On the positive side they had eliminated over four thousand men from their enquiry.

Murder investigations are usually solved with a mixture of good old-fashioned, painstakingly methodical detective work coupled with a slice of good fortune; detectives always believe that someone, somewhere, will unlock the whole investigation with a small but significant piece of information. This case would prove to be no different. A group of local bakers were having a drink in the Champions public house in August 1987; a woman overheard one of the men – Ian Kelly – boasting that he had taken a DNA test in relation to the murder enquiry posing as a friend of his called Colin Pitchfork who had paid him to do so. She reported this to the enquiry team and in September 1987 Colin Pitchfork was arrested at his home address in the nearby village of Littlethorpe; he was questioned about the murders of Lynda Mann and Dawn Ashworth. During his lengthy interview he admitted indecently exposing himself on many occasions, which had escalated into sexual assault and in these two cases, murder in order to protect his identity. A sample of Pitchfork's DNA was a match for the killer and he was charged and pleaded guilty to two counts of rape and two counts of murder and sentenced to serve life imprisonment with a minimum term of thirty years. On 2009 Pitchfork successfully appealed against the length of his sentence, which was reduced to twenty-eight years. The Parole Board may consider his release in 2018. These truly remarkable cases involving conviction and exoneration where the guilty party could have escaped justice and the innocent spend twenty to thirty years in prison have transformed the investigation of not only serious crime since, but crimes that have gone undetected going back many years. Many offenders who have so far escaped justice will be looking over their shoulders every single moment awaiting a knock on their door.

76. JUST WHEN YOU THOUGHT YOU'D GOT AWAY WITH IT (1989)

The procedural defence of 'Double Jeopardy' existed in this country for over eight hundred years preventing a person previously tried for an offence being tried again on the same or similar evidence following a valid acquittal. The Macpherson report into the death of Stephen Lawrence, murdered in a racial attack in south-east London in 1993, recommended that the double jeopardy rule be abrogated in murder cases and that it should be possible in law for a suspect acquitted of murder to be tried again for the same offence if new, fresh and viable evidence had come to light. The Law Commission produced a report entitled: *Double Jeopardy and Prosecution Appeals* in 2001 agreeing with Macpherson's proposals. A further report commenced in 1999 by Lord Justice Auld into the Criminal Justice system in England and Wales, suggested that exceptions to the double jeopardy rule be extended beyond murder to include such grave offences punishable with life and/or lengthy terms of imprisonment including manslaughter, rape, arson, kidnapping, armed robbery and serious drug offences whenever they were committed (including retrospectively). The 'Auld Report' got Parliamentary cross-party approval with Home Secretary Jack Straw leading the way. The recommendations were included in the Criminal Justice Act 2003 and became law in April 2005; for a case to qualify as an exception to the double jeopardy law two conditions had to apply. Firstly the Director of Public Prosecutions had to approve a retrial and secondly the Court of Appeal must agree to quash the original acquittal due to 'new and compelling evidence'. Three cases highlight the importance of this law change, two in England, and one in Scotland, which made a similar law change in 2011.

The ground-breaking case was the murder of Teeside mother Julie Hogg in 1989. For it was the incredible determination that justice must be seen to be done of Julie's distraught mother, Ann Ming, that pressurised politicians to act and change the law.

In November 1989 twenty-two-year-old Julie Hogg, mother of three-year-old son Kevin, went missing from her Billingham home just north of the River Tees in the north-east of England. At first, Cleveland Police treated her disappearance as a missing person. But eighty days after her disappearance Ann Ming discovered her daughter's decomposed and partially mutilated remains behind a bath panel in Julie's bathroom; a post mortem would conclude that she had been strangled and sexually assaulted. Following a murder investigation by Cleveland detectives a man called Billy Dunlop was suspected; on searching his house they discovered the victim's keys under his floorboards with his fingerprints on them. He was arrested on 13 February 1990 and charged with killing Julie. He stood trial for murder twice in 1991. On both occasions the jury were unable to agree a verdict; following the second failed attempt Dunlop was formally acquitted of Julie's murder by the trial judge. The law as it stood at the time meant that Dunlop could never be tried again for this offence.

In 1999 he was jailed for an assault and whilst serving his time he admitted to a prison warden that he was in fact guilty of the murder of Julie Hogg knowing full well that he could not be tried for the killing again. He was in fact charged with perjury in relation to the case but not the murder itself and he was sentenced to six years imprisonment. If Ann Ming ever had any doubts as to Dunlop's guilt she now knew Dunlop was responsible. This gave this extremely courageous woman a tremendous will to see her daughter's killer prosecuted for the crime and she embarked on a very difficult journey, which ultimately brought about (together with other cases of the time including the Stephen Lawrence case) a change in the law. Cleveland police were asked to re-open the case and as a result following the law change in 2005 Dunlop was again charged with the murder of Julie Hogg and the trial was transferred to the Central Criminal Court, Old Bailey, where on 6 October 2006 Dunlop pleaded guilty to the charge and was sentenced to life imprisonment with a recommendation that he serve a minimum of seventeen years – becoming the first person in eight hundred years of British criminal legal history to be retried for an offence following a valid acquittal. This was a change in procedural law with justice for victims and families very much in mind.

The next case is equally significant, as this would be the first under the new legislation that would actually go to trial and to a jury. Vikki Thompson, married with two young children, was attacked whilst walking her dog near her home in rural Ascott-under-Wychwood in Oxfordshire on 12 August 1995. She was found by her husband when her dog returned home without her; she had suffered severe head injuries and died six days later. Mark Weston, an odd-job man, was identified as the suspected killer and charged; he claimed that he was at home gardening at the time of the attack. He appeared at Oxford Crown Court in November 1996 but was acquitted of the murder. It was later claimed that the jury foreman wrote to Weston after the acquittal wishing him luck for the future and urging him to sue the police. Thames Valley Police Major Crime Team approached the Crown Prosecution Service (CPS) in March 2009 with new evidence in the Vikki Thompson case. With the advance of forensic science, in particular DNA, minute droplets of blood belonging to the victim were discovered on Mark Weston's boots seized following his arrest in 1995. The CPS referred the case to the Director of Public Prosecutions, Keir Starmer QC, who gave his consent for a retrial and for an application to be made to the Court of Appeal for the acquittal of Mark Weston to be quashed. During the trial it was alleged that Weston had attacked and killed Vikki Thompson because she had caught him masturbating as she passed him in the woods where she was walking the dog. Weston chased her down and hit her over the head and dragged her to a nearby railway line in an attempt to make it look like she had been struck by a train. Weston denied ever being in the vicinity of the murder but was unable to explain to the second jury the presence of her blood on his boots. Forensic scientists also informed the jury that the blood had been wet when it had come in contact with his footwear therefore rebutting any suggestion that his boots could have been contaminated following his first arrest. He was found guilty at Reading Crown Court and sentenced to life imprisonment with a minimum term of thirteen years.

The third case is a significant one for the people of Scotland, who passed the *Double Jeopardy (Scotland) Act 2011* on 22 March 2011, allowing the retrial of Scotland's most infamous killer – Angus Sinclair, suspected of murdering two young teenagers who disappeared from Edinburgh's Old Town on 15 October 1977. Christine Eadie and friend Helen Scott, both aged seventeen, were last seen leaving the World's End Pub in the company of two men whom they had met earlier. The following day Christine's naked body, hands tied behind her back, was discovered in Gosford Bay in East Lothian by hill walkers. Helen's body was later discovered in a similar state in a cornfield some distance from Christine's.

A huge murder enquiry took place with several witnesses coming forward stating they had seen the two girls in the company of two men in the World's End pub. By May 1978 the police had made no significant progress in identifying these two men and the enquiry was scaled down. Nearly twenty years later a cold case review team re-examined the case in light of major improvements in the use of DNA techniques. This resulted in the discovery of the DNA of a male present on both victims. The case was reconstructed on BBC's *Crimewatch* programme on 8 October 2003; researchers received over one hundred and thirty calls from members of the public. One witness, who hadn't come forward to police originally, stated that he had seen a works van being driven erratically in Gosford Bay the night the girls went missing. Detectives brought in the expertise of the Forensic Science Laboratory located in Lambeth, south London, in an effort to identify the DNA profile, which partially matched two hundred such profiles on the national database. On 25 November

2004 detectives at last felt they had enough evidence to detain and charge Angus Sinclair, who appeared at Edinburgh Sheriff's Court on 1 April 2005. Over two years later in August 2007 Sinclair's trial commenced at the High Court of Judiciary in Edinburgh. The details of the indictment and the opening facts were horrendous. It was alleged that Sinclair and his brother-in-law Gordon Hamilton (who had since died) either cajoled or forced the girls into their vehicle in St Mary Street near to the pub. It was alleged that he then drove Christine Eadie to Gosford Bay where he stripped her of her clothing, tied her hands behind her back then raped and murdered her before dumping her body. It was then alleged that he murdered Helen Scott in a similar way.

Sinclair pleaded not guilty to all the charges stating that any sexual activity between him and the two victims was consensual and Gordon Hamilton had been responsible for the murders. With Gordon Hamilton and the two victims dead it was a fairly logical defence for Sinclair to take and the prosecution struggled with what was – in the main – an evidentially circumstantial case. The vehicle owned by Sinclair at the time of the murders had been destroyed by him and therefore could offer no forensic evidence. The Forensic Science Service was able to give evidence that the semen found on Eadie and Scott shared the same DNA profile. Following the completion of the prosecution case the defence barrister Edgar Prais made a submission to the court that there was no case to answer due to the lack of any substantial evidence. He concentrated on the fact that the Crown had failed to substantiate that Sinclair had been involved in acting with force or violence against the victims and that the sexual activity between him and the girls had not been consensual. Lord Clarke presiding agreed with the submission and ordered that there was no case to answer and formally acquitted Sinclair, who walked from court a free man.

Following Sinclair's acquittal details of his previous convictions and the fact that he was serving two life sentences for murder and a series of sexual offences caused a huge outcry from the Scottish people and the media, which eventually led to the passing of the Double Jeopardy (Scotland) Act 2011. Within a year the Procurator Fiscal instructed Lothian and Borders Police to re-investigate the

Christine Eadie and Helen Scott murders. As a result of the further investigation and the new legislation the Procurator Fiscal's office applied for a retrial which was successful. Angus Sinclair stood trial for the second time at the High Court sitting in Livingston, West Lothian on 13 October 2014, two days short of the seventeenth anniversary of the deaths of Eadie and Scott. Sinclair was convicted one month later and sentenced to life imprisonment with a minimum term of thirty-seven years meaning he will be 106 before being considered for parole.

77. A VICTIM, NOT A KILLER (1989)

Domestic violence in Great Britain has been one of the most neglected, under-investigated crimes. What went on behind closed doors was private, accepted by society and often the victim. One case changed not only the law in respect of such violence, but society's attitude to it as well.

Indian-born Kiranjit Ahluwalia married her husband Deepak, left her home in the Punjab in 1979 and travelled with her new husband, whom she had only met once before the ceremony, to the United Kingdom. The next decade was a cycle of spousal violence and abuse; she turned to her family for help but was told in no uncertain terms it was a matter of family honour that she stay with her husband. The couple had two sons who were often witness to the appalling violence meted out to her but, through loyalty to their father and one would imagine a degree of fear, refused to give evidence to the police. She tried to run away but with no money she was found and brought home. Ahluwalia reached breaking point in the spring of 1989 following a particularly violent attack in which she alleged her husband had tried to break her ankles and burn her face with an iron. As her husband lay in bed asleep she mixed petrol with caustic soda to make a form of napalm. She poured the mixture over her husband's feet as he slept and set light to them. She told *The Guardian* (4 April 2007) newspaper some years later: 'I couldn't see an end to the violence... I decided to show him how much it hurt. At times I had to run away, but he would catch me and beat me even harder. I decided to burn his feet so he couldn't run after me.'

Five days later husband Deepak died of his injuries after contracting sepsis. Ahluwalia was arrested and charged with murder. The prosecution's main focus in proving her guilt was pre-meditation; they argued that although she had been beaten and threatened on the night of the incident she had waited until her husband was asleep before mixing a deadly cocktail, the making of which she must have researched, before setting him alight. Little of the abuse she had suffered for a decade was introduced by her incompetent legal team; she was even accused of being jealous of her husband's repeated affairs with other women. She was found guilty as charged and sentenced to life imprisonment.

Her case was taken up by the Southall Black Sisters, an all-Asian organisation based in the Southall district of west London. Originally established to protect the rights of Asian woman, it often turned its attention to domestic violence in Asian homes. The Southall Black Sisters pressed for a mistrial in the case as they argued Ahluwalia had not received sufficient legal advice from her counsel and was never informed that she could have pleaded guilty to manslaughter on the grounds of diminished responsibility. She was also found, understandably, to be suffering from depression at the time of the attack, which her new barrister argued would have diminished her decision-making capabilities that night. The appeal was successful and a mistrial declared, after which the Crown Prosecution Service decided it would not be in the public interest to order a retrial.

Kiranjit Ahluwalia's case was a benchmark in British criminal history not only for changing the law in its definition of provocation in cases of victims of domestic violence so as to reclassify such a crime as manslaughter and not murder, but in raising the awareness of non-English speaking immigrants about their human rights. Ahluwalia was honoured in 2001, in recognition of her achievements in the field of domestic violence, at the first Asian Women's Awards in London.

78. YOU'RE TELLING LIES, MY SON (1991)

It is commonplace for relatives or friends of loved ones who have gone missing to give an account of the last time that person was seen and to appeal publicly for them to return home or make contact, to let the family know they are safe. This is sometimes played out on our television screens. In most cases this is a genuine plea for information for the safe return of their loved ones; in other cases it can be used by detectives to examine the behavioural traits of a person they believe to be a suspect. Some may recall the profoundly disturbing interviews given by Soham child-murderer Ian Huntley in 2002, repeatedly appearing on various news channels expressing his concerns for the children's safety whilst demonstrating inconsistencies with his first account to detectives. The first time this was seen on our television screens was in 1991.

Rachel McLean was a nineteen-year-old student at St Hilda's College, Oxford. She met New Zealander John Tanner in August 1990 who was studying at Nottingham University. Rachel was last seen alive in the company of Tanner on the evening of 14 April 1991 by neighbours outside her rented accommodation. Following an argument in which Rachel confronted Tanner about his controlling ways, she admitted to him that she had been unfaithful. Tanner strangled Rachel with his hands and then forced her head down and tied a ligature around her neck. He concealed the body under the floorboards of the house and returned to Nottingham the next day. To cover his tracks he rang friends of Rachel's enquiring about her whereabouts and wrote letters to her expressing concern that he hadn't heard from her. Rachel's college were the first to contact the police about her disappearance; missing students were often reported to police in Oxford but nearly all would term up within a few days so the initial investigation was low-key. As time went by without any contact from Rachel the Criminal Investigation Department looked into the disappearance – searching her house they could find no evidence that any harm had come to Rachel. Police interviewed Tanner and went public with the appeal. Tanner told detectives that he had said goodbye to Rachel at Oxford railway station before returning to Nottingham. He also mentioned that they had shared a coffee before his departure with a man whom Rachel seemed to know well, describing him as having long hair.

Detectives started to suspect that Tanner was responsible for Rachel's disappearance and held a press conference on 22 April 1991 during which Rachel's parents made an appeal for information. Tanner was also present and made a similar appeal but detectives had briefed certain members of the press to ask questions they were not yet in a position to formally ask: such as did you kill Rachel. His manner and answers convinced detectives that he was indeed involved. The local scrublands and the River Cherwell were searched; a *Photofit* compiled by Tanner of the man he said they had shared a drink with at Oxford railway station was circulated.

On 22 April Tanner agreed to take part in a televised reconstruction of the period just before he claimed to have said goodbye to Rachel at the railway station. The enactment lasted for an hour with a policewoman dressed as Rachel; it incorporated the meeting he said they had with the long-haired male and the final kiss on the platform before his departure. Detectives now believed they were looking for a body rather than a missing person and the story of the meeting at the station had been completely fabricated by Tanner; they suspected that Rachel was already dead and was never at the station. Crucially, the scenario they believed to have taken place was gaining traction when two witnesses came forward, having seen the television reconstruction. They remembered seeing Tanner but not Mclean at Oxford station on the day in question. Detectives obtained detailed local authority plans for the houses in Rachel's road revealing previously undetected cavities under the floorboards. Rachel's body was discovered on 2 May wrapped in carpet. Tanner had dragged Rachel's body from the bedroom along the hall into a recess under the floor and pulled the body back toward the bedroom. John Tanner was arrested within hours of the discovery.

Tanner was charged with murder having broken down in an interview admitting the killing. Although he pleaded not guilty to murder he admitted Rachel had told him she wanted to end their relationship and that she had been unfaithful to him. He claimed that he flew into a rage placing his hands around her neck; he lost control but only had a vague memory of what happened after. He was found guilty and sentenced to life imprisonment although he was released after twelve years and returned to New Zealand.

79. BBC'S *CRIMEWATCH* – THE FIRST CASE (1994)

The appalling abduction and murder of sixteen-year-old trainee hairdresser Colette Aram near her home in Keyworth, Nottinghamshire, in 1983 would be a landmark case for two reasons: the formation and funding of cold-case review teams in the light of the advances in DNA and for featuring as the very first case on the BBC's *Crimewatch* programme.

On 30 October 1983 Colette left her home at 8pm to embark on the twenty-minute walk to her boyfriend's house. When she had not arrived by 10.30pm local police were called resulting in friends and family searching the route between her home and the boyfriend's address. Colette's naked body was found the following morning in a field a mile-and-a-half away from where police believed she had been abducted. Although detectives traced witnesses who heard Colette's desperate screams for help they never identified the killer and the case went cold, even though it was featured on the BBC programme in June 1994. Nottinghamshire police were one of the first police forces to receive funding for cold-case review teams and scientists were able to formulate a DNA profile of the killer from a letter he had sent to police, and Colette's clothes. The profile, created by using a more up-to-date technique called Low Copy Number (a more sensitive profiling technique where a profile can be obtained from only a few cells from skin or sweat), did not match any profiles on the national DNA database. The police had the breakthrough they needed in June 2008 when the son of fifty-one-year-old father of four Paul Hutchinson was detained for a driving offence and had a DNA sample taken. This sample flagged up as a match. His father Hutchinson was arrested and charged with the murder of Colette Aram twenty-six years previously.

At Hutchinson's trial the prosecution outlined the evidence. Hutchinson, a former electrician and now businessman, had left his house that day in 1983 with the intention of raping and murdering a female. Armed with a bread knife he spent the afternoon in a shed near to a riding school from where he intended to select a victim. When frustrated by lack of opportunity he stole a Ford Fiesta car and drove to Keyworth. He abducted Colette at 8.10pm as witnesses heard screaming and a car speeding off. Following the murder Hutchinson sent a letter to detectives mocking their slow progress: 'No one knows what I look like. That is why you have not got me.' He claimed that he was wearing a Halloween mask at the time of the abduction.

It would seem that Hutchinson returned to a normal life, marrying twice and fathering four children assuming he had got away with murder. Following his arrest he attempted to blame the murder on his deceased brother (as the DNA evidence was based on a familial match) but he changed his plea to guilty when police proved that his brother had a completely different DNA profile. Paul Hutchinson was jailed for life.

80. THE LAW CATCHES UP (1994)

The Criminal Justice Act 1996 provided a definitive definition of male rape as well as increasing the sentence for the offence, or an attempt at such, to life imprisonment. The first person to be convicted under the new legislation and therefore making British criminal history was multiple sex attacker Andrew Richards. He attacked an eighteen-year-old male in Regents Park, central London in December 1994. Richards had been drinking with his victim under the shelter of a tea bar when he indecently assaulted him before attempting to rape him. Having been found guilty medical reports revealed he suffered from a psychopathic personality disorder exacerbated by the use of glue, drugs and alcohol. He had a lengthy list of previous convictions and was sentenced to a minimum of ten years imprisonment.

81. DID YOU 'EAR THE ONE ABOUT... (1996)

In this volume we have discussed the incredible advances of forensic techniques to aid the identification and conviction of men and women who would otherwise have escaped justice and in many cases reoffend, together with those cleared of crimes of which they were innocent. Fingerprints, DNA, entomology, facial reconstruction and ballistics to name but a few, but one such technique is still a work in progress – identification by ear-prints.

In May 1996 an intruder broke into the home of ninety-four-year-old Dorothy Wood who lived alone at 32 Whitby Avenue, Huddersfield. Dorothy, who was profoundly deaf and suffered from severe arthritis, was fast asleep. The intruder gained entry to the premises by forcing a small window with a jemmy or screwdriver entered Dorothy's bedroom and smothered this defenceless old lady with a pillow – she would have put up little resistance. The examination of the crime scene revealed quite clearly four defined ear-prints on the glass of the window forced to gain entry; enquiries revealed that the windows had last been cleaned only a short time prior to the murder. Local detectives called in two renowned experts in ear-print comparison they were a Dutch police officer: Inspector Cornelius Van Der Lugt who had specialised in the comparison of ear-prints for over ten years and Professor Peter Vanezis, Regius Professor of Forensic Medicine at the University of Glasgow. There was no database for the comparison of ear- prints so detectives would have to identify and arrest a suspect before the ear-prints, left at the scene, could be of any use. Detectives turned their attention to known burglars in the area with a similar modus operandi in as far as method of entry into premises, time of day and victim classification; one of those on the list was Mark Dallagher. Dallagher was on bail for another burglary and was sentenced to a term of imprisonment in August 1996. Whilst in prison he allegedly shared information about the murder of Dorothy Wood with his cell mate including the use of a pillow to suffocate her – information that was not in the public domain. The cell mate, presumably shocked by what he had heard, informed the police and Dallagher was interviewed. He denied any involvement stating that he was with his girlfriend on the night of the burglary and murder. A controlled, sample impression was taken of Dallagher's ears whilst in prison; these were compared to the prints lifted from the glass of the window at the murder scene. Both Van Der Lugt and Vanezis were satisfied that Dallagher's ear prints matched those from the scene. The police and the Crown Prosecution Service believed they had enough evidence to charge Dallagher on the basis of the ear prints, his previous modus operandi and the evidence of his cell mate; he became the first person to be charged and successfully convicted of murder in the United Kingdom on the basis of such evidence.

At Dallagher's trial evidence was given by both Van Der Lugt and Professor Vanezis, surprisingly Dallagher's barrister, Mr David Hatton, did not seek to exclude their findings as having no real substance behind them. Van Der Lugt and Vanezis were cross examined, not on the basis that they had erred in making their comparisons, but such comparisons are necessarily imprecise, and cannot point with any certainty to Dallagher, who had voluntarily provided the controlled print, as being the person responsible for the ear prints found at the scene of the crime. Hatton did argue that Dallagher's previous convictions for burglary should be excluded from the jury but this failed. Dallagher offered evidence of his alibi but was convicted by the jury and sentenced to life imprisonment for the murder of Dorothy Wood.

It is beyond doubt that the conviction was secured in the main by the evidence given for the prosecution by Van Der Lugt and Vanezis which was never properly challenged by the defence. Dallagher's solicitors never gave up the cause and eventually secured evidence placing doubt on the reliability of ear print comparisons. Reports were obtained from Professor Moenssens in the United States, and Dr Champod of the Forensic Science Service in Solihull and a little later Professor Van Koppen from The Netherlands casting doubt on the reliability of the evidentially untested science behind ear-print comparisons. Dallagher's defence team were granted permission to appeal the conviction and sentence and the case came before the

Court of Criminal Appeal in 2002. The four grounds for appeal presented to the court were firstly the jury should never have heard the expert evidence on which the Crown relied because in law it is inadmissible. If defence counsel had available, at the trial, the expert evidence of Professor Moenssens, Dr Champod and Professor Van Koppen they would have been in a position to obtain from the trial judge, in the absence of the jury, a favourable ruling as to admissibility. Secondly even if the ruling had not been favourable the availability of the expert evidence challenging the reliability of such comparisons would have enabled defence counsel to cross examine more effectively. Thirdly in the absence of expert evidence for the defence the experts on whom the Crown relied were able to present their evidence in a way which was too favourable to the prosecution case and lastly in any event the judge was wrong to rule as he did in relation to the admissibility of evidence of previous burglaries.

Following the Court of Appeals judgement a re-trial was ordered and commenced at the Central Criminal Court, Old Bailey in June 2003. Following ten days of evidence the trial was abandoned and Dallagher released on bail while the Crown Prosecution Service (CPS) once again reviewed the evidence. In the meantime advances in DNA allowed scientists to construct a profile of the offender; the DNA was not Dallagher's and therefore the ear-prints left at the crime scene could not be his either. Dallagher, whose ordeal had lasted for seven years (six of those in prison), was formally cleared of the murder of Dorothy Wood in January 2004 when the CPS offered no evidence.

82. LONG ON MEMORY (1999)

The War Crimes Act 1991 was an Act of Parliament passed into British law by the House of Commons (the unelected House of Lords rejected it) under the provisions of the Parliament Acts of 1911 and 1949. These acts were constitutionally important for the United Kingdom as they limited the legislation-blocking powers (as in this case) of the House of Lords and asserted the supremacy of the elected House of Commons. The act allowed the United Kingdom to try people, in a British court of law, for war crimes committed in Nazi Germany or German-occupied territory during the Second World War who were not British citizens during the commission of these offences but had since become British citizens or taken up residency in this country. The only person to be tried and convicted under this act is Belarusian Nazi collaborator Andrei Abdreeovich Sawoniuk who was found guilty of war crimes in a landmark trial at the Central Criminal Court, Old Bailey in 1999.

Sawoniuk was born in Domaczewo, Poland (now Damachava, Belarus) on 7 March 1921. Sawoniuk's family were poor and there was doubt as to the identity of his father. His mother worked hard and supported the family by washing clothes whilst Sawoniuk and his brother helped out by selling firewood. Sawoniuk also earnt money by working as a Sabbath goy (an informal often offensive Jewish name for a non-Jewish person) employed by Orthodox Jews to carry out tasks they were not allowed to perform themselves on the Sabbath including manual work such as chopping wood and lifting of objects. During the Second World War Sawoniuk enrolled in the Nazi-supported Belorussian Auxiliary Police in which he rose to the rank of Commandant. In June 1941 the German Army occupied the town of Domaczewo which had a Jewish community numbering three-thousand. The Jews' property was seized by the Germans and they were forced to live in a ghetto. Sawoniuk's role with the Auxiliary Police involved the murder of Jews; several eye-witnesses would testify about Sawoniuk's personal involvement in the execution of at least eighteen Jews, most of them women. On 20 September 1942 on the eve of the Jewish holy day of Yom Kippur the occupants of the Domaczewo ghetto (some two thousand people) were rounded up by the Nazis and marched to a field at the edge of the town and massacred; it was believed to be one of the largest single-day massacres of the Holocaust. Andrei Sawoniuk was tasked with hunting down and executing those who had managed to escape the massacre. In 1944 when the German forces retreated following the advancement of the Red Army Sawoniuk also fled and joined the 14th Waffen Grenadier Division of the SS. Seeing the writing on the wall he deserted the SS in November 1944 and using his Polish birth certificate swapped sides joining the 10th Hussar Regiment of the Polish II Corps in the British Eighth Army.

Following the end of the war Sawoniuk came to England promoting himself as a Polish patriot; he settled there in 1946 having been awarded British citizenship. In 1951 he made his first big mistake, writing a letter back home addressed to his half-brother Nikolai. The Russian KGB, already suspicious that Sawoniuk was guilty of war crimes, intercepted the letter, which identified his new location in the United Kingdom. This information, due to the commencement of the Cold War, was not passed to the British authorities until the 1980s when the KGB started to share such information with their British counterparts. Eventually in 1997, following a mishap over the spelling of his name which allowed him to remain at large for longer than he should have, Sawoniuk, now aged seventy-six, was arrested on 26 September 1997 whilst employed on Britain's railway system. He was committed to stand trial at the Old Bailey; the first full Nazi war crime trial in British criminal history and the first occasion that a British jury had travelled to another country to examine the scene of a crime.

Sawoniuk appeared for his trial in 1999 and was charged on indictment with two specimen offences both concerning the killing of Jews in his home town during the Nazi occupation during the Second World War. During the trial the defendant accused all the witnesses of being professional liars having been told by the KGB what to say. He told the court that he was a: 'best friend of the Jews' and that 'these devils [the witnesses] came here with lies against me... I have done no crime whatsoever. My conscience is clear. I killed no one. I would not dream of doing it. I am not a monster I am an ordinary working-class poor man.' (*The Guardian* 23 March 1999). He also accused the Metropolitan Police of fabricating documents which proved his membership of the Waffen- SS and that they had conspired with the KGB in order to bring him to court.

On 1 April 1999 he was convicted on both counts; on the first count alleging that he murdered fifteen Jews, the jury returned a unanimous verdict, the second count accused him of shooting three Jews, the jury returning a majority verdict; he was given two life sentences. The following year he appealed his conviction on the basis that he was unable to receive a fair trial on charges involving events that occurred more than fifty years previously. The Court of Appeal rejected the application and upheld the conviction and sentence. Sawoniuk died of natural causes on 6 November 2005 in Norwich Prison, aged eighty-four.

83. A PLAN TO KILL HIS OWN PEOPLE (2000)

Britain's first convicted al-Qaeda-inspired terrorist was Birmingham-born Moinul Abedin who stood trial at Birmingham Crown Court in March 2002 charged under the Explosives Act of 1883.

Abedin and a co-conspirator, who was later cleared of all charges, was subject of a security service surveillance operation. In November 2000 a security service surveillance team followed the pair to a rented house in the Sparkbrook area of Birmingham. At some point the surveillance officers removed a bin bag left outside the address for rubbish collection. The contents of the bag were disturbing: wiring, packaging for electrical equipment, latex gloves, kitchen scales and most worryingly of all – traces of the highly unstable explosive Hexamethylene Triperoxide Diamine (HMTD). On 17 November the police – fearful that an attack was imminent – arrested Abedin who was discovered hiding in a neighbour's house. The jury at Abedin's trial were informed that a search of the Sparkbrook house, which Abedin rented under a false name for £95 per week, revealed a quantity of HMTD in a glass jar and five detonators as well as various documents such as passports, visas and immigration papers in several false names, protective clothing, surgical gloves and tools as well as credit cards and banking documents used fraudulently to raise funds. A search of a lock-up on a nearby industrial estate also rented by Abedin in an assumed name discovered a significant amount of HMTD. When questioned by detectives Abedin, a father of two children, claimed that he was in the process of setting up a firework business. His explanation for the rented property in a false name was to avoid paying tax and VAT. Abedin was convicted of committing an act with intent to cause an explosion using HMTD and sentenced to serve twenty years in prison.

This case stayed under the radar for several years and received little nationwide media coverage as the offences and the arrests were conducted prior to the 9/11 2001 attacks on New York's twin towers and the Pentagon when the world's attention was squarely focused on al-Qaeda and the ideology of Osama Bin Laden. Although detectives never evidentially linked Abedin with Mohammed Bin Laden's terrorist network there seemed little doubt he intended to cause an explosion that would have killed many innocent people and that his actions were probably inspired by Bin Laden's ideology. Following the New York attacks and the 2005 London bombings, Britain's terrorism laws were updated to cover such offences committed by Abedin and many others with more modern contemporary legislation.

84. AN EVIL UNCLE (2001)

Mobile telephone technology and design has progressed significantly from the late 1980s/early 1990s when mobile-phone users would try to look chic carrying something akin to a brick with an aerial. Now our mobile devices are so much more than a method of communication providing data beyond imagination. Of course whilst most mobile phone users are law-abiding citizens, the criminal element will always take advantage so crime detection methods in this field have had to move with the times as well. Today, the tracking of criminals and ultimately their undoing can often come down to technology; one of the first convictions reliant on mobile telephone technology was the landmark conviction of Stuart Campbell in 2001.

Stuart's niece, fifteen-year-old Danielle Sarah Jones, left her home in East Tilbury, Essex, on the morning 18 June 2001 and was last seen walking towards a nearby bus stop. The police were alerted when she failed to return home and suspicion fell almost immediately on her uncle Stuart Campbell. Campbell was interviewed by detectives but refused to answer any of their questions regarding Danielle and her whereabouts. Detectives were convinced that Danielle was dead and that Campbell had some knowledge of the circumstances of her disappearance. Campbell's house was thoroughly searched and significant evidence pointing to foul play was found: a pair of blood-stained stockings revealed the presence of both Danielle's and Campbell's DNA, lip gloss of a type used by the missing girl and a diary kept by Campbell, which revealed an obsession with teenage girls. A witness came forward following several public appeals with information that Danielle had been seen on the morning of her disappearance talking to a man in a blue Ford Transit van similar to the one owned by Campbell. Detectives turned their focus to the mobile telephones owned by Danielle and her uncle. They found a text message on Campbell's mobile which purported to be from Danielle thanking Stuart Campbell for being so nice and that he was the best uncle ever, all typed in upper case. Detectives were suspicious and they compared other messages sent by Danielle to other people, they were always in lower case. The triangulation of the mobile telephone positions of Danielle and Campbell's devices proved that when the message was sent both devices were in close proximity and destroyed Campbell's claim that he was half an hour away in Rayleigh when he received the message from his niece and consequently implying that Campbell may well have sent the message from Danielle's mobile to his own. Detectives successfully used, for the first time in a murder investigation, a form of linguistic analysis called forensic authorship, which examines the makeup and form of words and sentences, comparable in an electronic way to the more traditional handwriting analysis. The Crown Prosecution Service (CPS) took the brave decision that the police had enough evidence to prove the case and Campbell was charged with the abduction and murder of his niece, even though her body has never been found. Campbell was found guilty and convicted on both charges. He was sentenced to life imprisonment for murder and a ten-year sentence to run concurrently for abduction. Campbell did appeal his conviction on the basis that details of his obsessive relationship with Danielle and the evidence found in his diary should not have been introduced to the jury; the appeal was dismissed and Campbell will serve at least twenty years in prison before being considered for parole. Technological advances continue in relation to mobile devices and computers, especially with regard to social media, and form the basis of many criminal prosecutions in our courts today.

85. KILLED JUST DOING HIS JOB (2003)

Lorry driver Michael Little was travelling on the M3 motorway on 1 March 2003 when his life was ended by a drunken act of violence. Craig Harman, a teenage shop assistant, recklessly hurled a brick from a footbridge that crossed the motorway at Frimley, Surrey. The missile crashed through the windscreen of Little's vehicle striking him on his chest with such force that the fifty-three-year-old died of fatal heart injuries. When the cab was searched police discovered the brick baring traces of Harman's blood from a cut on his hand inflicted earlier in the day when breaking into a car. DNA testing on the blood revealed no trace on the database. However a new technique called 'familial testing' was used and formed the basis of a prosecution case for the first time; a process where the DNA profile matched Harman to the crime via a close relative's DNA. Harman was tried and sentenced to six years imprisonment for manslaughter.

86. WELL DONE, YOUR HONOUR (2005)

British justice can, at times, come to a grinding halt, barristers playing for time, defendants and witnesses deciding not to attend court, costs rising, and the Crown Prosecution Service throw in the towel declaring it not to be in the public interest to continue; step forward Judge Caroline Ludlow. Aftab Ahmed a forty-four-year-old taxi driver from Suffolk was due to appear at Ipswich Crown Court on

2 February 2005 to be sentenced for failing to disclose information when made bankrupt. He contacted court staff to report that he would be considerably late as he was stuck in traffic due to a fatal road accident. Judge Ludlow rang Mr Ahmed back and told him not to interrupt her as she sentenced Ahmed to one hundred and forty hours community service and ordered him to pay costs of £750. Now that's what you call justice!

87. A JUDGE BUT NO JURY (2009)

Trial by jury has been the cornerstone of English justice for many centuries so the decision of the Court of Appeal in 2009 that a criminal trial could be heard without a jury for the first time in over four hundred years was a contentious one. The legislation to enable such a decision to take place had entered the statute books in 2007 when the Criminal Justice Act 2003 came into effect allowing trial without jury on occasions where there were genuine fears jury tampering had or would take place, and if measures to protect jurors are deemed inadequate. The last time it was possible to have trial without a jury in the English judicial system was the Court of the Star Chamber (apart from the Diplock Court for terrorism offences to be discussed later) abolished in 1641. The Star Chamber was a court used by English monarchs against political opponents until the end of the English Civil War where people were regularly tried for indictable offences in the absence of a jury. It was so named after the star-patterned ceiling in Westminster Hall where the court would convene. King Charles I used the Star Chamber as a parliamentary substitute between 1628 and 1640 when he refused to call Parliament. The Long Parliament abolished the Star Chamber in 1641.

Consideration for suspending the right to trial by jury in Northern
Ireland was first aired during a report by Lord Diplock to Parliament
in December 1972, which sought to address the problem of dealing
with Irish Republicanism by other means than internment. The right
to a jury trial was to be suspended for certain 'scheduled offences':
offences defined in successive Northern Ireland (emergency provisions)
Acts and comprising those most likely to be committed by terrorists,
e.g. murder, manslaughter, firearm and explosive offences. These were
to be tried in front of a single judge. Diplock courts have been used
up to as recently as January 2012 when two alleged Real IRA men,
Brian Shivers and Colin Duffy, stood trial in such a court for the
murder of a British soldier at Massereene Barracks in Antrim Town
in 2009. Shivers was convicted and sentenced to life imprisonment
and Duffy acquitted. December 2005 witnessed the first Diplock
court to try a non-Republican or Loyalist case. The defendant
was Al-Qaeda terror suspect Abbas Boutrab tried for downloading
information on how to blow up a passenger aircraft. He was arrested
in Newtownabbey near Belfast over suspected immigration offences.
On searching his lodgings police found a cache of computer discs
containing bomb-making instructions; he was found guilty and
sentenced to six years imprisonment to be deported on his release.
The FBI constructed a bomb following the instructions in Boutrab's
possession and demonstrated its capability in bringing an aircraft
down.

The first British criminal trial in over four hundred years to take
place without a jury began in January 2010. Four men stood accused
of an armed raid at the Menzies World Cargo depot at Heathrow
Airport in February 2004. The men had anticipated a haul of about
£10 million but made off with a lesser, although still substantial,
amount of £1.75 million. During the raid sixteen employees were
taken at gunpoint and tied up. One man escaped and ran to raise the
alarm and was fired at by one of the gang. The bullet missed but the
gang member caught up with the escapee – several more shots were
fired but caused no injury. The four men who were to stand trial in
this unprecedented manner creating modern British criminal history
were John Twomey, Peter Blake, Barry Hibberd and Glen Cameron. It
had been a very long and expensive road to get to this position costing

the taxpayer £25 million, over ten times the amount stolen. The first trial was heard at the Old Bailey in 2005, when Twomey appeared in the dock with other alleged defendants; the trial was stopped due to Twomey becoming ill. When a second trial started in 2007 Twomey had been joined in the dock by Blake and Hibberd. The trial lasted for five months, by which time the jury were down to ten members but they indicated to the judge that they had reached a majority verdict on all three defendants. The trial judge decided not to accept a majority verdict at this stage and sent the jury home for a long bank holiday weekend. When they returned they were down to nine as one jury member refused to return claiming stress. The jury were unable to reach a unanimous verdict and were discharged. A third trial started the following year, Twomey, Blake and Hibberd were now joined by Cameron. Again with the trial nearly five months old proceedings were brought to a halt when the trial judge revealed that an attempt had been made to nobble two of the jury. The historic fourth trial started in the January of 2010 at the Royal Courts of Justice in front of a lone judge with no jury. Twomey, Hibberd and Cameron were found guilty of robbery and having a firearm with intent to commit such. Blake, in addition, was found guilty of attempting to cause grievous bodily harm and possession of a firearm with intent to endanger life. They were jailed for a total of sixty-four years: Twomey received twenty years and six months, Hibberd seventeen years and six months, Cameron fifteen years and Blake ten years nine months.

88. BATS RULE THE ROOST (2011)

Following the introduction of the Proceeds of Crimes Act onto the statute books in 2002 very few would imagine it could or would be used following the destruction of a bat roost in Matlock, Derbyshire. In 2010 a Birmingham-based property developer purchased some vacant properties in Matlock which they intended renovating for residential use. Before work could start a survey was carried out in the loft space in March 2011 for the presence of bats – a protected species in the United Kingdom under the Conservation of Habitats and Species Regulations 2010. The survey identified the presence of a roost in the loft of one of the properties belonging to the brown long-eared bat, this was followed by a further report which announced that work on the roof and loft space could only take place under licence and if appropriate mitigation was in place. Over a year later the ecologist who had carried out the survey and stipulated the conditions for work to be completed noticed that the roof of the building had been replaced. He reported this to the Derbyshire Police, who despatched a member of their National Wildlife Crime Unit to visit the site; they found that the roost had been destroyed. The officers interviewed one of the directors of the company who denied knowledge of the bats until it was pointed out that he had in fact commissioned and paid for the survey as a condition of the original sale. Both the company and the director were summoned to appear in front of magistrates in Chesterfield where they denied the charge of destroying the roost – they were convicted and the case sent to the Crown Court for a Proceeds of Crime Act (POCA) hearing during which time the director and the company appealed against the conviction. By the time the case came before the Derby Appeal Court in March 2016 the appeal had been dropped, as were the individual charges against the director. The company was fined £3000 and ordered to pay £2000 costs. A further order was made under POCA of £5737 against the company, the first occasion in a British court such an order was made in relation to the destruction of a bat roost. The organisations involved in the case were very satisfied with the outcome, the head of the National Wildlife Crime Unit – Chief Inspector Martin Sims – commented that: 'This is a landmark case and we will explore opportunities to use the Proceeds of Crime Act in future cases, people who act outside the law cannot be seen to profit'.

A spokesperson for the Bat Conservation Trust commented after the conclusion of the case:

> It is our view that this case is the most significant conviction for bat crime ever recorded. Not only is it the first occasion where such a case has been heard in the Crown Court but to our knowledge it is the first time that a proceeds of crime application has been heard in relation to any wildlife crime not involving the illegal trade in endangered species. A strong message is being sent to developers to the effect that they cannot, in future, expect to benefit from criminal behaviour.

89. MURDER ON THE SMALL SCREEN (2013)

We are familiar with the detective shows that appear on our screens becoming ever more violent and less believable as they battle for viewers in the television ratings war. However, in 2013 Channel Four broadcast a ground-breaking television documentary of a real murder case when its cameras were allowed, for the first time since photography was banned from British courts in 1925, to follow the trial of a man accused of the murder of his wife. The two-hour documentary, filmed from six remotely controlled cameras, was first shown on Channel Four on 9 July 2013. The case was the re-trial of Nat Fraser who was accused of the murder of his wife Arlene, whose body was never recovered, which took place at the High Court in Edinburgh. The cameras recorded the moment on 30 May 2012 when Fraser was found guilty following a majority verdict and sentenced to serve seventeen years in prison. The documentary titled *The Murder Trial* won the award for best single documentary at the 2014 British Academy Television Awards.

90. BERLINGO BINGO (2014)

Driving in the middle lane of a motorway is consistently voted by Brits as one of the most annoying habits. This inconsiderate trait is not only frustrating for those who wish to drive safely and with respect for other road users it is also downright dangerous, often leading to uncharacteristically reckless manoeuvres such as undertaking and tailgating. This practice of sitting in the middle lane of a motorway – often exercised by drivers oblivious to the problems they cause to the traffic flow – was deemed so dangerous to road safety it was outlawed in 2013 under the term 'careless driving', which also incorporates other reckless offences such as tailgating, undertaking and driving too slow. The first landmark prosecution and conviction for middle lane driving was recorded at Leeds Magistrates Court and resulted in a fine of £940 for a forty-two-year-old painter and decorator after he was observed by police to drive his white Citroen Berlingo van at sixty miles per hour in the central lane along a stretch of the M62 motorway between Rochdale and Huddersfield on 25 August 2014. A traffic police officer gave evidence to the court that he had seen the offending driver drive his vehicle in an 'inconsiderate manner' for several miles, causing inconvenience to other road users. The officer added that six drivers were forced to brake and swerve to overtake the vehicle. PC Nigel Fawcett-Jones from the Road Policing Unit of West Yorkshire police said lane-hogging was dangerous and caused congestion and inconvenience to other road users: 'It reduces the capacity of roads and motorways, and can lead to dangerous situations where other drivers "tailgate" the vehicle in front to try and get the lane hogger to move over. Members of the public regularly tell the Road Policing Unit that lane hogging and tailgating are real problems on our roads and this conviction shows that the police and the courts understand the public's concerns and take this offence seriously.'

91. I JUST CAN'T REMEMBER (2015)

In an allegation of serious sexual assault such as rape the case often comes down to the subject of consent – did the victim agree to the sexual act? There has been a lot of concern within the legal profession and indeed at ministerial government level of the way the criminal justice system was dealing with cases where victims are incapacitated by either drink or drugs at the time of the crime. A case tried at Lincoln Crown Court in early 2015 went a long way to clearing the muddied waters in this very sensitive area. The three men on trial were Michael Armitage, Rafal Segiet and Pawal Chudzicki. The twenty-three-year-old victim was having a night out in a nightclub in the town and consumed up to twelve shots of vodka. She met the three men accused of rape sometime during the evening and agreed to get into a taxi with them and go to a flat. She drank more alcohol before each of the men had sex with her. They claimed that the sex was consensual but the victim said she was so drunk that she could not remember anything about the relevant time. When the victim didn't get home the following morning concerned family members reported her missing to the police; she was located later the following evening in a distressed and confused state and making allegations to the police that she had been raped.

The case was tried at Lincoln Crown Court in front of Judge John Pini QC. The young victim endured a vigorous cross-examination and admitted that the sex could have been consensual but she just couldn't remember anything about the incident. His Honour Judge Pini terminated the trial on the grounds of insufficient evidence to prove the victim could not have agreed voluntarily to have sex. He made it clear that he was not saying a victim who had been drinking could not say no or that a lack of memory equates to giving consent.

The Judge's decision was appealed against by the Crown Prosecution Service (CPS) and the case appeared before the Court of Appeal. The three judges – Lord Justice Treacy, Mr Justice Walker and Mr Justice Thirlwall – listened to the submissions by the Crown and watched video footage of one of the three men having sex with the victim and agreed with the CPS. Part of their judgement read:

> It appears to us that [the victim] is depicted throughout as being sufficiently inert and unresponsive as to leave it open to a properly directed jury to be sure that she was not consenting and that she did not have the freedom and capacity to do so. The issues of consent and capacity to consent should normally be left to a jury to determine.

This case gives clear guidance for judges when summing up to juries in the future and sets a precedent for a victim's capacity to give sexual consent. The three men were subsequently convicted and received six years imprisonment each.

92. A TALE OF TWO WOMEN (2015)

The Anti-social Behaviour, Crime and Policing Act 2014 became law in June 2014 following campaigning by Jasvinder Sanghera, who formed a charitable organisation called Karma Nirvana, which provides support and training to help prevent forced marriages and honour based abuse within the United Kingdom and beyond.[33]

The act makes it an offence for any person to use violence, threats, or any other form of coercion, for the purpose of causing another person to enter into a marriage and who believes, or ought to reasonably believe, that the conduct may cause the other person to enter into the marriage without free and full consent. The first breakthrough against this form of criminality came with a landmark prosecution and conviction of a male businessman in the Welsh city of Cardiff.

The trial took place at Merthyr Crown Court in June 2015 during which the terrible circumstances of the case were outlined. The accused was a thirty-four-year-old man who claimed to be a devout Muslim who had tricked a twenty-five-year-old virgin, with whom he had an obsession, into a house on the pretence that they were to meet friends. The house was in fact empty. The offender drew the curtains and locked the door, he bound and gagged her before raping her whilst playing loud music in order to drown out her screams for help. He then allowed her to take a shower during which he filmed her. He then showed her the footage and threatened to make the footage public unless she married him. He also made threats to murder her parents if she did not agree to his demands. Although originally pleading not guilty to charges under this legislation as well as four counts of rape, bigamy (as he was already married) and voyeurism he changed his plea just before his victim was about to give evidence and was sentenced to sixteen years imprisonment.

---

33 www.karmanirvana.org.uk

The trial judge Daniel Williams praised the victim for her courage and fortitude. Iwan Jenkins, Head of CPS Wales Rape and Serious Sexual Offences Unit, said:

> Forced marriage wrecks lives and destroys families. We hope that today's sentence sends a strong message that forced marriage will not be tolerated in today's Britain. It is a testament to the strength of the case which we constructed with the police that we secured a guilty plea for the offences in this case. The victim has shown great courage and bravery in reporting these matters. This conviction illustrates the seriousness in which these crimes are treated and investigated by the Crown Prosecution Service and South Wales Police. I hope today's sentence brings some closure for those who have suffered as a result of these particularly nasty and invasive crimes.[34]

Jasvinder Sanghera commented after the sentence:

> It became law in June last year in the face of a lot of opposition, we had barristers' chambers arguing for it not to be law, you had campaign groups saying it will not encourage victims to report, we have had a lot of people wanting it to fail. What we've noticed [since] the change of the law is an increase in the number of police forces wanting to engage with our organisation ... the law brings with it a shift in accountability and a shift in attitudes. We still have to raise awareness that this law even exists. Some victims don't know it exists – some professionals don't know it exists.[35]

This exceptional and inspirational woman was voted the Woman of the Year 2007, awarded a CBE in 2013 and names as Legal Campaigner of the Year in 2014.

---

34 www.cps.gov.uk
35 www.telegraph..co.uk 10 June 2015

93. THERE'S A LOT OF MONEY IN VEG (2015)

A terrible event occurred on a beach in Morecambe Bay, Lancashire on 5 February 2004 when twenty-three undocumented Chinese cockle-pickers were drowned when a fast-flowing tide came in cutting them off from the mainland. The labourers had been smuggled into England via shipping containers through the port of Liverpool and were hired out by local criminal gangs. They were paid just £5 per twenty-five kilograms of cockles they collected. Twenty-one bodies were recovered, two of which were women; all the dead were aged between eighteen and forty-five. Gangmaster Lin Liang Ren was convicted of the manslaughter of the twenty-one people whose bodies were recovered and he was sentenced to twelve years for manslaughter, six years for facilitating illegal immigration and two years for conspiracy to pervert the course of justice. This terrible loss of life prompted the government to introduce new worker's safety law resulting in the Gangmasters Licensing Act 2004, which also created the Gangmasters Licensing Authority in order to protect in particular the vulnerable workers often employed in the shellfish and agricultural industries.

On 26 June 2015 two Lithuanians became the first people to be convicted under a previously unused section (s.12(2)(b) of the act: being in possession of a document know to be obtained improperly with the intention of leading people to believe they were properly licensed under the Gangmasters Licensing Act. In a landmark conviction Stasys Skarbalius was sentenced to two-and-a-half years imprisonment, his wife Virinija Skarbaliene received three years. Following their conviction at Sheffield Crown Court the trial judge Simon Lawler QC described the conviction as: 'the first of its type in the UK'.[36]

Both defendants had entered Britain illegally; they built up a lucrative property empire on the back of a successful – but illegal – vegetable picking business in the east of England. Skarbalius used a

---

36 *Fresh Produce Journal* 26 June 2015

stolen Dutch identification in the name of Charles Luske, the same identity he would use in an attempt to escape from the country when he became aware the Gangmaster Licensing Authority was closing in on him. The judge went onto comment when sentencing the couple:

> The sentence is not just a reflection of the public view that serious dishonesty resulting in financial gain should be discouraged but it also sends a clear and unequivocal message that dishonesty in this important area will not be tolerated.

94. THIRTY YEARS OF MISINTERPRETATION (2015)

The Common Law doctrine of 'Joint Enterprise' goes back several centuries and has allowed more than one person to be charged or convicted for the same crime. For example: a group of people surround a victim, one of whom stabs the victim, under joint enterprise all present could be charged and convicted of the resulting offence – serious assault or murder – regardless of the role they played. The Supreme Court in London, when examining the case of Ameen Jogee who was sentenced to life imprisonment at Leicester Crown Court in 2012 for encouraging another to harm a third party resulting in the death of a young man, ruled that joint enterprise had been misinterpreted by trial judges since Supreme Court rulings thirty years back.

This ruling had a significant effect on a murder trial at the Central Criminal Court, Old Bailey, about the same time when four defendants stood trial for the murder of twenty-four-year-old Ahmed Ahmed, who was fatally stabbed several times in the leg when he walked out of a block of flats in Plumstead, south-east London, on 10 August 2015. All the attackers wore headscarves three of the four held him down whilst the fourth stabbed him with a kitchen knife. A submission to the trial judge on behalf of two of the defendants Khalid Hashi and Hamza Dodi argued that there was no case to answer reflecting on the very recent ruling by the Supreme Court in the case of Ameen Jogee. The Crown Prosecution Service again considering the recent ruling did not oppose the submission and Hashi and Dodi became the first people accused of murder to be acquitted following the landmark ruling on the joint enterprise law. A third defendant was also acquitted by the jury but a fourth – Osman Musa Mohamed – was convicted and sentenced to a minimum life term of twenty-two years imprisonment.

95. A HUMILIATING CRIME (2015)

The Criminal Justice and Courts Act 2015 addressed the disturbing phenomenon of 'revenge porn' in which ex-boyfriends would upload indecent images or videos of previous partners in sexually compromising situations without their permission with the intention of causing distress. The law had fallen behind the advances in social media and such cases were unsatisfactorily dealt with under the Protection from Harassment Act 1997 and parts of the Malicious Communications Act 1988 and the Communications Act 2003. Several high-profile celebrity victims focused law-makers and the general public's awareness; further investigation revealed many children and young adults were suffering this crime. The first person to be convicted under the new legislation covered under an amendment to the Criminal Justice and Courts Act 2015 was twenty-one-year-old Jason Asagba, sentenced at Reading Magistrates Court on 1 September 2015 to six months imprisonment suspended for eighteen months and required to carry out one hundred hours unpaid community work, attend a probation service behavioural programme and pay costs of £300 and finally made subject of a four-year restraining order instructing him not to contact the victim or her family or go to her home or her family's home or anywhere she may reside. Asagba, who lived in Romford, Essex, contravened the new legislation on 16 April 2015 only three days after it became law when he threatened to post intimate pictures of a Berkshire woman on social media before subsequently carrying out his threat posting the material on *Facebook* and sending it to several members of the woman's family.

Following the sentencing the Director of Public Prosecutions Alison Saunders commented:

> Revenge pornography is a particularly distressing crime for the victim, which is often, but not always, brought about by the vengeful actions of former partners. It is a violation of trust between two people and its purpose is to publicly humiliate. Prior to the new law, crimes were dealt with by using other areas of legislation such as the Malicious Communications Act 1988. I am pleased that these crimes can now be prosecuted as an offence in their own right, reassuring victims that it is a recognised offence and it is being taken seriously by the authorities.[37]

It is often assumed that most offenders under this legislation are men but this is not always the case. The first woman to be convicted for revenge porn was twenty-four-year-old Paige Mitchell who received a six-week term of imprisonment at Stevenage Magistrates court in September 2015 suspended for eighteen months for posting intimate images of her girlfriend online. Following a violent argument with her partner Mitchell allegedly assaulted her before posting the images on *Facebook*, which were live for

---

37 www.cps.gov.uk

thirty minutes. Mitchell pleaded guilty to an offence of disclosing private sexual photographs and films with intent to cause distress and one charge of assault. The magistrate commented that 'posting the photos on the internet was a highly vindictive invasion of privacy... It was done with the intention of humiliating and hurting your victim.'

96. LOOK BEHIND YOU AND SMILE FOR THE CAMERA (2015)

How many times have you sat in your car, having witnessed a dangerous piece of driving, and thought: 'There's never a copper around when you want one'? With the introduction of high-quality cameras installed in mobile telephones and more recently the ever-growing use of dashboard cameras in motor vehicles, often to negate spurious insurance claims, more of these idiots of the road are getting their comeuppance. The first person to be convicted using a 'dashcam' was twenty-four-year-old James Stock from Tilson in Cheshire when he was recorded recklessly overtaking vehicles on the A495 in Shropshire. The footage showed him driving his black Volkswagen Polo at high speed and overtaking a Ford Ka on a blind bend causing a transit van travelling in the opposite direction to take evasive action by swerving onto a grass verge in order to avoid a catastrophic head-on collision. He later repeated the same manoeuvre approaching a blind bend, just avoiding another collision with a Vauxhall Insignia. The footage had been recorded on a dashcam in a vehicle that Stocks had overtaken in a dangerous manner; the driver of this vehicle posted the footage on the website *PoliceWitness.com*, founded by a retired police officer in 2011, which holds bad drivers to account by bringing such driving to the attention of the police in an evidential format. This can lead to prosecution and in this case, imprisonment, as Stocks pleaded guilty at Mold and Caernarfon Crown Court in December 2015 to dangerous driving and received a custodial sentence of eight months. He also received a fine and was banned from driving a motor vehicle for two years and four months, as well as having to re-sit an extended driving test.

Following the successful prosecution the chairman of the PoliceWitness website – Matt Stockdale commented that:

> To date, nearly 1,000 motorists up and down the country have faced positive formal police action following the submission of dashcam footage by those who call themselves police witnesses. These have resulted in fines and points, through to driver re-training, vehicle seizure warnings and even prosecutions, where drivers have been banned from driving altogether. Being banned from driving, or even losing your job following a moment of madness has often been described as the ultimate price to pay having been caught on video by a dashcam. But this case has resulted in a driver losing their liberty and freedom – and in my view rightly so.[38]

---

38 www.motoringresearch.com

97. HAVE YOU NEVER HEARD OF THE MINIMUM WAGE?
(2016)

No subject is so frequently thrown back in the faces of the British than the abhorrent slave trade, even though the country led the path to its abolition in 1807. In modern times the nation is rightly proactive in disrupting and halting the disturbing international criminal practice of 'modern slavery', which can range from women forced into prostitution, child slavery, forced labour and people trafficking.

The United Kingdom introduced the Modern Slavery Act 2015 in order to combat such practices within her borders. One of the first people to be convicted for an offence under this act was businessman Mohammed Rafiq in February 2016. Rafiq ran a company called Kozee Sleep, a successful bed manufacturing business in Ravensthorpe, Dewsbury, West Yorkshire. Rafiq employed a large contingent of Hungarian workers whom he accommodated in squalid conditions, made them work for up to eighty hours a week whilst only paying them £10 a week and a packet of tobacco, after promising them good wages, housing and food. He was sentenced to twenty-seven months imprisonment at Leeds Crown Court.

98. AN ILLEGAL HIGH (2016)

On Wednesday 20 July 2016 Daniel Kelly became the first person to be convicted under S.79 of the Serious Crime Act 2015 which states that it is an offence to throw, or otherwise project, any article or substance (not already specified by the Prisons Act 1952 such as controlled drugs, firearms, explosives, alcohol and mobile telephones etc.) into a prison without authorisation. The law was updated to combat the supply into prisons of so-called legal highs.

On 25 April 2016 Kelly was seen in a car parked near to HMP Swaleside near Leysdown on the Isle of Sheppey in Kent. When approached by police he drove off; however, his car was traced to a caravan park where Kelly, following a search of his vehicle, was arrested. In the boot of the car police found a drone that had its lights blacked out with tape and had been spray-painted black. When the Drone's flight recorder was interrogated it was discovered that it had also been in the vicinity of two other prisons. Police stated that Kelly had used the drone to fly items such as the psychoactive drug known as 'Spice' into the prisons. He appeared at Maidstone Crown Court and admitted to conspiracy to project an article into prison under the new legislation and was sentenced to fourteen months imprisonment.

99. BLINKS INTO WORDS (2017)

An astonishing conviction for a crime was secured in March 2017 at Bournemouth Crown Court. A former vicar was sentenced to four years imprisonment for sexually assaulting a young choir boy on three occasions between 1978 and 1982. The offender was seventy-eight-year-old Cyril Rowe who indecently assaulted his victim in a church in the Borough of Tower Hamlets, after which he paid the boy £1 to maintain his silence. What made this case ground-breaking was the manner in which the evidence against Rowe was delivered to the court.

The forty-seven-year-old victim was diagnosed with motor neurone disease in 2015 but was determined to see justice done.

He was at a stage where he could no longer communicate by speech so gave his evidence, for the first time in a British court, using eye-tracking technology called Eyegaze, which turned the blink of his eye into a word. He told the court that Cyril Rowe had abused him on twenty occasions between 1978 and 1982 at the vicarage of the church and in the choir practice room, after which he would be paid to maintain his silence. The evidence was presented to the court via a taped interview and a video-link from a south London hospice where the victim was gravely ill; unfortunately, the victim could not hang onto life long enough to learn of the 'guilty' verdict.

The trial Judge Peter Johnson underlined the bravery of the victim when sentencing Rowe:

The victim was diagnosed with motor neurone disease in 2015 and wished to see justice done. Despite the ravages of that incurable illness he was, thanks to modern science, finally able to tell the court what happened to him at your hands. He wanted to see justice done, but tragically that was not the case as he died shortly before an officer arrived to deliver the news. He was sadly deprived of the news that justice had been served...You have shown absolutely no remorse and very little insight into the harm you caused to a little boy.[39]

---

39 *London Evening Standard* 10 March 2017

100. BRITAIN'S LONGEST-RUNNING TRIAL (2017)

Edwin and Lorraine McLaren from Renfrewshire in Scotland were convicted of property fraud amounting to an estimated £1.6m following this country's longest criminal trial, which commenced at Glasgow High Court in September 2015 and concluded on 16 May 2017 – a total of three-hundred and twenty days of evidence. The total cost for the trial including legal fees is said to be in excess of ten million pounds. Over the course of the trial the jury had been reduced from the original fifteen (under Scottish law) to the minimum of twelve. During the trial there were several interruptions including a three-week break for one juror to get married, sickness and pre-booked holidays. Another first for this case was the giving of evidence by a witness who was too ill to travel to the court; her house was set up as courtroom enabling her to give her evidence from her own home. The judge continued to the end of the trial even though he officially retired on his seventieth birthday in December 2016. The case involved a property scam in which the defendants preyed on the vulnerable. Edwin McLaren was found guilty of twenty-nine charges whilst his wife Lorraine was found guilty of two charges of mortgage fraud in relation to their own home. Edwin and Lorraine McLaren returned to court in June 2017 and were sentenced to eleven and two and a half year's imprisonment respectively.

ACKNOWLEDGEMENTS

I would like to take this opportunity to thank the British Newspaper Archive (www.BritishNewspaperArchive.co.uk) for the abundance of information available for writers of social and criminal history. I would also like to thank Ayah Al-Rawni from BT Heritage and Archives in High Holborn, London (archives@bt.com).

BIBLIOGRAPHY

Newspapers/Magazines/Journals

Aberdeen Evening Express
Aberdeen People's Journal
Bells New Weekly Messenger
Berkshire Chronicle
Blackburn Standard
Burnley Gazette
Cambridge Independent Press
Carlisle Patriot
Chelmsford Chronicle
Clare Journal and Ennis Advertiser
Daily Telegraph
Derby Daily Telegraph
Dover Express
Dundee Evening Telegraph
Fresh Produce Journal
Greenock Telegraph and Clyde Shipping Gazette
Hartlepool Evening Daily Mail
Hendon and Finchley Times
Illustrated Police News
Independent Whig
Kent and Sussex Courier
Lancaster Gazette
Lancaster Guardian
Leicester Journal
Lichfield Mercury
Liverpool Echo
Lloyds Weekly Newspaper
London Courier and Evening Gazette

London Daily News
London Evening News
Morning Herald
Morning Post
Norfolk Chronicle
North Devon Journal
Northampton Mercury
Northern Echo
Northern Whig
North London News
Nottingham Evening Post
Nottinghamshire Guardian
Paisley Herald and Renfrewshire Advertiser
Post Office Telecommunications Journal
Preston Herald
Rugby Advertiser
Scots Magazine
Sheffield Independent
Shoreditch Observer
Sunderland Daily Echo and Shipping Gazette
Tamworth Herald
Taunton Courier and Western Advertiser
The Guardian
The Lancet
The Times
Western Daily Press
Worcester Journal

Online

British Newspaper Archive: www.BritishNewspaperArchive.co.uk
British Transport Police: www.btp.police.uk
Crown Prosecution Service Online: www.cps.gov.uk
Daily Mail Online: www.mailonline.co.uk
Daily Telegraph Online: www.telegraph.co.uk
MI5: www.mi5.gov.uk
Motoring Research: www.motoringresearch.com
Old Bailey Online
Police Witness: www.policewitness.com
The Guardian Online: www.theguardian.com

Books

Baxter, Carol, *The Peculiar Case of the Electric Constable* (Oneworld Publications 2013)

Cullen, Pamela, *A Stranger in Blood: The Story of Dr Bodkin Adams* (Elliott and Thompson 2004)

Fairfield.L and E Fullbrook, *Trial of John Thomas Straffen* (W.Hodge 1954)

Lovill, Justin, *Notable Historical Trials Volumes II and III* (Folio Society 1999)

Powell, Gary. *Death Diary: A Year of London Murder, Execution, Terrorism and Treason* (Amberley 2017)

Sereny, Gitta, *The Case of Mary Bell: A Portrait of a Child Who Killed* (Pimlico 1995)

Simpson, Keith, *Forty Years of Murder* (Harrap Limited 1978)

Soanes, Catherine, *Compact Oxford English Dictionary* (Oxford University Press 2000)

Swinney, Christopher, *The Beast of Birkenshaw* (R. J. Parker Publishing 2016)